After the Korean War

Following his prizewinning studies of the Vietnam War, renowned anthropologist Heonik Kwon presents this groundbreaking study of the Korean War's enduring legacies seen through the realm of intimate human experience. Kwon boldly reclaims kinship as a vital category in historical and political inquiry and probes the gray zone between the modern and the traditional (and between the civil and the social) in the lived reality of Korea's civil war and the Cold War more broadly. With captivating historical detail and innovative conceptual frames, Kwon's moving and creative analysis provides fresh insights into the Korean conflict, civil war and reconciliation, history and memory, and critical political theory.

Heonik Kwon is Senior Research Fellow in Social Science and Professor of Anthropology at Trinity College, University of Cambridge. He is the author of *The Other Cold War*, *Ghosts of War in Vietnam*, and *After the Massacre: Commemoration and Consolation in Ha My and My Lai*.

Studies in the Social and Cultural History of Modern Warfare

General Editor
Robert Gerwarth, *University College Dublin*
Jay Winter, *Yale University*

Advisory Editors
Heather Jones, *University College London*
Rana Mitter, *University of Oxford*
Michelle Moyd, *Indiana University Bloomington*
Martin Thomas, *University of Exeter*

In recent years the field of modern history has been enriched by the exploration of two parallel histories. These are the social and cultural history of armed conflict, and the impact of military events on social and cultural history.

Studies in the Social and Cultural History of Modern Warfare presents the fruits of this growing area of research, reflecting both the colonization of military history by cultural historians and the reciprocal interest of military historians in social and cultural history, to the benefit of both. The series offers the latest scholarship in European and non-European events from the 1850s to the present day.

A full list of titles in the series can be found at:
www.cambridge.org/modernwarfare

After the Korean War

An Intimate History

Heonik Kwon

University of Cambridge

CAMBRIDGE
UNIVERSITY PRESS

University Printing House, Cambridge CB2 8BS, United Kingdom

One Liberty Plaza, 20th Floor, New York, NY 10006, USA

477 Williamstown Road, Port Melbourne, VIC 3207, Australia

314–321, 3rd Floor, Plot 3, Splendor Forum, Jasola District Centre, New Delhi – 110025, India

79 Anson Road, #06–04/06, Singapore 079906

Cambridge University Press is part of the University of Cambridge.

It furthers the University's mission by disseminating knowledge in the pursuit of education, learning, and research at the highest international levels of excellence.

www.cambridge.org
Information on this title: www.cambridge.org/9781108487924
DOI: 10.1017/9781108768313

First published 2020

A catalogue record for this publication is available from the British Library.

Library of Congress Cataloging-in-Publication Data
Names: Kwon, Heonik, 1962– author.
Title: After the Korean War : An Intimate History / Heonik Kwon.
Description: Cambridge, United Kingdom ; New York, NY : Cambridge University Press, 2020. | Series: Studies in the social and cultural history of modern warfare | Includes bibliographical references and index.
Identifiers: LCCN 2019041202 (print) | LCCN 2019041203 (ebook) | ISBN 9781108487924 (hardback) | ISBN 9781108768313 (ebook)
Subjects: LCSH: Korean War, 1950–1953 – Social aspects. | War and society – Korea. | Kinship – Political aspects – Korea. | Social ethics – Korea. | Collective memory – Korea. | Cold war – Social aspects – Korea. | Korea – Foreign relations – 1945–
Classification: LCC DS921.5.S63 K96 2020 (print) | LCC DS921.5.S63 (ebook) | DDC 951.904/21–dc23
LC record available at https://lccn.loc.gov/2019041202
LC ebook record available at https://lccn.loc.gov/2019041203

ISBN 978-1-108-48792-4 Hardback

Contents

Acknowledgments

This book would not have been possible without the support and encouragement of many interlocutors. Among others, I thank the village elders in Andong who so generously tolerated my intrusive inquiries into their shared yet divisive past trajectories. Special thanks are also due to members of the Hagui Village Development Assembly in northern Jeju, who made my research in the village possible, as well as many others elsewhere in Korea who kindly shared their family histories with me. My research in South Korea received generous support from the Academy of Korean Studies (AKS-2016-LAB-2250005). Seoul National University's Department of Anthropology kindly provided a space, in the form of a distinguished visiting professorship, during a crucial stage of writing. I am indebted to numerous other institutions for giving me opportunities to discuss – with students, colleagues, and the general public in Asia, Europe, and North America – on the one hand, different ways to rethink the history and legacy of modern civil warfare, and, on the other, the fate of *communitas* in modern politics. This book has grown out of the thoughts we exchanged in these two separate investigative spheres, which I set out to bring together in this book. The present book also grows out of my earlier engagement with Vietnam War history. Marilyn B. Young, a towering scholar of the Vietnam War and US foreign policy, offered unfailing support while I was struggling to migrate from one gigantic historical milieu of human struggle against political violence to another. When I first met her, Marilyn was preparing a similar journey, having started her eminent career from the study of China in civil war. We shared the conviction that this move was necessary for coming to terms with the living ruins of the global civil war, which we habitually call the Cold War. This book is dedicated to her memory.

Introduction

An elderly woman keeps shaking her head each time she encounters a stranger. She has no control over her unusual bodily reaction, which originates from an incident in the early days of the Korean War that tragically claimed her son's life. Her only son was in hiding in a nearby village. A group of armed men suddenly confronted his mother while she was tending to the family's rice paddy. Taken by surprise, she began to shake her head vigorously as a way of saying that she had no knowledge of her son's whereabouts. She believed that these men were after him, and this was what her young daughter-in-law had asked her to do if such a situation should arise. The young woman knew that her mother-in-law was not good at lying. When the petrified woman recovered her senses shortly afterward, she came to the painful realization that she had made the gesture of denial before the men even began questioning her about her son.[1] A middle-aged woman is on a visit to a Buddhist pagoda together with her frail mother, with whom she shares a secret relating to their family's war experience in Seoul. Keeping this experience a secret was necessary for the family's survival during the war; however, now that the war was over, to keep doing so had become a source of mutual estrangement for the two women. The daughter knows that her mother is trying to find some solace in the realm of the Bodhisattva. Each time she witnesses this, she wishes that she could console her mother, but it feels as though something is trapped in her throat, and this alien object is blocking the words that she is trying to say. She calls this fierce little lump her Korean War memory.[2]

Kim Sung-chil, a history professor, kept a diary of North Korea-occupied Seoul from June 28 to September 28, 1950.[3] He wrote about a neighbor who joined the occupying power as a local recruit. The neighbor's wife was worried about her husband's pro-communist activity and what this might bring to her family if the world changed hands. She confided in Kim's wife, the one person in her neighborhood she genuinely trusted. The historian's wife wished to comfort her but didn't know how. She also knew that if she said the wrong things to her neighbor and the woman's husband heard about what she had said, it might bring calamity to her family. Park Wan-suh, an eminent South Korean writer, gives a similar account of the breakdown of neighborly trust. In her autobiographical writings, Park remembers her uncle's family, whose three-room traditional house in Seoul was requisitioned by the Northern forces to provide an eating house for their army officers.[4] Because of this, her uncle was arrested and summarily executed when the tide of war changed and South Korean and US troops recovered the town. His arrest was triggered by a neighbor who had denounced him for being a collaborator. Park's elder brother, a schoolteacher, had been active in a radical political movement before the war. Yielding to family pressure, however, he later signed up to the Alliance of Converts, the prewar South Korean public organization that was intended to reeducate the former radicals in the "right way" of anti-communist patriotism. When Seoul was under the occupation of the communist North, the schoolteacher was pressured by his former comrades to join the town's civil support activities for the revolutionary war and was subsequently conscripted into the North Korean People's Army as a Southern "volunteer." When the tide of war changed and Seoul had new liberators, her brother's past career and his absence from home became a life-threatening liability for Park's family. In a desperate attempt to survive, Park Wan-suh, then a first-year college student of literature, joined the anti-communist paramilitary youth group as a secretarial clerk.

Many years after the chaos in Seoul ended, the effects of the changing waves of violence that had caused it can still be felt in corners of the vibrant cosmopolitan city today. A house in the city's old quarter is distinct from the neighboring houses. The owner of this house has refused to renovate it for the past six decades, defying the general trend in his hillside neighborhood for fear that his elder siblings might not be able to find their way back home. All of his brothers and sisters left northward during the war and have not yet fulfilled their promise of a prompt return to their then eleven-year-old youngest sibling. Amid the recent belligerent standoff between Pyongyang and Washington involving claims of a nuclear armed state and threats of preventive strikes against it, the celebrated South Korean writer Han Kang tells a story about a man in Seoul who lost all his money.[5] The man cashed out all his life savings only to misplace the money on his anxious journey home from the bank. He had hoped to help his grandchildren survive, being faithful to his own experience of survival from the 1950s war.

These are harrowing experiences. The wounds of war depicted in these stories may not be the same as those familiar from the cultural history of modern warfare – for instance, the war neurosis caused by trench warfare, which preoccupied one of modern anthropology's early intellectual ancestors, W. H. R. Rivers. Rivers was a pioneer of the comparative method in kinship studies, trained in both social psychology and social anthropology. During the First World War, he worked at the Craiglockhart War Hospital for Officers near Edinburgh as a psychopathologist. It was partly through Rivers's clinical engagement with Siegfried Sassoon and other British officers who were troubled by their trench experiences that the idea of shell shock later became widely recognized and accepted.[6] Rivers considered shell shock a real illness, and believed that the driving force behind this war neurosis was the instinct of self-preservation, thus departing considerably from the then prevalent theory of neurosis that emphasized early sexual experience and related latent anxieties. Korea's civil war wounds also differ from the post-traumatic stress disorders, or what Allan Young calls the culture of psychiatric science in the United States during the 1970s, which initially focused exclusively on symptoms experienced by American veterans of the Vietnam War.[7] The literary, biographical, and testimonial accounts of the grassroots Korean War experience that have become available in recent years make it abundantly clear that this war was a profoundly injurious experience not merely for the combatants but also for many more people who had no professional role in the three-year-long conflict. Moreover, many of these war injuries experienced by the civilian population were *social* wounds – both in their distinction from combat traumas, and, equally importantly, because they were experienced by relational beings rather than isolated individuals and their individual bodies.

Indeed, "relations," or "web of relations" (*gwangye* in Korean), appears as a keyword in the literary renderings of Korea's civil war experience told in South Korea.[8] The relational suffering refers to the ways in which the violence of the Korean War induced brutal and enduring effects into the milieu of communal and family relations. It is also testament to the fact that the main thrust of the war's political violence targeted not only the enemy soldiers' physical bodies and their collective morale but also the morality and spirituality of intimate human ties. Moreover, the concept of relationship evoked in this context addresses a three-dimensional phenomenon. It speaks of intimate, concrete interpersonal ties, but also interactions between impersonal political entities and the abstract ideals these entities harbored. The concept points further to the reality of relatedness between these qualitatively different forms of relations – between the fate of human relationships in their immediacy and the imperatives of impersonal political forces on a national and global scale.[9] Hence, the philosophy student Myung-jun, in Choi In-hun's classical Korean War story, *Gwangjang* (The square), undergoes a violent interrogation by the security forces of the nascent South Korean state about his ties to his absent father, whom they believe is sympathetic to the communist regime in the North. Myung-jun finds that for his interrogators, these ties are, at once and indistinguishably, family ties and political connections. He discovers that being a child of a communist is equivalent to being a follower of Kim Il-sung and Joseph Stalin, and that the life of such a human being born with the wrong genealogical background is freely disposable. It may be argued that such an assault against human relatedness is committed in all forms of warfare and, especially, in the king of all wars in terms of the brutality of war – the modern civil war. There is truth in this view, and I believe that there is merit in placing the Korean War experience in a broad comparative historical context of modern civil warfare. However, the Korean War's social, human-relational sufferings illustrate not only the general human condition in the wars of the twentieth century but also the particular character of the Korean conflict.

The Korean War (1950–1953) was not a single war but rather a combination of several different kinds of war. Above all, it was a civil war fought between two mutually negating postcolonial political forces, each of which, through the negation, aspired to build a common, singular, and united modern nation-state. It was part of a global conflict waged between two bifurcating international forces with different visions of modernity, commonly known as the Cold War, which some astute observers today prefer to define as a "global civil war."[10] The Korean War was also an international conflict fought, among others, between two of the most powerful political entities of the contemporary world, the United States and China. Since the end of the Cold War in the early 1990s, the Sino-American dimension of the Korean War has been the subject of prolific investigations. This is in part because of the growing availability of previously inaccessible archival sources held in the former Soviet Union, China, and elsewhere in former Eastern Bloc countries. The trend involves new sources and new interpretations of existing sources held in the United States and elsewhere in the West. The growing attention on the Korean War as a pivotal episode in US-Chinese relations is also because the implications of this particular dimension of the war reverberate strongly in the unfolding of contemporary world politics.[11] The end of the Cold War as a prevailing geopolitical order of the past century has made it possible to see the realities of the Korean War from yet another perspective and dimension. Hidden beneath the relatively well-known characteristics of the Korean War as a civil and international conflict, recent studies have shown that there was another kind of war being waged in postcolonial Korea.

The 1950s war in Korea was principally a war against society, according to the Canadian historian Steven Hugh Lee.[12] South Korean scholar Kim Dong-choon delves into the reality of what he calls "another Korean War" in a similar light, focusing on the relentless assault against the civilian population during the conflict. Kim points out that the civilian sufferings of the Korean War are not well known to the outside world, or for that matter, even the Koreans themselves.[13] The historian Park Chan-sung throws a microscopic gaze on the war's societal reality. He calls this reality "a war that moved into a village," thereby highlighting the disparities between Korean War history as national or international narratives and those remembered by local communities.[14] The present book adopts an even more microscopic view, approaching the history and memory of the Korean War within milieus of intimate interpersonal relationships. It will do so in part with reference to the idea of *societas* (an order based on persons and their relations), understood as distinct from *civitas* (civic and political society based on territory and property), a conceptual contrast that was once central to the anthropology of kinship and politics (see later discussion).[15] Among people to whom the Korean War was a "village war," it is often recalled as the era "when the heavens suddenly collapsed" or "when both the laws of the heavens and the laws of humanity were no longer."[16] These expressions speak of the extremity of the human condition and the intensity of social chaos generated by the politics of exclusive political sovereignty in violent means, which, when pursued by both parties to the war, characterize the civil war dimension of the Korean War. The allusion to heavenly laws also points to a crisis of morality: how radically a modern civil war can violate our fundamental sense of human goodness, and the profound wounds it leaves behind in the normative fabric of interpersonal lives.

The 1950–1953 war resulted in astonishing death tolls. Most disturbing is the number of civilian deaths estimated to be more than two million, a higher number than the total combat casualties of all the different armed forces involved in the three-year conflict.[17] Arguing that destruction on this scale cannot be written off as collateral damage, Lee advances the view that the reality of the Korean War is not intelligible without taking into account the struggle for survival by unarmed civilians against the widespread, indiscriminate violence perpetrated by the armed political forces of all sides. The South Korean state committed preemptive violence on a massive scale in the very early days of the war. Directed against people whom it considered sympathizers or hypothetical collaborators with the enemy, this state action set in motion a vicious cycle of violence against civilians in the ensuing chaos of war. It radicalized the punitive actions perpetrated under North Korean occupation against individuals and families who were classified as supporters of the Southern regime, which in turn escalated the intensity of retaliatory violence against the so-called collaborators with the communist occupiers when the tide of war turned. When the North Korean forces left their briefly occupied territory in the South, they acted in the same way as the South had before, committing numerous atrocities of preemptive violence against people whom they considered to be sympathizers with the Southern regime. This chaotic, generalized violence against society generated a mass exodus of the terrified population from their places of origin, both southward and northward, and, thus, is greatly responsible for one of the most critical issues regarding the human condition of the postwar Korean peninsula that still remains unresolved today – the plight of divided families across the 38th parallel. After the war ended, missing family members – those who were suspected of having moved to the enemy's territory or those who were killed during the war after being accused of anti-state sympathies – became a critical liability for the entire surviving family.

These two phenomena – family separation and collective liability – induced acute existential and moral crises in family and kin groups, who struggled in the postwar years with the desire to reunite, on the one hand, and, on the other, the fear of being deemed guilty by association. Families everywhere experience moments of disappointment and conflict as well as times of amity and solidarity; this actuality does not diminish the basic meaning of kinship, the human condition of having to mutually nurture each other and mutually participate in each other's lives.[18] In the theater of Korea's civil war, this world of kinship, broadly defined, was far from being a private realm existing more or less independently from the public world, or a shelter to which one can retreat from the world of anonymous associations among self-interested individuals. Instead, it became a field of vigorous struggle throughout the long Cold War era, between the powerful forces of bipolarizing global politics and the fragile moral integrity of intimate human sociality.

Knowledge of such moral and political crises and conflicts became a public taboo after the war was over. South Koreans were not able to publicly share their experiences of the politics of collective culpability until recently, while living in a self-consciously anti-communist political society. The same is true for people in North Korea who, living in a self-consciously revolutionary political society, are obliged to follow the country's singular official narrative of war, which is a victorious war of liberation against American imperialism. North Korea's *sŏngbun* system classifies the place of its citizens varyingly, based on their family's political background, within a vast concentric hierarchy consisting of a pure core group, a peripheral adversarial group, and groups that fall in between these two extreme poles. The politics of associative guilt continues to be a powerful instrument of societal control in this system, pointing to families of people who had left home southward during the war and now involving those whose members joined the recent wave of defections to the South. Despite the tight lids put on the stories of these families, across the 38th parallel memories of the Korean War's violence against society persisted throughout the long postwar era: in whispered conversations among family and village elders; quiet talk among trusted relatives during family ancestral death-day ceremonies; in the silent agonies of parents who couldn't tell their children the true story of how their grandparents died during the war; and the anxieties of aging parents who don't know how to meet death without knowing about and hearing from their children, whom they still want to believe are surviving on the other side of the bipolar border. They are also found in the furious self-expression of some forgotten ancestral spirits who intrude into a shamanic rite, thereby startling the family gathered there; in the anxieties of two young lovers in a village, who do not understand why their families so furiously object to their marriage without providing any intelligible reason; and in the curiously un-renovated house that looks frozen in time in the middle of a bustling neighborhood.

These accounts make up a tiny fragment of the gigantic iceberg of the Korean War-related human dramas still unfolding in Korea. Today, some of these dramas also involve courageous and ingenuous efforts to confront the war's hidden wounds. The rise of these communal initiatives since roughly the mid-1990s is closely intertwined with forceful changes of an era on a global scale, which we customarily call the end of the Cold War. The end of the global bipolar political order did not entirely materialize in the Korean peninsula. The two-state system that was created during the early Cold War remains entrenched. Although there have been considerable changes in the relations between Korea's two states since the 1990s, the once globally meaningful confrontation continues to be waged now in a uniquely localized way. Whereas the end of the Cold War is still a prospect rather than a thing of the past in the region, the epochal global change has, nevertheless, radically transformed how the history of the Korean War is told and understood at local and communal levels. A flood of information has recently been made available on the grassroots Korean War experience in South Korea, and it is becoming increasingly possible to begin to understand what this war meant in the framework of social experience. Many communities are finally coughing up their long-trapped foreign objects of intimate Korean War memories. In this state of convulsion, the lived history of the Korean War, which was one of the earliest and most formative episodes of the global Cold War, has suddenly appeared as a powerful subject of contemporary history, after having been long kept away from the public light, since the end of the Cold War. This book is a response to this curious phenomenon of an old history of destruction that has suddenly erupted into the present time, more than a half century later when this history was about to part with the living memories of destruction, only to invite ethnographic attention. At the vortex of this development is the voice of human kinship demanding to recover its fundamental right to stay related, both among the living and with those lost, without fearing the consequences of doing so.

Bellum sociale

Moral conflicts between families and the state are a subject of enduring interest in the tradition of modern political thought. In the Hegelian philosophical heritage that explores the subject with reference to the domain of death commemoration, it is assumed that families are morally disposed to remember all the dead, including the war dead, equally and comprehensively, as long as they are part of the family tree. Whereas it is the imperative of the modern state to remember and honor only the sacrifice of citizens that it deems meritorious. The state's actions may involve excluding from the public sphere the memories of those it regards as unworthy or treacherous. Drawing upon Sophocles' epic tragedy of *Antigone*, Hegel famously defined the ethical foundation of modern political life in terms of a possibility to resolve clashes between these two moral imperatives, which he called the law of the state and the ethics of kinship.

Debates in this philosophical tradition, however, tend to overlook the very specific context in which the state and the family come to confront each other within the epic drama, along with their separate, diverging moral claims. This context is the condition of a civil war, which creates the moral hierarchy of death and the politics of exclusion in the first place.[19] Antigone's defiance of the state's edicts is not merely about her wish to commemorate her dead siblings, but specifically about her act of remembrance that is torn between what is right (for her hero brother) and what is not (with regard to her other brother considered a traitor). Related to this problem is the tendency to regard the family as a "natural" or pre-political entity. This rendering of the law of kinship as a natural law contradicts the idea of kinship familiar in the tradition of modern anthropological research, in which it is an eminently *political* concept. The idea of kinship addressed in this book relates to both of these traditions in the theory of politics – one in which kinship is pre-political and the other in which it is not – although it is closer to the latter. Kinship in this book does not necessarily entail a web of relationships existing discretely as a given unity of natural love, as Hegel defines it, which can confront, if obliged, the power of the state externally and in a seemingly coherent voice that represents the interests of its natural unity. Instead, this book explores the zone of modern political life in which human ethical relationships in their immediacy are brought to confront the politics of sovereignty from within their lifeworld – that is, in the specific state of siege after the apocalyptic wind of civil war "knocked loudly" at the door of the house, as Francis Lieber, the Prussian-born American lawyer, said about the American civil war.[20] The knocking was the moment when *bellum civile* transformed into *bellum sociale* for Lieber, whose family fought for both the North and the South. In this zone of *bellum sociale* that exists as part of *bellum civile*, but which nevertheless is unique to the space of civil war for reasons to be explained later, the claims of the state are not merely external to what Hegel calls manifestations of family feelings. Rather, the power and efficacy of these claims are, in a crucial aspect, grounded in the appropriation of familial sentiments as a vital element in the state's disciplinary politics. The politics of collective culpability is a lucid example of the assimilation of the ethics of kinship into the law of the state. The picture concerns contradictions between the ethics of kinship and the politics of sovereignty, becoming a constitutive property in both kinship and politics. Accordingly, the idea of kinship in this book addresses two interrelated questions about the fate of intimate human relations in modern politics. One concerns the political life of kinship, the way in which kinship relations are made to confront the imperatives of impersonal political forces from within, namely, kinship as a locus of global politics. The other question relates to the politics of the morality of kinship – how modern politics appropriates the very idea that kinship relations have unique ethical properties.

Returning to Hegel, it is important to note that in his scheme, moral claims by the state and those made by the family are *both* exclusionary. The state excludes those whom it deems unworthy or treacherous; the family is, by its own nature, indifferent to the memories of those unrelated to them. In between these two separate types of exclusion, however, a powerful, inclusive moral practice may arise – especially against the backdrop of civil war that turns a community inside out by forcing it into bifurcated paths of mutual negation and organized reciprocal violence in the image of the larger political society in a state of siege. The family's commemorative practice has to go beyond the prevailing friends/enemies contrast in order to do justice to its ethical integrity, which involves paying attention to the identities that the state regards as strangers to the political community. The family's pursuit of this moral objective cannot be realized unless it develops into a wider civic action, and these actions, if generalized, can bring about a significant change to the existing parameters of the state's exclusionary politics. Key to this process is how an individual family's self-conscious and even self-centered moral claims can transform into shared concerns and a concerted voice of *bürgerliche Gesellschaft* (i.e., civil society). Hegel himself was pessimistic about this possibility, believing that claims such as Antigone's are ultimately unable to overcome their narrow, self-interested basis of natural love. In this book, we will consider similar possibilities in a more optimistic spirit and in an empirically grounded way that does not lose sight of the very context, from which such moral conflicts between the family and the state arise in the first place. This historical context is the condition of civil war, as noted earlier, that can tear apart a multitude of communities in the image of the larger society at war with itself. In mass-mobilized modern civil warfare, unlike the ancient wars between the city-states such as the background to *Antigone*, moral conflicts as addressed by Hegel are not isolated episodes but, instead, make up a generalized, universally shared predicament. In other words, in such historical backgrounds, the distance between the voice of kinship and that of civil society may be much narrower than the eighteenth-century philosopher imagined. It may even be argued that unresolved legacies of civil war can only be properly confronted if these two voices can meet and develop into a concerted chorus of claims. Indeed, this book will show how communal voices can turn into powerful civic awakenings and actions in relation to Korean War experiences, and the importance in this constructive process of revealing publicly unknown historical realities of war that were kept secret in the milieu of intimate human relations. The idea of kinship in this book is, therefore, a *political* concept in the specific historical sense that addresses how the milieu of human intimacy became the primary target of the politics of the Korean War, and how it continued to be a vital site of the state's disciplinary actions throughout the long Cold War.[21] It is also a *public* concept in the sense that it is open to possibilities that the morality of kinship plays a meaningful role in the public world and even in reshaping this world into a more democratic form.

Political Life of Kinship

The relationship between kinship and politics has been a theme of great prominence not only in the tradition of political philosophy but also in that of social anthropology. In some ways, it can even be said that modern anthropology was born as a study of politics through a study of kinship, as demonstrated by the career of the American jurist and anthropologist

Lewis H. Morgan in the era of the American Civil War. Morgan approached the evolution of political systems and that of kinship systems as coactive processes, suggesting two forms of government in human history: one is based on "persons, and upon relations purely personal" (which he named *societas* or "social organization"), and the other founded upon territory and property (which he called *civitas* or "political society").[22] His idea was that the form of politics that is familiar to the moderns, grounded as it is in the institution of the state as the guarantor of their territorial security and private properties, is far from universal in human history. He postulated that politics can exist as aspects of human relations without the benefit or the burden of the state, embedded in the ways in which people measure distances to one another, in their customary rules about close and distant relations, and in how these rules are manifested in their rituals. Morgan's *societas* versus *civitas* distinction greatly influenced scholars of subsequent generations, especially among those who, during the interwar era, sought to describe political systems in the language of kinship.[23]

With a particular emphasis on Africa, scholars in this tradition investigated how in societies without central state apparatuses, kinship norms play a pivotal role in regulating political relations and allocating rights, entitlements, and obligations. The key idea in this development was the contrast between state societies (close to Morgan's *civitas*) and stateless societies (close to his *societas*) in terms of how basic principles of political life are understood and implemented.[24] While it may appear untenable to imagine, in the context of a complex state society, that kinship relations are coterminous with political relations, these anthropologists believed that it would be necessary to suspend this impression while dealing with forms of human relations in other societies. During this crucial period in the development of modern anthropology, therefore, the study of kinship was not about charting who was related to who in family trees, as the moderns would imagine is the meaning of kinship. On the contrary, in the interwar-era anthropology of kinship, it was advanced as a science of politics and law meaningful for societies in a greater part of the human world that exists without centralized state institutions. They had an even greater ambition – to turn kinship studies into a scholarship of comparative politics, whose scope was meant to be much broader than what the then emerging disciplines of political science and international politics could handle. These early anthropologists asked that if kinship norms and relations are central to the political orders of many societies, past and present, it follows that a theory of politics grounded on an understanding of these norms and relations should be equal in relevance to the theories of politics and law that permeate the modern world, which are narrowly focused on worldly affairs in and between state societies. The dominant theory of international politics since the mid-twentieth century has considered the relations among states in the international system in the image of individuals in modern society – as autonomous, sovereign subjects that are destined to pursue their self-interests relentlessly. In contrast to this trend, the interwar-era anthropology of kinship advanced a normative theory of politics, highlighting the imperative of relational norms (pointing to ties of kinship and friendship) in the making of a political order, both domestic and foreign (within and between tribal entities).

In this regard, *African Political Systems*, published in 1940 by Meyer Fortes and E. E. Evans-Pritchard, was a landmark work that aspired to advance a comparative analysis of kinship rules to comparative politics and comparative political theory. Evans-Pritchard regarded his enquiry into the Nuer kinship rules in southern Sudan as a way to understand the group's political order. He characterized the Nuer as a "nation" ("although in a cultural sense," as he says) and explained their "foreign relations" with neighboring groups such as the Dinka in terms of "structural distance" – the idea that a political system consists of an inner entity of thick solidary relations, which expand into outer circles of increasingly distant senses of solidarity.[25] For Fortes, too, an understanding of the Tallensi descent system in northern Ghana was equal in meaning to that of the Tallensi's legal and political system. He understood that a comparative study of kinship rules and norms (as regards traditional societies) would be equivalent to comparative law and politics (in relation to modern state societies). Throughout his career, Fortes advocated that politics and kinship are inseparable, mutually constitutive orders. He also tried to define kinship in a way that distinguished it from other types of human associations, coining expressions such as "the axiom of amity" and "the ethics of generosity," although he was well aware of duplicity in the moral character of kinship – that it was rife with potential conflicts and relationships of enmity while harboring a pronounced ideology of amity and unity. In this respect, he took an interest in the coexistence of contradictory images of ancestors among the Tallensi – benevolent and generous in some contexts, while threatening and menacing (to their descendants) in other situations. The concept of amity, which appears prominently in Fortes's essays on kinship and polity, has an interesting etymological background. Its meanings in old English incorporate both the mutuality of kin relations and the intimacy among people or groups who consider one another as friends. It can be said that the important heritage of this concept lies precisely in the fact that it does not discriminate between kinship and friendship.[26] Similar observations can be made with respect to the Sino-Korean idiom of propinquity or proximal relationship, *ch'in*, which applies equally to the idea of kinship and that of friendship, including international friendship. During the first half of the twentieth century, the term "amity" was forcefully brought back as an important concept in international relations. In this context, amity denoted certain normative dispositions and ideational orientations toward international solidarity, as shown in such expressions as the amity of nations, which was sometimes used interchangeably with the older idea of the family of nations – both denoting the ideal and impera- tive of international peace.[27]

It is not clear whether Fortes was conscious, while writing about the axiom of amity, of the concept's other emerging meanings at the time, especially those relating to the threats of war and rising public aspirations for international peace. However, by the end of the Second World War and the onset of the Cold War, some anthropologists of kinship and politics were clearly mindful of the need to find a way to relate the morality of human kinship relations to questions of international peace. Notable was the South Africa-born anthropologist Max Gluckman, who sought to advance some of the key issues on kinship relations and political orders raised in *African Political Systems* to a challenging perspective on broader questions of war and peace. In his essays published in 1955, Gluckman argued that the segmentary descent system in traditional Africa can drive constituent units into competing relations, which might involve occasional crises, such as feuds or even a war.[28] The broad world of African kinship has other relational spectrums, however, such as those established through marriage or trading ties. During times of an immi- nent threat of war, these can be brought forward as forceful diplomatic, reconciliatory initiatives between warring groups. In presenting this pic- ture of traditional Africa that he called "peace in the feud," Gluckman was conscious of the disparity between Africa's traditional kinship-based political system and the radically bipolarizing global political system of his time. The African political system was structurally prone to the risk of war, but it also had a structural capacity for peace due to the fact that it was built on networks of concrete human relations. In contrast, the Cold War political system was based on competitive politics of absolute align- ment, allowing no space for crosscutting ties between the contending groupings. Gluckman's essays were based on his six BBC lectures that he delivered in the spring of 1955, shortly after the Korean War in which his native country of South Africa participated as an ally of the United States – and as part of the South African National Party's relentless efforts to justify the making of a racialist political order in anti-communist rhetoric.[29] Another notable initiative emerged in the late 1980s against the backdrop of the generalized chaos of the time in Africa, the Middle

East, and other parts of the postcolonial world, which some historians call the Second Cold War.[30] Entitled *Societies at Peace*, anthropologists involved in this project confronted head-on the Hobbesian assumption about the drive for self-preservation as humanity's natural quality, which led to his theory of the state. They did so by highlighting the peaceable and sociable nature of archaic and contemporary hunting-and-gathering societies.[31] Seen from a different angle, early social anthropology's distinct kinship-based political theory forged a way for an innovative view of the Cold War world order. Several scholars of international politics took an interest in the way in which Evans-Pritchard characterized the Nuer political system as an "ordered anarchy," finding in it a mirror image of the condition of the international order in the mid-twentieth century, which was also "stateless" in the sense that it consisted of an increasing number of sovereignty-claiming political entities without the benefit of a world government.[32] Similar interests are found in Hedley Bull's *The Anarchical Society*, a work regarded as a foundational text in the so-called English school of international relations theory.[33] Bull challenges the then prevailing idea of international politics as an anarchical power struggle between states pursuing their narrow interests, arguing instead for the existence of an international society with norms and rules.

During the Cold War era, early anthropology's interest in kinship evolved into an innovative view of modern politics, especially in the theory of international society. In the era's development of the anthropology of kinship itself, in contrast, the dominant trend was to decisively turn against the earlier disciplinary heritage in which kinship studies aspired to be comparative studies of political systems. These new developments had complex and diverse backgrounds. Here, it suffices to say that the propensity to make a break with the past was not merely due to academic paradigmatic reasons; it was also closely intertwined with momentous changes in the broad political circumstances of the post-Second World War era. Most notable of these circumstances was the global process of decolonization. The advent of decolonization in Africa and elsewhere made it increasingly difficult for anthropologists to consider a traditional world as a discreet entity that can be considered separately from wider political and social changes on a global scale. A key aspect of the process was the rise of the idea of nation and the related decline of kinship. Decolonization meant the achievement of self-determination free from colonial subjugation and that of equal status in the new postcolonial international environment. In the domestic sphere, however, the key question was instead about integrating the multitude of existing communities into a unified national political society. This was the era in which the keywords were *nation* and *national unity*; there was little space in this world for the idea that human beings can have meaningful political lives simply by being related to one another – and, worse, without the institution of the state. With the end of the Second World War, moreover, the gravity of anthropological research shifted from Europe to the United States geographically, and thematically, from traditional kinship-based societies (usually those found within the imperial sphere) to the newly emerging nations in Asia and Africa. Research funding from the Rockefeller and Ford Foundations played a pivotal role in driving this shift.[34] In this broad milieu, the concept of "politics" in anthropological research subsequently became increasingly indistinguishable from the idea of politics familiar in disciplines such as political science – that is, an idea of politics anchored in the institution of the state. Fortes resisted this development, reiterating in his 1969 work *Kinship and the Social Order* the merits of the political theory of kinship. This was when decolonization in an institutional sense was being completed in Africa, however. By then, despite his resistance, there was not much Fortes could do to dispel the prevailing sense both within the discipline and the wider public world that the so-called kin-based political orders had become a thing of the past. The era's attention was on the future of the imagined community of the nation and the nation-state, not on the art of politics without the state.

In this turbulent milieu, the subsequent anthropology of kinship began to take on several different developmental routes, which were, while diverse, commonly based on critical reflection on the earlier interwar-era orientation.[35] A particularly strong critique came from scholars who advocated a theory of practice. These scholars took the view that the traditional approach of kinship had been too narrowly focused on sets of formal rules and norms of descent, thereby ignoring how kinship relations were actually acted upon in everyday, practical lives. From roughly the late 1960s, the argument in favor of practical kinship and against normativity of kinship advanced as part of a broader shift of focus in social research from interests in systems of norms to those in practical actions – according to the French sociologist Pierre Bourdieu, from what people say they do toward what people actually do. Calling the earlier research trend in kinship studies "abandoned roads on an old map," Bourdieu says in his *Outline of the Theory of Practice* originally published in 1972:

Representational kinship is nothing other than the group's self-representation and the almost theatrical presentation it gives of itself when acting in accordance with that self-image ... Official kinship is opposed to practical kinship in terms of the official as opposed to the non-official; the collective as opposed to the individual; the public, explicitly codified in a magical or quasi-juridical formalism, as opposed to the private, kept in an implicit, even hidden state; collective ritual, subjectless practice, amenable to performance by agents interchangeable because collectively mandated, as opposed to strategy, directed towards the satisfaction of the practical interests of an individual or group of individuals.[36]

Bourdieu's call for practical, informal kinship in action, as opposed to formal rules of kinship as the representation of the collective self, had considerable influence. In the subsequent development of kinship studies, kinship increasingly came to denote the process in which ties of intimacy and propinquity are produced and reproduced through acts of sharing food and other substances; namely, what people do to create and recreate relations rather than the rules and norms that supposedly govern these relations. The emphasis shifted to individual actors and their strategies, moving away from supra-individual entities and structures.[37] In this atmosphere, questions regarding the relationship between ideas of kinship and forms of political order became an increasingly outdated, outmoded subject to be overcome, a problematic past legacy that is biased toward structural order and oblivious to human agency. Consequently, the study of kinship as comparative politics became an increasingly unpopular subject of inquiry, existing as a defunct past legacy against which new, supposedly more appropriate paradigms of kinship studies were to take shape. In this development, kinship came to mean a fluid field of practical actions (or diverse systems of meanings, in another developmental trajectory), rather than a system of norms and relations meaningful in shaping the structure of political reality. These formative changes in kinship studies were grounded on the critical awareness that the political concept held in earlier kinship studies had been too narrowly based on an overtly rigid conceptual separation between stateless and state societies. In the post-Second World War milieu of decolonization, which not only meant the disintegration of existing imperial state entities but also a rapid incorporation of formerly "stateless" societies into newly forming national state entities, as noted earlier, the conceptual contrast was considered no longer tenable empirically. These critical considerations later extended to the fact that the so-called stateless societies, even before the time of decolonization, had been already under the strong influence of the system of indirect rule by European imperial state politics. Relatedly, challenges were made against the orientation in interwar-era kinship studies to view politics in traditional "kin-based" societies as stable and static, without taking into full consideration the impact of the political and economic forces of colonialism on the constitution of indigenous political order. Bourdieu was particularly well placed in advancing these challenges, having started his intellectual career in the mid-1950s as an observer of social transformations among the Kabyle (meaning "tribe" in Arabic), the large Berber-speaking population in northern Algeria, while Algeria was swept into the whirlwind of a war (1954–1962) as part of its struggle against France's colonial power. He was also a keen observer of the social and political crisis that the Algerian crisis provoked in France.

What I intend to say with this brief and obviously highly skeletal account of the history of modern kinship studies is, first, that the idea of kinship, as it is discussed in the discipline of anthropology today, is not a coherently controlled concept, but rather a concept that keeps a history of currents and countercurrents within it.[38] Second, the concept's turbulent historical trajectory within the discipline, as previously mentioned, is closely intertwined with the transformation of global society in the mid-twentieth century. The end of colonial rule and the subsequent process of postcolonial state and nation building, above all, have profoundly affected the conceptual order of the idea of kinship. It is through this process that the idea of kinship came to lose its original relevance as a political concept. From the perspective of global history, it is important to recall at this point that the history of decolonization is substantially intertwined with the history of the Cold War. These two global processes – decolonization of the political order and the bipolarization of politics – were largely coeval phenomena, and in many parts of the decolonizing world, were much like the two sides of the same coin, inseparable from each other while signifying different historical and historically meaningful dynamics. The progression of the Cold War involved the eruption of radical political crises in the decolonizing territories, including convulsive civil war as part of the very process of postcolonial state and nation building. Manifested first in East Asia and waged between ideologically polarized postcolonial political forces, these civil wars brought extreme moral and existential crises to the milieu of human relationships in their immediacy. The eruption of these wars was closely intertwined with the process of decolonization. However, these wars were significantly different, in character and in form, from wars of independence from colonial domination such as the Algerian conflict of the 1950s. In the latter, the battlefront consisted of a relatively discreet dividing line between the foreign colonial power and its representatives, and the indigenous communities and the organized political forces that claimed a mandate over these communities. In the context of the postcolonial Cold War, however, the fault line was not merely between the indigenous and the foreign political forces. Rather, it became an increasingly entrenched internal property of the indigenous community itself.

The irony is, therefore, that while efforts were being made in kinship studies to make a clean break with the past intellectual tradition, including this tradition's central premise that, in the words of Fortes, kinship and political order "represent correlative and interdependent institutional complexes,"[39] it was precisely the time when the milieu of kinship, in a broader world, was transforming into a vital site of power struggles of a global proportion and magnitude. This was the epoch in which families and kin groups in the decolonizing world were thrown into tumultuous conditions as part of decolonization amid the bifurcating global political system. Moreover, as we will see later in this book, the construction of the international Cold War political order drew upon, in a significant way, a new ideology of kinship and new ideas about what constitutes a proper "family of nations." Thus, the main problem with critiques of interwar-era political studies of kinship is that these criticisms advanced exactly when comparative kinship studies should have reengaged with questions as to the place of human kinship in modern politics and how new ideas of kinship are invented in the making of modern political systems.

Issues of kinship and politics emerging from such a chapter of global history may not be what the authors of *African Political Systems* had in mind.[40] For Fortes, kinship relations are a defining feature of the public political arena, but only to the extent that these relations make up a reasonably stable social order. In the historical process discussed here, in contrast, kinship relations stand as a locus of a tumultuous power struggle between clashing ideological visions asserted by powerful state forces, both domestic and foreign, amid a fluctuating and precarious socio-political environment. Fortes proposed "the axiom of amity" as the constitutive property of kinship: "Kinship predicates the axiom of amity, the prescriptive altruism exhibited in the ethic of generosity."[41] In his understanding, kinship makes up a distinct domain of human relationships and is a primary example of morally social relationships, in contrast to the contractual relationship between self-interested social actors that characterizes modern industrial and commercial society.[42] As one observer noted, for Fortes, "the moral character of kinship is unique and marks off kinship relations from all others."[43] Contrary to this characterization, the political life of kinship in our discussion is not an entity existing independently from the forces of enmity that exist in the broad political world, but rather one that struggles with these forces that have penetrated deep into their milieu. Finally, the idea raised in early kinship studies that political relations are coterminous with kinship relations is meant to address conditions in specific social systems that are referred to as stateless. It was in these societies where observers believed kinship relations functioned as an organizing force of the political order, that is, as a substitute for the role of government in state societies. In contrast, the political lives of kinship discussed in this book relate to complications in the process of state and nation building within the specific global and local environment of decolonization and the postcolonial Cold War – a process that often involved extremely excessive coercive powers of the states.

Despite these disparities, I believe that the basic premises of the inter-war-era kinship studies in anthropology are still meaningful for this book's general inquiry into the human experience of the Cold War at the frontier of the global conflict – the idea that kinship and politics can be intertwined in a mutually constitutive relationship. Earlier, I mentioned how the "web of relations" appears as a critical idiom in recent accounts of Korea's civil war and its long aftermath. Similar idioms are found in the historical and literary renderings of other civil war conflicts. Seen broadly, these idioms sit uneasily with the debates on the war experience of today. These debates have a strong tendency to approach the experience of modern war from the perspective of the individual subjects, be they combatants or civilians. This is largely in critical reaction to the mechanics of war-making, which necessarily involve radical empower-ment of the rhetoric about collective destiny and the polemic against individual choices and beliefs.[44] The emphasis on individual war experi-ences also aims to strike a balance with the traditionally dominant mode of telling modern war histories, in which national perspectives and pro-jected collective voices take center stage. Seen in a broader perspective, however, our understanding of modern war experiences should not ignore the fact that the destruction caused by modern war may be experi-enced by the modern individual subject and, at the same time, by a "traditional" social subject. This is especially the case when we deal with a war waged as part of postcolonial nation building, whose ultimate purpose is to turn the traditional social subject into a modern political subject through violent means. If this war takes the form of a fratricidal civil war, the way to become a proper political subject involves the imperative of the self to make an assault against its own social selfhood. This self's war experience does not provide a critical distance from the war's reality, if rendered merely and singularly as an individual experi-ence. This is because this individual is exactly who was expected to be born through such a historical process to merit membership in the larger political society, not the person who actually lived through the turbulent and violent history. In order to obtain that crucial distance, it is necessary to recover the voice of the self's hidden social self – the very entity against which the coercive power of the postcolonial states and their wars are concentrated.

We may approach these voices in terms of Morgan's *societas* and *civitas* distinction, and the related idea of war experience as a mixed reality in which the subjectivity of war experience has both traditional-social and modern-civil properties. It is this question of the duplicity and plurality of the modern war experience that this book hopes to bring to the reader's attention. It is hoped that careful attention to this question will help enrich the concept of *social* in the social history of modern war. In addition to this aim, this book has a more specific objective relating to the history of decolonization and the Cold War. This book boldly argues that the politics of decolonization and the politics of the Cold War were both – in part yet in crucial ways – *politics of kinship*. Postcolonial state building advanced the idea of political community as a family writ large rather than necessarily a society of individuals, as we will see, in which an act to resist the particular mode of state building became equal in meaning to that of betraying the family and punishable accordingly. The construction of the global Cold War order at large also invented an idea of familial feelings in the international sphere, for the purpose of forging a new transnational alliance in the postimperial age. These abstract political ideas of kinship were part of the environment in which concrete milieus of human kinship, such as those focused on in this book, came to undergo such radical existential and moral crises. In this light, this book will consider the politics of kinship in the postcolonial Cold War era with a two-pronged approach – both as an intimate social experience and as an element of powerful impersonal political forms in operation.

Pursuing these goals to bring kinship back to the history and theory of politics, this book hopes to contribute to mending the broken intellectual tradition in the anthropology of kinship, and to do justice to the important legacy whose powerful understanding of kinship as a locus of comparative politics faded away from history precisely when such understandings were most needed to come to terms with the human condition. Meaningful to these efforts is the idea of *amity*. We will approach amity, following Fortes, as a constitutive property of human kinship – the property of human sociality that even the most vicious violent acts of war cannot destroy entirely. Amity also means the way of peace – that is, true to the idea's ancient roots.

1   Massacres in Korea

In the sweltering July heat of 1950, Daegu's railway station was jam-packed with people arriving in freight trains with bundles of bedding, food, and household utensils. These war refugees had hastily left their homes shortly before the arrival of North Korea's armed forces, which, less than a month into the war, were already closing in on the strategically important town in Korea's southeast region after capturing Seoul only four days into the all-out conflict. On the outskirts of the city, South Korean and US troops were fortifying their defense lines along the Nakdong River. Although feeling triumphant and claiming total victory by mid-August, the North Korean People's Army suffered heavy losses to US firepower, especially during their unsuccessful offensives against the Nakdong perimeter. By the beginning of September 1950, the Northern army had lost nearly half of its personnel and was relying heavily on the labor of Southern youths and students whom it had hurriedly mobilized in the areas of South Korea under its control. Meanwhile, the vicinity of Daegu's railway station had become a huge refugee shelter area. In the public square south of the station, youth groups were assembled on a regular basis – sometimes to protest against "the communist enemy's treacherous ambition to turn the Korean peninsula to a red territory," and, at other times, to stand in line, surrounded by their anxious families, before they were hurriedly hauled to the front line.[1]

These scenes are familiar from the existing public accounts of the Korean War and as part of the permanent displays in the National War Museum in Seoul. The following is not, however. Ten years later, on July 28, 1960, about 2,000 people were gathered in the same public square. They came from all corners of Daegu, some from nearby, and others from the distant countryside. By 10 a.m., the station's public square was crammed with people, many of whom were women in white traditional dresses. The meeting began at 10:45 a.m. When a schoolgirl came up to the podium and started reading a letter that she had prepared for her father, there was a tremendous stir in the crowd. The girl's father went missing during the early days of the 1950–1953 war. Her letter was followed by a woman's invocation to her husband who also went missing in July 1950: "You, the broken name; a name that departed to the empty air, name belonging to an unknown, and a name I shall keep calling upon until I myself meet death. Here and now I am summoning your name!"[2] While these initiatory actions were underway, several white-clothed women in the crowd started to wail, which was soon joined by the voices of many others and developed into a deafening collective lamentation. According to a local newspaper the lamentation shook the city center that day, attracting sympathy from many onlookers. People who assembled in the railway square on that day in July 1960 had different concerns from those who had crowded the place in July 1950. The purpose of this second assembly was not to bid farewell to the loved ones who were called to join their compatriots' collective struggle against communist aggression. However, it was related to the country's struggle for survival in 1950 and how this struggle began with a brutal assault against civilian lives. The grievances expressed by these families were widely reported at the time, both locally and nationally. In the subsequent era, such acts of public grieving came to be regarded as a threat to national security and remained outlawed until recently.

The State of Exception

The July 1960 assembly was concerned with a specific class of casualties of the 1950–1953 war. These casualties were not fallen soldiers of the civil war, either on the Southern or on the Northern side; nor were they considered innocent civilian victims at the time. Even today, the inclusion of these casualties of war in the category of innocent civilian victims of war, commonly referred to as *yangmin* (meaning literally "benign subjects" or "benevolent people"), provokes strong objections from certain sectors of the South Korean public. By the time of the Korean War, the category of civilians, as stated in the 1949 Geneva Convention relative to the Protection of Civilian Persons in Time of War, primarily addressed people inhabiting territories occupied by hostile state powers or those exposed to belligerents' artillery fire or aerial bombardment – that is, the lives of unarmed people potentially under threat, in the condition of war, from the acts committed by armed adversaries.[3] The victims of war addressed by the Daegu assembly did not belong to either of the two principal categories of casualties of modern warfare – combatants or innocent civilians. Instead, they were victims of a specific form of political violence perpetrated prolifically at the outbreak of the 1950–1953 war, which, although it had taken place as part of the broader reality of a national and international crisis referred to as the Korean War, was nonetheless distinct from the forms of violence familiar from the existing public knowledge of this formative conflict of the twentieth century. The violence perpetrated against them was not the same as the destructive powers exchanged between the two defined state entities and their international allies. It also differed from the coercive violence exercised liberally by both of these entities for the purpose of mobilizing the population behind their respective war efforts. This violence was committed not "in the hands of the adversary,"[4] but by the very state power to which the victims stood as its subjects. The targets of this violence were not armed enemy combatants or unarmed civilians in enemy territory, but people "whose mere presence was deemed to threaten the security of the state and the war effort."[5]

Such violence of the state against its own society was first unleashed as part of the state of emergency measure implemented throughout the territory of South Korea, following the beginning of the Korean War on June 25, 1950, and before the war transformed into a full-blown international conflict. Mass arrests and killings took place first in areas that were under the threat of occupation by the advancing communist forces. The South Korean combat police and military police carried out killings in remote valleys or in abandoned mines. The victims were mostly people who had been earmarked before the war as harboring some sort of sympathy toward communism or socialism, and they included prison inmates arrested during the prewar political unrest in parts of South Korea. The decision to eradicate these individuals en masse was on the pretext of a preventive measure, allegedly to stop them from providing support to the enemy. It was also a reaction to North Korea's revolutionary war strategy that combined a frontal assault against South Korea's defense with popular revolutionary uprisings from within enemy territory. It is believed that about 200,000 lives succumbed to this whirlwind of state terror unleashed at the outset of the Korean War, although the exact number of victims remains unknown to date. Such wanton destruction of civilian lives continued throughout the war, later changing in character to punitive violence (committed against alleged collaborators with the enemy forces), once the tide of war changed and the North Korean forces were pushed back. This followed atrocities committed by the retreating communist forces in their briefly occupied zones, against people who they believed were sympathizers with the Southern regime. The violence committed by one side radicalized the intensity and scale of the violence committed by the opposite side, and this vicious cycle of terror perpetrated against the civilian population devastated countless local communities to the extreme.

These waves of violence that came with the changing tides of war involved not only an extreme abuse of the states' coercive powers but also the self-destruction of traditional communities. Villages were turned inside out, becoming a crucible of destruction in the image of the wider theater of war, but in the hands of people who had lived together for generations. In an account by the late Korean writer Park Kyung-li, Ji-young speaks of the situation in her village in September 1950:

The United Nations troops set up tents on the school grounds. Soon, their ration boxes began to flood into the village marketplace. Meanwhile, inside the village, people who had played moles for the past ninety days came out and shouted, "Kill all the reds! Their children and their parents, too! Dry out their seeds!" Then, Ji-young recalled what she had overheard some ninety days ago: "Kill all the reactionaries! Destroy mercilessly the enemies of the people, the puppets of U.S. imperialists!" The village river and hills were speechless in face of these terrifying human voices, the echoes of the blood spilled earlier that return to claim more blood.[6]

In the words of Park Wan-seo, "As the frontline moved back and forth, the order of the world changed as if someone was flipping his hand. Each time the world changed, accusations were made against 'collaborators' or against 'reactionaries'. Then, innocent lives were lost. The villagers underwent this madness repeatedly."[7] Park Chan-sung, a historian who investigated local histories in an island community off the southern coast, describes what he encountered in the islanders' Korean War memories: "These small village wars are not a thing of the past in the affected communities. These wars lasted only two to three months, whereas their shadows are still vigorously alive in these communities sixty years after."[8]

Similar conditions are referred to in the existing literature as the privatization of violence.[9] Stathis Kalyvas investigates, primarily with reference to events during the Greek civil war, what he calls the zone of ambiguity in civil war conflicts – the murky arena in which the violence committed by states or other organized political forces meets with the violence initiated from within local communities. Kalyvas calls the latter a civil war's "intimate violence" to distinguish it from the impersonal violence executed by the coercive forces of the state hierarchy.[10] These two forms of violence – impersonal and intimate – proliferated in the theater of Korea's civil war. They were closely intertwined in local realities and remain sometimes indistinguishable in collective memories. In many testimonial accounts recently made available, it is often impossible to tease out traces of impersonal political violence from those of intimate communal violence. It is also difficult to discover the details of intimate violence in a community where both the victims and the perpetrators of this violence still share the space of communal life today. However, it is clear that these details, rather than necessarily those of impersonal violence, constitute especially vexing memories within the community. In such milieus, people still struggle with the radical disparities between their distant memory of sharing food and child-minding with a neighboring family before the war broke out, on the one hand, and, on the other, the ever-present memory of their neighbor turning his or her back on them at a time when they needed the latter's support most desperately. If that neighbor also happens to be a relative, bitter memories of betrayal are brought back, for instance, at a gathering for ancestral remembrance. On such occasions, the act of making food and alcohol offerings to some ancestral graves becomes a poignant reminder of the family's wartime division and its enduring, unspoken divisiveness – rather than, as tradition has it, a moment of togetherness and rediscovering the comfort of closeness.

In the initial chaos of war, catastrophic conditions also confronted those who joined the exodus to Daegu and elsewhere in the southeastern corner of the peninsula. Steven Lee insists that the reality of the Korean War is unintelligible if it is approached only from the perspective of conventional military history that focuses on the interaction between organized armed groups.[11] In support of this point, Lee explores how the different armed groups of the conflict related to the confused civilian population. He focuses on the assault by the South Korean state against its citizens, the mobilization of civilian labor for the cause of national liberation carried out by the Northern forces in their occupied Southern regions, and the difficulties faced by the US forces in distinguishing allies from foes, and civilians from enemy combatants. Concerning the last, several recent studies convincingly show gross failures on the part of US military commands in the Korean conflict in protecting the unarmed civilian population.[12]

One well-known example in this regard is the tragedy of Nogun-ri near Daejeon, which was en route from Seoul to Daegu. The massacre of war refugees in Nogun-ri was one of the first incidents of civilian killings in the Korean War to become public knowledge in the mid-1990s, which has since attracted wide attention internationally.[13] It resulted in the killing of several hundred refugees over three days and began with a US warplane opening fire on the refugee columns, which forced them to take shelter underneath a nearby railroad bridge. The refugees were cornered by machine-gun fire from a unit of a US cavalry division that had prepared a defense line there against the advancing People's Army forces. After three days of shooting, only ten out of an estimated 400 refugees – mostly children, elders, and women – survived. The investigation carried out by a group of Associated Press journalists found that the incident was not simply the tragic collateral damage of a military action, resulting from

difficulties in distinguishing genuine civilians from enemy fighters infiltrating the rear line disguised as civilians.[14] Instead, the investigation
concluded that the tragedy was the result of a systemic failure in the
military command that blatantly disregarded, in the name of
a condition of emergency and in that of efficacy in a military operation,
the obligation to discriminate unarmed civilians from armed
combatants.[15]

The exodus of war refugees was a widespread phenomenon by the time
the massacre in Nogun-ri took place in July 1950. The widely executed
assaults against refugee groups, most often by aerial actions, made their
movements highly precarious. For this reason, among the most common
episodes that appear in the testimonial histories of the Korean War are
those concerning unintelligible attacks by allied planes against the refugees. This also explains why it soon became general knowledge among the
Korean War refugees that in order to stay alive, it was imperative that they
move during the night and along rugged mountain paths to remain
invisible to American planes, which often meant following the same
routes as those taken by the Northern communist forces. This was indeed
the case in the experience of five students, whose stories I had the privilege
to learn. Consisting of two female high school students and three male
junior high school students, all from the same rural area near Daegu, the
group joined the exodus to the South toward their birthplace on June 27,
1950. They narrowly escaped the strafing against the refugee boats by US
warplanes while crossing the Han River that cuts across Seoul. The
North's expeditionary forces were advancing ahead of them, and following advice from other refugees, the students tracked behind the communist troops along the central mountain ranges, traveling only in the dark.

Close to their home village, along a mountain footpath, the students
were stopped by a group of armed communist partisans. Although the
partisan leader was intent on reeducating the young refugees and recruit-
ing them for the revolutionary war, he let the group of five go free. It
turned out that the leader had recognized one of the students. He spoke to
this student with these words, which she remembers vividly today: "I am
letting you go. Your father is a rightist but I know he is a decent man. You
go home and tell him to be kind to my family back home, just as I am kind
to you now." By the time the five students reached their home village after
eleven days on foot, the area was already under Northern occupation. The
parents of one girl were waiting for their daughter, and on the night she
arrived, they left the village to join their family who had already evacuated
to Daegu. On their way out of the village, they took with them one of the
three boys who, having discovered that no one was at his home, happened
to come to her place in the late evening to ask for news. The other girl also

found her home empty and went to see the village chief the following morning. There she was greeted by members of the village's hastily organized revolutionary women's association. She later joined the village's revolutionary youth organization together with the two other boys in her group from Seoul. When the girl who moved to Daegu returned home a few months later, she heard that the two boys had left the village, heading north shortly after the communist troops had evacuated the area. The villagers had not heard of their whereabouts since. A year later, she was shocked to see a picture of her dear friend, the girl with whom she shared the arduous journey home, on the front page of the local newspaper. The news was about a female student communist mountain guerrilla fighter captured alive, together with three dead male comrades. In the picture, the captured friend looked exhausted and heavily pregnant.

While these refugees were heading to Daegu and elsewhere further south during a time of great hardship, a state of emergency was declared throughout the territory of South Korea. The presidential decree issued on June 28, 1950 ordered the suspension of the judicial procedure for crimes that concerned national security. The decree specified that these crimes were acts that benefited the enemy in terms of material assistance, and of providing information and voluntary assistance to enemy troops and authorities. However, by the time this executive order was endorsed by the country's parliament and subsequently developed into a formal declaration of a state of emergency on July 8, 1950, the country's police and military police forces had already arrested a large number of individuals on charges of potential collaboration with the enemy and executed them without any due court procedure. The mass execution targeted prison inmates classified as "ideological criminals" as well as members of the so-called Alliance of Converts (*bodo yŏnmaeing*), the nationwide state-run organization established in 1949, whose stated objective was to bring the former members of the South Korean Communist Party and other alleged sympathizers of communism to "the right way of patriotism and anticommunism."[16] Many of these ill-fated prison inmates and so-called ideological converts were survivors of South Korea's earlier, prewar state-of-exception politics. These locally confined emergency measures were first implemented by the US Military Government in Korea (from September 1945 to August 1948), which targeted specific areas that experienced outbreaks of popular revolt and armed partisan resistance against the Military Government. The politics of the state of emergency continued after the South Korean government was established on August 15, 1948.

The state of emergency that was declared in 1948 in Yŏsu, amid the crisis of a mutiny in this southern coastal town, ruled: "Individuals who conceal traitors or those who communicate with the latter shall receive the punishment of death." The state of emergency declared in June 1950 was, in form, an extension of this and other earlier measures on a national scale. In its character, however, the June 1950 decree was distinct from the prewar varieties in that it was intended principally to justify preemptive violence, which targeted presumed, hypothetical collaborators ("suspected traitors"), rather than actual crimes of treason.[17] These measures were imbued with a profound historical irony, too. It has been observed that the 1948 constitution of the Republic of Korea (South Korea) had no provision for martial law, which obliged the country's lawmakers, during the political crisis of 1948–1950, to refer back to the Meiji constitution of the colonial era in justifying the state's right to institute a state of emergency.[18] This observation highlights the critical ambiguity in South Korea's constitutional power in this sphere, which was, on the one hand, an extension of the power of the US Military Government in South Korea, and, on the other, a restoration of Japan's imperial constitutional order.[19] As the Korean War developed into an international conflict, involving the intervention of United Nations forces, the rule against collaboration continued to take effect, changing in character from preventive to punitive action. When the territory that had been briefly occupied by the Northern army was recovered by South Korea's national army, the country's police, military intelligence, and paramilitary anti-communist youth groups conducted brutal cleanup actions against individuals who were thought to have assisted the occupying Northern political authorities and military forces. These actions were typically indiscriminate, with the punishment falling not only on the individual suspects, but also on the individuals' families, and sometimes on the entire village community to which the accused individuals belonged.

The behavior of the North Korean occupation forces was overall relatively more restrained during the early days of occupation. This was in part because their war was nominally a revolutionary people's war, the success of which relied heavily on earning the hearts and minds of the local population. The relative calm did not last long, however. When the communist units were forced to retreat northward in September 1950, they committed a number of atrocities including summary civilian killings in their occupied areas.[20] These killings targeted "the civil servants [of South Korea], members of the rightist organizations, and wealthy farmers," and were based on the order issued by North Korea's politburo to remove "all elements that might turn out to be potential supporters of the United Nations forces."[21] As such, they constituted preemptive violence, the same in nature as the violence committed earlier by their Southern adversary. The victims of this preemptive violence included prison inmates in

North Korea's occupied territories and, in some areas, members of local churches. In the city of Daejeon, 150 kilometers south of Seoul, the UN troops discovered that the withdrawing Northern units had left behind a prison compound where the cells were stacked with several layers of corpses. This atrocity was widely reported at the time in both the South Korean domestic press and the international press. One report described the incident: "More than a thousand patriots were brutally murdered by the communist puppets." These reports did not mention, however, that two months prior to this incident, the same prison had been widely mentioned in the North Korean press and in the international press of the Eastern Bloc countries as the site of a major atrocity committed by "the puppets of American imperialists."[22]

In the southwestern region of the peninsula, the advancing South Korean forces met fierce resistance from the remaining North Korean troops and their local recruits, some of whom had by then transformed into partisan groups entrenched in the surrounding hills. In the village of Gurim, at the beginning of October 1950, the communist partisans set fire to the local school and the village's ancestral assembly hall and Protestant church. On October 7, 1950, according to the local annals prepared by the villagers in 2006:

Part of the remaining forces of the [North Korean] People's Army, together with some elements of the communist partisan forces who had operated during the period of the People's Republic [the occupation regime] and who had lost their senses of reason, arrested the remaining families of the [South Korean] army and police, people who had been wrongly accused of being reactionaries under the rule of the People's Republic, and the followers of the Christian god.[23]

The annals continue that the arrested were subsequently locked up in a private home, which was then set on fire, not knowing "what crimes they had committed to deserve such a cruelty."[24] Soon after this incident, on October 17, the village suffered once more. The village annals mention the second massacre only fleetingly. Hence, I quote from a different source, the report of a local history project conducted in the area in 2000–2002:

In Gurim, another civilian massacre was committed, this time by the [South Korean] police, on October 17, 1950. Hearing that the police were closing in on the village, those villagers who had previously worked actively for the People's Republic had already evacuated the village. The police surrounded the settlement and ordered the villagers to come out of their houses. Those who followed this order were people who believed that they had not done anything wrong. As soon as they were out, however, the police fired at them, and this resulted in seventy-eight casualties. The incident is therefore, rather than a punishment against leftist activists, a mass execution of innocent people who were, despite the fact that they

maintained a neutral position during the conflict, accused of being leftist activists. [25]

The memoir of Park Wan-seo speaks of the precarious living conditions
in Seoul at the time of its liberation from the North's occupation. Park's
family failed to evacuate the city before the Northern army took control of
it. This was hardly unusual for residents of Seoul at that time, many of
whom, although feeling confused and uncertain about the future, did not
feel compelled to abandon their homes. [26] In fact, of the city's population,
amounting to a million and half, less than a third joined the exodus to the
South. Of those who did, eight out of ten were refugees who had left their
homes in Northern Korea during the prewar partition period of
1945–1950; that is, people whom the communist forces were likely to
define as harboring hostility to the state. Park's elder brother,
a schoolteacher, had a background in working with progressive intellectuals and leftist groups before the war, which resulted in a host of problems for the family. The activity he was involved in was, according to his
mother, "the business of the red" and a sure sign of a forthcoming
catastrophe for him and for the family. [27] The son's actions met resistance
from his family, particularly from his mother, who moved the family's
residence each time their house became a meeting place for her son's
entourage. Influenced by his mother's insistent protests, Park's brother
eventually abandoned his political activity, found a teaching job in a rural
school, and married. The family later found out that before taking up the
job, he was forced to sign up to the Alliance of Converts to prove that he
had abandoned and renounced communism. Immediately after the
North Korean forces took over the town, her brother was approached
by his old comrades, who urged him to join the revolutionary youth
organization and the patriotic front in support of the People's Army.
Park herself was drawn to a similar initiative organized among her college
friends. Meanwhile, the liquor store of her paternal uncle and aunt was
transformed into a gathering place for North Korean military officers,
where the couple had to prepare meals for their new clients. Park's mother
saw the family's growing incorporation into the politics and economy of
the communist occupation as an ominous sign of a dark future for the
family. She was particularly worried about her son's unstable, deteriorating mental condition, which Park believed was related to his bifurcated
mind – between his obligations to family as the eldest son and his political
commitments as a conscientious intellectual – as well as the shame of
embracing an ideology after having renounced it.
      The liberation of Seoul was not a celebratory event for Park's family,
whose living conditions became even more precarious thereafter. Having

witnessed the roundup of people classified as counterrevolutionaries or supporters of the Southern regime during the early days of the North Korean occupation, this time Park was shocked to hear of the arrest and summary execution of neighbors and other residents, now being branded as *buyŏkja* or "collaborators." Park's paternal uncle and aunt were among those arrested, denounced by one of their neighbors as having fed and entertained the enemy combatants. Park Wan-seo herself endured a humiliating interrogation at the hands of an anti-communist paramilitary group, together with other family members accused of being collaborators. Her brother escaped this round of violence because he had already been conscripted into North Korea's armed forces, and Park struggled to persuade her interrogators that her brother did not volunteer for the enemy's armed forces but was simply forced to join. Park learned through this experience that in the eyes of her interrogators, the residents of Seoul who experienced North Korea's occupation were all collaborators with the communists and "people who offered their labor to the enemy." She realized that the population of the liberated Seoul was divided between the returning refugees and the nonreturnees, depending on whether or not they had evacuated the town before the communist occupation, and that those who failed to leave the city before the occupation were not regarded as proper citizens of the South Korean state and, instead, as disposable elements having no civil or human rights. Hence, she writes, "The life of a 'red' is like the life of an insect; the family of the 'red' has a destiny no better than that of worms."[28] Coming to the understanding that the only possible way to preserve life in the liberated city was to join the struggle against communism, Park Wan-seo took the initiative to seek employment with an anti-communist youth organization as a secretarial clerk. She understood the prevailing logic of violence at the time: if her family as a whole faced the threat of appearing impure to the jealous persecutors as an extension of a family member, whom the latter regarded as a seditious and impure element, the only possibility for the family to shake off this life-threatening appearance and to survive was for someone in the family to join the interiority of anti-communist militancy. Also notable in Park Wan-seo's accounts of vulnerable life in wartime Seoul is the breakdown of communal trust in a state of siege. The summary killing of her uncle was triggered by his neighbor's accusation. Her own arrest by a paramilitary group was also caused by information about her brother provided by her family's long-time neighbor. Park's mother lamented the situation: "How in the heavens' name is this possible? What happened to the food we used to share? Have people forgotten how we, the rich or the poor, had all taken turns to care for our grandchildren?"[29] The general vulnerability of life and the fear of complicity influenced close kinship groups, too. Park introduces the following as one of the most painful episodes of the time. While her aunt and uncle were in jail, Park's mother wished to deliver clothes to them, so she asked a favor of a relative who worked as a prison guard. She was shocked to hear him remark sternly that he wished to have nothing to do with a family that was an enemy of the state.

The distortion of communal relations caused by the politics of retributive violence often took a more radical form in rural communities. It has been observed that the Korean War "permitted two antagonistic state powers to penetrate deep into the communities and thereby played a constitutive role in disintegrating these communities."[30] Indeed, recent studies show how the states' systematic terror against civilians developed into a spiral of tragic intimate violence perpetrated within and between communities in which "the victims of violence turned into the perpetrators of violence and the perpetrators to the victims" – a situation that was repeated following the movement of the frontier.[31] These studies show that in many rural communities, the Korean War is remembered primarily as a village war, as briefly noted earlier, a conflict that took place within the community and between local groupings. Two challenging questions arise from the investigation of the Korean War's intimate violence. One of them concerns the circumstances in which the politics of civil war brought a civil war-like crisis into a village community, and correspondingly, the extent to which the violence waged within a local community was related to locally specific historical conditions. The investigators who raise these questions also find considerable diversity in the experience of communal violence across places and even between physically close communities.

The anthropologist Yun Taik-lim's study based in Yesan, a rural area near the city of Daejeon, for instance, asks why between the two neighboring villages she investigated, retaliatory communal violence erupted only in one particular village, not in the other (see later discussion). Other recent studies raise similar questions as to how social groupings within a community, such as lineage groups, came to experience the war's violence in markedly different ways.[32] Similar observations are made in the recent reports prepared by South Korea's Truth and Reconciliation Commission (see Chapter 6) on its investigation of several dozen incidents of mass civilian killings during the Korean War. The Commission's richly documented reports amply show considerable variance in the patterns of state and communal violence. In a district near Kongju, in the south-central region, for instance, the Commission found that although residents of this area suffered from the preemptive violence perpetrated against alleged communist sympathizers in the early days of the war, the region was fortunate to avoid a subsequent escalation of violence, unlike other nearby places. According to one local villager who provided testimonies to the Truth Commission's investigation team, this was due to the fact that "the retaliation against the Right rarely took place during the time of People's Republic [in our area], so no retaliation against the Left followed after the recovery [of the village by South Korea]."[33] The Commission's investigation also notes a geographical factor in explaining the relative absence of communal violence in this area – that the evacuation of the North Korean troops and their local supporters involved fewer of them turning into locally based partisan resistance groups, unlike in other places in wartime South Korea, as the region lacks wooded mountains and hills that could shelter partisan insurgents.[34]

The diversity of war experience is observed not only between regions but also within the same locale and even within the same village community. Notable in this respect is Yun's accounts of a village in the Yesan district mentioned earlier. The village was the birthplace of several locally prominent intellectuals, who assumed leadership roles in the wider region's radical social reform movement and political organizational activities during the early postcolonial years. Due to this legacy, the village earned, during the war and afterward, the designation of "Yesan's Moscow" or "another Moscow" among the locals (see Chapter 3).[35] Although the village as a whole was viewed by outsiders as a hotbed of radical politics, relations were more complicated within the village, which consisted of two residential clusters, Gamgol and Bamgol. Even before the outbreak of the war, according to Yun, conflicts were intense in Bamgol. The hamlet was divided between the returning former veterans and labor conscripts of Japan's imperial army from various parts of the Pacific War theater and, on the other, a village notable and his supporters. The latter played a role in conscripting the village youths into Japan's war ventures, so the returning veterans had legitimate grudges against the man and his entourage, who continued to exert influence in village affairs after the end of Japan's colonial occupation of Korea in 1945. By the time the Korean War broke out in 1950, animosity between these two groups of villagers was magnified and took on, according to Yun, "the façade of a left versus right ideological struggle."[36] What Yun means by this remark is, from my understanding, that the polarization of village politics, according to the terms of the Cold War, was partly rooted in the colonial-era conflicts between the collaborators with colonial politics and the victims of these politics. These intra-communal conflicts were less prominent in the village's other settlement of Gamgol, however, according to Yun, who associates this community's relative peace in 1945–1950 with strong leadership within the hamlet provided by two prominent anticolonial activists and radical intellectuals.[37] These two men enjoyed great moral authority in Gamgol, not only due to their anti-colonial credentials, but also because they were from families that had long enjoyed prominence within the settlement.

These two settlements reacted to North Korea's occupation politics quite differently. Gamgol was incorporated into the revolutionary administration swiftly and relatively peacefully, and some of its residents were recruited for important positions in the village and district-level war administrations of the occupation power. In Bamgol, by contrast, the occupation generated a tumultuous local situation. The villagers who were classified by the occupation authority as counterrevolutionaries had to run for their lives, and their properties were confiscated. Those who failed to escape were put before a panel of summary justice, called the People's Court, and five of them were subsequently beaten to death. Yun observes that this violent episode at the outset of the occupation later led to vicious retaliatory violence against the villagers who had participated in the People's Court, when the North Korean forces left the area, and the people who had escaped the occupation returned to the village triumphantly in advance of the South Korean government forces. This time, the villagers who had taken part in the local administration during the occupation were forced to evacuate the area. People who failed to do so were executed, and their properties were taken by villagers who claimed to be anti-communist patriots. These lethal actions extended to the families of the accused individuals. Although both settlements suffered retributive violence during this time, Bamgol's experience was far more destructive than Gamgol's. In Gamgol, acts of retribution were mainly conducted by the South Korean military forces. In contrast, residents of Bamgol were persecuted not only by the military but also by vengeful villagers who had suffered under North Korean occupation. The latter is remembered by the villagers as the most painful episode of the war, according to Yun, and it continues to haunt village life to this day.[38] A village elder in Gamgol said:

We did not know who was right at that time, whether the Left was right or whether the Right was right. It was only after the war was over that we were taught that communism was wrong ... Both the Right and the Left were wrong. Each side claimed that only their side was right. Looking back, it occurs to me that both sides were wrong. They both were wrong in what they had done to us.[39]

When the UN forces crossed the 38th parallel, the prewar frontier that partitioned Korea into two separate states, and charged through the territory of North Korea, it is reported that the troops found numerous traces of mass killings. The withdrawing North Korean political and military authorities continued their violence against civilians on the grounds of guilt by suspicion, but this time against their own citizens whom they suspected might collaborate with the Southern forces. In certain areas, the violence specifically targeted members of local church groups.[40] When the northward advance of the UN troops was halted by the Chinese and North Korean forces along North Korea's border with China, which then began to roll back the UN forces from the territory of North Korea and further back to the central region of South Korea, a new whirlwind of violence was unleashed.

China's military intervention in the Korean conflict is a subject of intense investigation among historians of the Korean War today, together with the US decision to cross the 38th parallel, which triggered the intervention. China's involvement changed the character of the Korean War from principally a civil war with elements of an international war to a full-blown international war with a diminishing dimension of civil war. Militarily, it altered the form of the Korean War from a chaotic mobile-territorial war in the second half of 1950 to stagnant trench warfare and hill fighting along the 38th parallel that would last two more years. However, the radically changing conditions of the Korean War at the end of 1950 politically and militarily meant, in terms of social experiences, a return of the chaos of July 1950. During the retreat of the UN forces in the early months of 1951, numerous civilians in the central region of South Korea succumbed to a revived storm of preemptive violence, and these included people who had survived the earlier storm of political violence. It is known that communities in North Korea were also affected by this wave of violence, although details are yet to emerge.[41] A number of rural communities in the environs of Seoul, including those on the island of Kanghwa and in the district of Koyang, were almost completely destroyed during this time by the indiscriminate violence of summary killings committed by South Korea's combat police troops and paramilitary youth groups. In Koyang, local paramilitary groups arrested villagers suspected of having assisted the North Korean occupying forces, executed them en masse on a hill, and threw their bodies into an abandoned colonial gold mine. The paramilitary groups in Kanghwa gathered the islanders who they had previously earmarked as collaborators and conducted a series of executions along the seashore.

In both cases, violence often fell upon the family members of the accused individuals according to the scheme that the locals remember as *daesal*, "substitutive killing."[42] The gruesome logic of substitutive killing was that someone in the family had to take the place of the suspected collaborator if the latter was not available, so that the number of targets in the prepared list of suspects should be identical to the number of people executed. For instance, in January 1951 on the island of Kanghwa, close to the 38th parallel, paramilitary violence against suspected communist collaborators fell heavily on the families of people whom the perpetrators believed had escaped to the northern part of Korea. The casualties of this "substitutive killing" make up nearly half of the Kanghwa victims.[43] Substitutive killings were widely practiced in other parts of wartime Korea, and the ruthlessness of this violence left particularly deep scars among the survivors. This is evident in the prison diary of Lee Won-sik, a practitioner of traditional herbal medicine who played a pivotal role in organizing the bereaved families' rally in Daegu in July 1960. Lee received a death sentence in 1961 in a military court, charged with an alleged seditious activity "to characterize leftist elements [victims of massacres] as patriotic individuals," "to create and assist an anti-state organization [of bereaved families]," and thereby, "to benefit North Korea."[44] He had joined the bereaved families' association in his capacity as the spouse of a victim of state violence – his wife had succumbed to substitutive killing in August 1950 in the vicinity of Daegu while Lee was away from home. Lee Won-sik's prison diaries, kept by his son, abound with his remorseful feelings toward his wife, his regrets over failing to do justice to her innocence, which he knew better than anyone else, and his disbelief over "how I became a prisoner condemned to death because of my love for you who died without a grave." Lee was found "not guilty" posthumously in a hearing at a district court in Seoul on June 25, 2010. The verdict was later sealed, following the rejection of the prosecutor's appeal, at a hearing in the country's Supreme Court on May 25, 2011. Although a similar reinstatement is yet to be extended to Lee's wife, their children believe that the court decision helped to bring about a closure to the family's long-held grievances. Shortly after the 2011 verdict, the family held an annual death-anniversary rite for their parents. While Lee's son was standing up after making a closing bow to the ancestral tablet, his sister urged him, in a hurried voice, to take a look at the table of food offerings. Doing so, he marveled at the scene as the two spoons, each of which he had inserted into the separate bowls of cooked rice meant for his mother and father, were slowly beginning to incline toward each other. The movement stopped when the tips of the handles touched.

Impossible Citizenship

The Korean War's terror against civilians changed in terms of its perpetrators as well as in its character, from preventive to punitive violence and back to the former. As the frontier of the war moved, first to the southern reach of the peninsula and then to Korea's northern border with China and then again southward, new waves of organized terror were unleashed against civilians. Each side in the war defined their action as an act of liberation. From the perspective of the local community, however, each act of liberation was hardly a liberating and joyous event, but one that generated an extremely precarious situation. Families who had lost their loved ones to the "white terror" were coerced into the propagation of the subsequent "red terror" and vice versa. Communal relations were distorted and strained to breaking point with the imposition of the binary order of "families of patriotic individuals" versus "red families" (by the Southern authority), or "democratic families" versus "counterrevolutionary families" (by the Northern authority). The war's changing tides of violence induced the civilian population, caught in the cross fire, into an impossible position of having to survive in between the two ideologically opposing yet structurally identical forces that commonly hammered society with a zero-sum logic. Each side in the war defined the other as an illegitimate authority and as an "antinational grouping," thereby making any act of accepting or even acknowledging the authority a crime against the national community. North Korea's postcolonial state authority initiated the war, among other reasons, primarily on the basis of the belief that only it had the mandate to represent the entire nation, and the same idea governed the leaders of the South Korean state before and during the war. As a civil war, the Korean War was a conflict waged between two nascent postcolonial national states that hoped to become a singular nation-state worthy of the name by negating the competing state's claim to sovereignty through violent means. As a global conflict that was waged in the form of a civil war, it was fought between two opposing international forces, whose mutual ideological negation was brought to bear in the form of an armed conflict in Korea. In the arena of the war's violence against civilians, the global dimension of mutual ideological negation and the national dimension of exclusive sovereignty formed a lethal fusion, turning it into an unimaginably uncivil conflict, tearing apart the moral fabric of numerous traditional communities.

For those people who survived the waves of impersonal and intimate violence that came with the changing tides of the war, the preservation of life often meant radical displacement from home (see Chapter 2). The result was, when the war was over, a widespread dispersal of family and kin across the bipolar political border, which remains to this day one of the most enduring human legacies of the Korean War.[45] The mass exodus of war refugees southward to escape the communist occupation became frequent images in the international reportage of the Korean War. Popular songs in postwar South Korea feature the sorrow of witnessing loved ones in the columns of prisoners being forcibly marched to the North, or of having to part with their family during the evacuation of residents in North Korea to the southern regions.

Episodes of wartime family separation continued to be a main theme in the art, music, and literature of postwar South Korea. Most of these episodes are related to escaping from communist occupation or rule. When they are about human displacement in the opposite direction, the drama of separation is typically featured as one of coercion, such as in the above song about prisoners on the forced northward march. In reality, however, the Korean War's human displacement took place prolifically in both directions. The move to the South was not always "in search of freedom"; many residents of North Korea who fled to the South did so not necessarily from fear of communism, but principally from fear of the United States' massive aerial bombardment campaigns, including the threat of thermonuclear destruction – a threat that remained real from the early days of the Korean War.[46] As for people who joined the exodus to the North, they were not always coerced by the Northern communists but often conditioned by fear of retributive violence by the opposite side. The Korean War's human displacement and family separations were products of the reciprocal actions committed by both parties in the conflict to contain the civilian population away from the influence of the enemy side through violent means. Within the ideologically charged, mass-mobilized civil war, control of the civilian population was not a secondary issue to military action but rather constituted the main objective and instrument of war. Ideological purity was the necessary property for the preservation of life in this milieu; for the civilians, it was impossible to attain such purity within the war's chaotic, shifting frontiers.

Against this historical background of generalized terror and assault against civilian lives and communal moral order, kinship relations in postwar Korea rarely constitute a discrete, genealogically unbroken, or politically homogeneous entity. This is amply demonstrated in the biographical and literary accounts of the Korean War in South Korea, which typically depict the reality of war in terms of an acute domestic and communal crisis. The choice of political positioning that individuals and groups made during the war was sometimes voluntary, based on moral and ideological commitments, but it was much more often one of coercion, imposed on the family and the community by forces beyond their control or comprehension. The politics of civil war brought a radical crisis into the moral community of kinship and the traditional village community; yet, existing kin- or place-based solidarities were also made into instruments of war, as we will see in the following chapters, mobilized to collective political actions in the service of the business of war-making. The violence of war left scars in local communities not merely in terms of the brutality of violence but also because of the forms it took; in particular, the measures of collective punishment it enforced upon the communal world, in which the community as a whole was to take responsibility for an individual action believed to benefit the enemy. Death and separation were common in the dynamic theater of a mass-mobilized total war with prolific foreign interventions, and these included the death events of close relatives, whose stories remain a taboo subject within the family and the local community because they involved the actions of neighbors or relatives as the immediate cause. How to remember these deaths and to account for their histories is, therefore, not a simple question, and this has been one of the most challenging questions for the moral survival of a community in the postwar era. Many separated families and families with missing persons from the war continued to face a testing time even after the war ended. They lived with the risk of being considered politically impure groups within society, due to the possibility (or the reality) of being related to someone who had moved to the opposite side of the bipolar border. Whether people crossed the border voluntarily or against their will mattered a great deal, and many postwar families took the view that their relative's move had been purely one of coercion. In actuality, people's "voluntary" crossings were typically coerced moves, made in fear of the retributive violence against their lives, as we will see in the next chapter, and often in the hope that their departure might help their remaining family members escape from the violence.

The grassroots experience of the Korean War was, therefore, primarily about an extreme existential crisis in intimate social relations. The crisis took a number of concrete forms: the burden of collective culpability, and the division and dispersion of families and local communities into separate political paths and state entities. Yet, these diverse forms were all related to a single most important issue in the lived social reality of Korea's civil war: "the impossibility of performing the business of citizenship in this land," as one historian wrote in his wartime diary on September 23, 1950, while living in Seoul under North Korean military occupation and when the city was about to be recovered by South Korean and US forces.[47] The history of the Korean War, in this sphere, is also about what ordinary people, such as the author of this diary, did to survive the war and how they set out to take on the impossible task of performing citizenship under the two states that vehemently negated each other's *raison d'être*. These people struggled to carve and recarve niches of innocence in the war's turbulent, changing waves of violence and shifting loyalty claims that systematically destroyed the spaces of physical and moral survival. Each time the front line changed and the identity of the occupying (or liberating) forces changed accordingly, the very possibility of moral innocence was under threat, as the new liberators viewed the community they had just liberated with extreme suspicion, as being collectively culpable for having colluded with the enemy. They questioned how the community could have otherwise survived the enemy's occupation. For the author of the diary, the question was not merely about what he had done during the occupation, such as changing the national flag of South Korea to that of North Korea on the flagpole on the door of his family home or having to attend public meetings in order to avoid the risk of being labeled reactionary. Rather, it concerned his entire bodily being and his entire relational world of family, relatives, friends, colleagues, and neighbors. Under North Korean occupation, he felt that his family in Seoul and his father and other relatives living down in a Southern region became the subjects of different states. After South Korean troops recovered Seoul, he discovered that the townspeople became tainted and impure as a whole: having breathed the air of North Korea's People's Republic, they were unfit for life in the Southern republic.[48] Everyone was deemed guilty, he recognized, and the only way to assert innocence seemed to be by joining the machinery of accusation. Even in this extremely precarious condition of a radicalized zero-sum logic of civil war threatening to overwhelm the possibility of personal and communal survival, the villagers and townspeople of wartime Korea set out to find ingenious pathways and niches of survival, and to confront the war's consuming ideology and physical force in remarkably inventive ways. Very often, the road toward physical and moral survival was paved on the basis of existing communal ties.

The Right to Be Related

Many did find small alleyways of survival and helped one another along the way; others were less fortunate and joined the yet unrecorded list of numerous nameless victims of one of the most brutal wars of the twentieth century in Asia. Across the widely variable spectrum in the structure and agency of survival, however, the experience of the Korean War had a single common consequence for a great number of Koreans in the war generation. Histories of survival typically involved coping and living with the claims and demands made by two political forces that vehemently negated each other's moral grounds. Histories of nonsurvival were mostly related to the same difficult existential conditions, only with added elements of higher structural rigidity within the given structure of enmity and of disempowered agency for survival coerced by that structure. Both streams of history were closely intertwined in their unfolding, and they both involved painful episodes of separation in familial and communal lives. Many histories of survival include the displacement from home of family members whose presence at home threatened the survival of the family as a whole; the life histories of individuals who did not survive the war often have an unspoken dimension within the surviving family, in which the family, during and after the war, strove to sever its ties to those individuals whose historical and genealogical presence threatened the family's collective survival. The history of survival also involves, as shown by the family gathering in 1960 at Daegu railway station, the long and arduous efforts of families in the postwar years to reinstate the status of their dead relatives to that of innocent victims of war and state violence, away from the dark zone of the law of the lawless war, according to which the dead were neither enemy combatants nor innocent civilian victims. Family and kinship ties were, therefore, an important site of a struggle for life in the theater of Korea's civil war, and this struggle continued, for many, long after the guns went silent.

Before the assembly at Daegu railway station in July 1960, some family representatives joined a public hearing in the presence of the commander of the provincial military forces, from whom they hoped to solicit permission to hold their memorial gathering. In this meeting, the commander argued that he would not consider the assembly to be about *yangmin* ("innocent civilians"), pointing specifically to the family of Mr. Shin, one of the organizers of the railway gathering, to prove his point. Mr. Shin's son had joined the Alliance of Converts before he was killed in July 1950, the commander said, and his younger brother later escaped to the North during the war. These actions made it impossible, according to him, to consider Mr. Shin's family as one of innocent civilian victims of war and, therefore, the activities of the assembly of the bereaved families that Mr. Shin was part of as innocent activities.[49] In response, the family representatives argued that the military commander's distinction between innocent civilians and noninnocent civilians was purely of his own imagination. The intention of their assembly was instead, they said, to achieve the right to commemorate the dead. In order to do so, it was necessary to find out the date of their death and to recover their scattered remains.[50] They also demanded "resolving complications in family records" and "an end to the police surveillance of bereaved families" based on these records – that is, an end to the practice of associative guilt and collective culpability (see Chapter 4).[51] The newspaper column that reported the July 1960 meeting said that the deafening lamentation of women in white clothes dwarfed the ear-piercing whistles of a steam-powered locomotive that day. For those who took part in the collective lamentation, the day is remembered as a rare liberating experience, when they were free from the fear – the fear that a family's act to remember the dead may make the family as a whole an outcast from political society as an extension of the dead. The distant echo of their voices still rings true today, and the confrontation between the ethics of commemoration and the politics of sovereignty is not over yet, two generations after the war ended. The same is true of disputes over what constitutes innocent death in the ruins of that old yet unfinished war.

2   Bad Gemeinschaft

On a gentle hillside in the southwest of Jeju Island, a local cemetery in Sangmo Village has a unique name and history. The history of this cemetery relates closely to the assembly of families in Daegu in July 1960 that we saw in the previous chapter. After the meeting at the railway station, these families joined efforts to open the suspected sites of mass killings and burials hidden in the town's suburban hill areas. The results of this work are now traceless. One mass grave that they had started opening in the fall of 1960 was closed down in the summer of 1961 – by the order of the military leaders immediately after they took power following a coup in May 1961. The place is part of a valley south of Daegu, known as the site of one of the largest-scale killings of civilians of the Korean War and is now submerged underneath a reservoir. Another site disappeared during the construction boom of the 1980s, now buried beneath a block of high-rise residential apartments. Ironically, this place is a stone's throw from the city's prominent memorial dedicated to fallen soldiers of the Korean War. Only one site remains more or less intact today, in part thanks to the fact that it was left untouched in 1960. This place is an old colonial-era cobalt mine in the east of Daegu, where more than 3,000 prison inmates and suspected leftists are believed to have been executed in July 1950 and their bodies dumped. The old mine has emerged in recent years as a focal point of disputes among family groups, property developers, and local authorities. The cemetery in Jeju is unique in that it has survived the turbulent postwar years of political repression and subsequent public oblivion, unlike numerous other Korean War mass graves in Daegu and elsewhere in mainland South Korea. Therefore, it offers rare glimpses into the tumultuous postwar political life of people who are related to victims of the Korean War's state violence.

The cemetery in Sangmo-ri overlooks the Pacific Ocean and, in the back, is surrounded by extensive fields of reed that abound on this beautiful island near Korea's southern maritime border. It consists of a large stone-walled compound where tens of dozens of modest mound-shaped, well-tended graves lie in a neat order. Visitors to this cemetery can easily recognize that the place is not an ordinary burial ground. The cemetery is different from the traditional hillside family ancestral graveyards familiar to the mainland Koreans, or from the stone-fenced individual and family tombs typical of the Jeju islanders' burial tradition. There are simply too many graves concentrated in one place in this cemetery to be deemed a family graveyard. Moreover, none of them are marked by a gravestone or stone tablet where the visiting family can place food and alcohol offerings to the dead, according to their traditional custom of tomb visit and death commemoration. The graves in this place are nameless; they stand in a strangely ordered fashion along tidily organized lines – an organization that one would expect to encounter in a military cemetery, such as the national cemeteries on the mainland or the many smaller district-based cemeteries for fallen police personnel scattered around the island, but not in a village graveyard.

The locals call the Sangmo-ri cemetery "Graves of One Hundred Ancestors and One Single Descendant." A dark granite memorial stands at the center of the compound, on the top of which is engraved an image of South Korea's national flag. The image is confusing, again making the place resemble a military cemetery. The cemetery's name is also unfamiliar, going against the conventional idea of genealogical continuity and prosperity emphasized in Korea's traditional mortuary and commemorative culture. In ordinary circumstances, as in other places where the aesthetics of genealogical continuity take on great cultural significance, this continuity should be expressed in the opposite order, using the language of reproductive prosperity and family expansion from one ancestor to many descendants.[1] Neither does the name correspond to the forms of family genealogical order familiar in anthropological research. This usually takes the shape of a pyramid, with a single apical ancestral figure on the top, followed by increasingly numerous members of the genealogical group in descending lines. How is it that only a single descendant survives from the historical community of a hundred ancestors? What happened in this community's past history that its order of descent has fallen to the anomalous situation of minimal existence today?

One Hundred Ancestors

The cemetery contains objects that, upon closer examination, begin to offer clues to some of these questions. Near the shining granite memorial stone is kept a glass vessel that contains some broken remains of what originally appears to have been a sizable tombstone. These stone fragments are from the original ancestral memorial erected in 1960, according to the annals prepared by a local scholar,[2] and they were unearthed from scrubland near the cemetery a few years after the current memorial stone was erected in 1993. The annals explain that in June 1961, the families who had prepared the original memorial stone were summoned by the district's police chief, who ordered them to remove the stone. When the families protested against the order, the police sent a convoy of officers and hired laborers to take down the stone.[3] The police also intended to obliterate the gravesite and ordered the families to unearth the remains from the graves and then to cremate them. Several families felt threatened and removed the coffins of their relatives from the gravesite. Others went on to protest against the order. They contested that the police order was a blatant violation of customary laws, which prohibited the act of opening someone's grave without obtaining consent from the entombed person's close kinsmen (and also from the spirit of the dead through an appropriate rite). The district police chief argued that the removal order had come from the highest state authority, saying also that the construction of the cemetery and the memorial stone violated state law, posing threats to public security.[4]

For many years after this incident in 1961, the police forces in the environs of Sangmo-ri were given a distinct, disreputable identity by local islanders – as the desecrators of family ancestral graves. Confrontations between public authorities and families on the question of burial were not unusual at the time. Elsewhere in Korea, such as in Daegu as well as in Ulsan and Geochang, other localities that suffered large-scale civilian killings during the Korean War, the assemblies of bereaved families were judged by military tribunals to be "pro-communist organizations benefiting the enemy."[5] The incident in Jeju took place during a critical transitional period for postwar South Korea, when its political order changed from the previous autocratic anti-communist regime headed by the Princeton-educated president, Syngman Rhee, to an administratively more effective anti-communist political order led by a group of military elite in the subsequent decades. The transition between these two forms of authoritarian politics was initially made possible by the student-led mass uprisings in April 1960, which helped bring down Rhee.[6] The uprisings subsequently paved the way for a short-lived period of democratic rule before it was toppled by a military coup in May 1961. The destruction of the family graveyards, such as the incident in southern Jeju and those on the outskirts of Daegu, occurred during South Korea's postwar transition from civilian to military-led rule, and it targeted places that arose locally during the short-lived democratic rule or in the last years of Rhee, when the government's anti-communist drive became relatively more moderate compared to the immediate postwar years. This brief period was the first time since the end of the Korean War in 1953, according to a former member of the Korean War bereaved family group in Daegu, that he was able "to freely lament over the dead" and "to say in public that my parents were not communists."[7] The assault against family graveyards and other related local sites of memory was, in fact, one of the first major policy directives, among other disciplinary actions against society, taken by the military coup leaders as part of their drive for what some observers call the "politicization of national security."[8] The Jeju police chief understood the urgency and gravity of these actions when he ordered the removal of the gravesite, and when he argued that the existence of these sites of memory was not a private matter for families but constituted a question of state and national security. The coup leaders declared a new constitutional order for South Korea founded on the principle of anti-communism; this order was manifested first in the culture of commemoration – just as local grievances against the consequences of radically militant anti-communism during the war had been expressed using this cultural form.[9]

The Sangmo-ri ancestral memorial stone was dedicated to the victims of a tragic incident that had taken place on the island immediately after the Korean War broke out on June 25, 1950. In this incident, the provincial police and military forces arrested several hundred islanders and executed them en masse in several remote highland areas on Jeju and elsewhere on the island. Numerous similar orders were carried out elsewhere on mainland South Korea, as we saw in the previous chapter, while the country's military forces were failing to stop the advance of the North Korean invasion, and its government was forced to hastily relocate southward, having abandoned Seoul, the country's capital. These atrocious actions targeted people whom the administration had earmarked before the war as harboring sympathy for communism or having a history of doing so. The killings also targeted the inmates held in state prisons – the so-called ideological prisoners – who were being held in custody on charges of political crimes relating to the earlier prewar social unrest and political conflicts of postcolonial Korea (after Korea's liberation from Japan's colonial rule in August 1945 at the end of the Pacific War) and the subsequent division of the nation between the Soviet-occupied North and the US-occupied South. The author of the annals of the Sangmo-ri cemetery, Lee Do-young, clearly understood the connectedness of these incidents. Being a native of Jeju, Lee's father was in the Daejeon prison in the central part of mainland South Korea at the outbreak of the Korean War. He was killed, together with other prison inmates on July 5, 1950, on a hill on the outskirts of Daejeon. Among the notable events of South Korea's prewar political crisis was the popular uprising in Jeju in 1948 against US military rule of South Korea (1945–1948), and especially against the Military Government's attempt to establish a separate anti-communist state in the southern half of Korea. The uprising is commonly referred to as "the incident" by the locals, similar to what the Taiwanese call the violence committed by the Kuomintang forces in 1948 or how the Columbians remember their long era of state terror.[10] The uprising quickly invited devastating counterinsurgency actions by the nascent South Korean military, police, and paramilitary forces under US military authority, claiming numerous lives (see Chapter 6). Many of the prison inmates held in mainland Korea at the dawn of the Korean War were, in fact, Jeju islanders captured and incarcerated during "the incident." People interred in the Sangmo-ri cemetery were survivors of the earlier wave of violence that hit the island in 1948–1949.

After the killings in July 1950, the sites of massacres became no-go zones. During the war and for a period after the war ended in July 1953, although exceptions did exist, the families of victims were forbidden from approaching these sites and were unable to identify and recover the bodies of their relatives from the shallow mass graves. The postwar South Korean state authority considered the bodies in these mass graves to be the bodies of traitors, and even those of nonbeings that are less than human, and, by extension, the act of touching them (especially for the purpose of giving burial to them) as an act of treason. Despite these draconian measures, a number of families risked recovering the bodies of their relatives, which was often done through a wider communal effort involving several bereaved families and their kindred.[11] These included some of the families who later took part in building the Sangmo-ri cemetery. It was several years after the end of the war, in 1956, that these families cautiously approached the provincial military authority for permission to open the mass grave. When they finally opened the grave, in a valley where an old munitions depot of the Japanese colonial army had existed before 1945, the corpses had decomposed and the families found it nearly impossible to identify the remains they had unearthed. The families then joined forces to separate the tangled remains and to put them back together, according to a village elder who participated in the excavation, in the hope of helping the dead have a "minimal human shape with a head, two arms and two legs."[12] This communal initiative resulted in approximately 100 more or less complete skeletons. The bereaved families then jointly prepared a communal ground for 132 graves (the rest were taken to other existing family-based graveyards), buried the remains separately in these nameless graves, and gave the collection of graves the name, "One Hundred

Ancestors and One Single Descendant." Several years later, the families once again joined forces to erect a memorial stone, which became the original stone that is kept today in the glass container in broken pieces.

War and Democracy

Observers of Korea's modern history commonly point out the early 1960s and the 1980s as the thresholds of South Korea's political development. It is observed that in each of these times, South Korean society took an important step toward a participatory political democracy against many odds – through the student protest of April 1960 against the autocratic postwar political rule and, then, the popular uprisings in May 1980 and in June 1987 against the decades-long military rule. There is no doubt that these events constituted a historic momentum for the growth of public political consciousness and the maturation of civil society in the country. Bruce Cumings's seminal work on the origins of the Korean War adds yet another era to the genealogy of political democracy in Korea – the immediate postcolonial period of 1945–1946, when Korea experienced an outburst of forceful popular aspiration and mobilization for democratic self-rule and economic justice throughout the country.[13] This brief period marked a transition from the colonial rule of 1910–1945; it was also conditioned by the growing entrenchment of Cold War politics following the partition of the peninsula into the Soviet-occupied North and the US-controlled South. The time is crowded with critical questions of decolonization and the Cold War, a subject that has been discussed prolifically in recent Cold War historical scholarship. An understanding of the texture of this era has also been the subject of intense debate by historians of the Korean War. In South Korea's historical scholarship, the time is referred to as "the liberation space" (*haebang gongkan*), the subject of long-running debates on complications caused in the process of decolonization by the bipolarization of global politics. These debates typically involve controversies over the character of American power in the early Cold War; in particular, how it shifted from being a member of the anti-Axis alliance to a leading anti-Soviet, anti-communist power with the end of the Second World War, and what this change meant for the process of decolonization in Korea and in northeast and southeast Asia more broadly. Cumings reflects on these questions with reference to the idea of parallax visions.[14] The parallax effects are an important concept in astrophysics. They refer to the phenomenon that the formation of stars in the night sky appears to change over the seasons, which is due to the shifting positions of the earthbound observer and not to any actual changes in the objects in view. Drawing upon this idea of a cosmological parallax, Cumings explains the change in the US approach to Asian politics passing the threshold of 1945, in terms of a geopolitical parallax, from a moral alliance with nationalist forces in the region to an increasingly hostile position toward the latter's claims; that is, it was primarily as a result of the shift in the United States' own positioning rather than a substantive change in the course of Asia's postcolonial politics.

This parallax shift had far-reaching consequences in social as well as geopolitical terrains. In the transition from the end of colonial rule in 1945 to the establishment of two separate states in 1948, the United States came to see the indigenous social mobilizing efforts in the southern half of Korea under its control through the prism of its broader containment politics against the Soviet power – that is, increasingly as a menacing left-leaning development that was beneficial to the Soviets. The social mobilization in the southern part of Korea in 1946–1947 had a strong bottom-up character; political assemblies were taking place at the local county level and even in villages. The American intervention in this situation, with a policy set to crush the widespread locally-grounded indigenous political activism, was close to a declaration of war against the postcolonial society. The worst part of the US Military Government's occupation politics at the time was its decision to revive the coercive mechanisms of the past, especially the structure of the colonial-era police forces, which generated waves of shock and disillusionment across communities. This measure was principally responsible for the escalation of tensions, such as those in Jeju leading up to the crisis of 1948.

The events in the late 1980s were a success story, as the civil protest of the time ultimately paved the way for the thriving political democracy that we see in South Korea today, whereas those in the early 1960s and in the late 1940s were not. The popular mobilization of 1945–1946 was thwarted by the onset of the early Cold War, within which the US military authority in southern Korea came to increasingly identify these mobilization efforts as communist-driven social forces and, subsequently, set out to suppress them, first using its own coercive might and later by bringing in the services of native police forces and paramilitary organizations. The student-led uprising of 1960 broke the will of the postwar authoritarian regime, only to be replaced shortly afterward by stronger military-led anti-communist authoritarian politics.[15]

It is interesting to note that in each of the two great momentums toward political democracy in the postwar era, in the early 1960s and at the end of the 1980s, there was an eruption of public interest in the hidden history of the Korean War. Examples from the beginning of the 1960s were illustrated earlier. The decade of the 1990s witnessed an explosive "flooding of memories" of the Korean War (see Chapter 6). The stories that emerged in this milieu typically focus on the societal realities of the Korean War, seen from the perspective of a displaced family or a rural community or urban neighborhood under siege: as a conflict between siblings who stumble on opposing political paths or as violent struggles between neighboring settlements or even between different family groups. Noticeable in this development is the emergence of family and community relations as a principal subject of war experience.

This new focus is, without doubt, partly in critical reaction to the public narrative of war that prevailed during the earlier postwar eras in which communities' memories and voices were silenced. We may understand the situation with reference to George Mosse's critique of the sublimation of the falsely homogenized, collective experience of war – what he calls "the myth of the war experience."[16] Since myth-making in this context is designed "to mask war" and "to displace the reality of war,"[17] it is understandable that critical reactions against the rendering of war experiences as those of national society should involve efforts to recover individual experiences. In this light, Christine Sylvester advocates placing the human individual and the human body at the center of critical war studies.[18] Others argue that thinking of war on a personal level is a "whole different realm of thinking than considering war as something that is between states."[19] This rising interest in the individual's experience and memory of war is part of the broader effort to clarify the places and textures of individual and collective memory in political analysis.[20] The idea of the individual experience of war as an analytical category, understood as distinct from "the myth of war experience," is particularly prominent in the sociocultural history of the First World War, in part because the power of myth-making in this sphere was particularly forceful during the interwar era, especially in Weimar Germany, although not exclusively. The idea was put into practice with powerful results in many literary works on the trench war; notably, in Erich Maria Remarque's 1929 novel, *All Quiet on the Western Front*. It continues to be meaningful today, as demonstrated by the scholarship of *culture de guerre*, which advances a powerful account of the aftermath of the Great War based on careful micro-historical attention to the multitude of individual works of grieving.[21]

Drawing upon these orientations, Christopher Goscha and Vatthana Pholsena note that the idea of war as experience, while increasingly prominent in the social and cultural studies of modern warfare in the context of Europe, has not yet found its proper place in the scholarship of Asian wars.[22] They point out that the study of war as "reflections on societies at war and the combatant's experience of battlefield violence" has much to offer to the advancement of war studies in the modern Asian context. In this regard, they take note of a recent encouraging development in the scholarship of the Indochina Wars. Edward Miller and Trung Vu also note a recent paradigmatic shift in Vietnam War studies.[23] With the end of the Cold War, it has been increasingly possible for students of the Vietnam War to consider Vietnam's perspective of the war, using the sources available within the country. This has contributed to partially moving away from the previously predominant mode of narrating the war based primarily on sources held in US archives. The end of the Cold War has also enabled empirical access to the Vietnamese socio-historical milieu and, thus, facilitated an investigation of the legacies and memories of the Vietnam War in Vietnam. Several noteworthy intimate accounts of war have been made available in Vietnam. Although these accounts often take the form of fiction, these personal testimonies to the brutality of war by former Vietnamese veterans of the Vietnam War, such as Bao Ninh's *The Sorrows of War*, come quite close to what Goscha and Pholsena had in mind when invoking the idea of war experience.[24] Other recent works explore the experience of the Vietnam War from the perspective of those who lost the war (former veterans of South Vietnam) as well as from those civilians who were seized under cross fire.[25]

Some cautions are due, however, in extending the idea of war experience from the context of the Great War, which had a relatively clear demarcation between the battlefield and the home front, to the chaotic reality of total civil war such as the Vietnam War or the Korean War, in which such demarcations were much less evident. The experience of war in such divisive realities had aspects that run counter to what a "mythical" rhetoric of collective experience can deliver. However, it also had dimensions that cannot be properly understood if the idea of war experience is narrowly focused on the individual subject. In this context, experience can be a deeply social phenomenon in which the personhood of the experiencing subject goes way beyond what the concept of the individual entails. This is well illustrated in Robert Brigham's work on the South Vietnamese soldiers' experiences of the Vietnam War.[26] These soldiers had a duplex identity, according to Brigham. They were part of a modern army in which the actors were supposed to construct a relationship of fraternity, away from their traditional identity based on family and village origins. However, according to Brigham, it is impossible to understand these soldiers' lived world from this perspective only. In their combat mobility, these soldiers were accompanied by their families, who themselves had been uprooted from their home villages, due to the generalized, unbearably violent conditions in rural South Vietnam. Brigham concludes, therefore, that the subjectivity of these soldiers was both modern and traditional, and that it is not intelligible if seen from a perspective that is oblivious to the work of traditional identity in the unfolding of modern history.

Brigham discusses the meeting of the traditional and the modern in the context of a powerful modern institution – the mass-mobilized modern army. We may approach the same question in yet another context. The experience of the Vietnam War, for the Pham family in the south of Da Nang, central Vietnam, for instance, was at once a personal, communal, and political experience. Of the seven brothers and sisters, the eldest son was a decorated partisan fighter, now buried in the state cemetery of revolutionary martyrs. Three of his younger siblings also joined the National Liberation Front. Although their reasons for doing so were complex and unique, they were also all connected to the influence of their eldest brother: the second eldest of the seven joined the revolutionary war to stay close to his elder brother, whereas his younger sister later joined the local partisan group in part to escape from the intimidation by South Vietnam's police that her family had to endure due to her eldest brother's prominence on the opposite side of the war. The same was true for one of the younger Phams, who joined South Vietnam's elite paratroops, thanks to whom the rest of the family became relatively free from harassment by the local police. The youngest Pham also joined the Saigon army, but he did so as a covert contact whose true loyalty was to his eldest brother. The Pham family today has gripping stories to tell about how their paratrooper brother helped to protect their youngest sibling's life on several occasions, sometimes risking his own life, and how he still has not made peace with the fateful day in the dry season of 1970 when his youngest brother, as a soldier in the Saigon army, then exposed to South Vietnam's intelligence nets, failed to make a run to the other side. The experience of war for these humble actors of history is as much about how they related to one another and what these relationships meant to each of them or to them as a whole, as it is about how each one of them experienced that turbulent time in his or her own unique way and how they understand what the war means for the Vietnamese nation as a whole.

These vignettes are intended to show that for an understanding of human experience in the context of a mass-mobilized modern civil war, it is important to keep in mind that, in the unfolding of this experience, two analytically distinct forms of sociality can coexist. Earlier, we explored this distinction, following Lewis Henry Morgan, in terms of *societas* and *civitas*.[27] A broadly related distinction is discussed in the sociological literature regarding the language of the private versus the public or that of community and society (see later discussion). In the tradition of anthropological literature, similar questions are often discussed in terms of the distinction between moral personhood and modern individuality.[28] The debate on the category of the person, understood as distinct from that of the individual, involves observations on the way in which human beings are, in the words of Clifford Geertz, "intimately involved in one another's biographies."[29]

Similar ideas exist in the literature about the Korean War experience in which the subject of war experience appears often as a relational being or even the *relation* itself. A prominent writer speaks of his lifelong effort to "see the world [of violence] in webs of relations."[30] In Park Wan-suh's biographical accounts, the "I" that narrates the experience of war shifts from a sister (to a brother who is active in a radical political movement and to whom she is sympathetic) to a daughter (to her mother who commits all her energy to protecting her only son's life by trying to dissuade him from getting involved in dangerous politics). It moves from a niece (to her aunt and uncle who are accused of collaborating with communists) to an employee in an anti-communist youth organization (a decision she made in order to protect the rest of the family from falling into the same fate as that of her uncle and aunt). Ultimately, her selfhood evolves into one that tries to somehow bring all these different relational selves together into the space of the historical events they share through the act of writing.

For these eminent storytellers of the Korean War experience, the "relations" that shape their literary worlds are both intimate human relationships and relations of high politics (such as the relations between the two divided political entities of Korea). These relational persons are not the same as "selfless persons," who appear in certain renderings of cultural and religious traditions in Asia.[31] Nor are they to be confused with the idea of moral personhood (as against that of modern individuality) that is discussed prolifically in the tradition of modern anthropology primarily with reference to small-scale traditional societies.[32] The relational person addressed here is a *political* concept, inseparable from the particular milieu of modern political history within which it finds meaning. The concept is principally about the connectedness of two qualitatively different domains of relations, and how these personal and impersonal relations are tightly woven together in shaping the unfolding of human dramas in modern history. The idea of relations in this context resonates, instead, with what the American sociologist, C. Wright Mills, advocated in his 1959 work, *The Sociological Imagination*.[33] For Mills, the power of sociological imagination consists in connecting personal troubles to critical public issues. Like Mills's call for a leap of imagination, the idea is intended to bring to the fore how, in certain historical contexts, the constitution and unfolding of intimate human relations come to be caught up with the formation and evolution of geopolitical relations.[34] It also closely communicates with an important stream of thought existing in anthropology as well as in social psychology, represented most forcefully by Keith Hart in today's anthropological community, who finds merit in modern social science, above all, with its capacity to connect the personal with the world-historical.[35]

This mode of representation is, in postwar South Korea, far from a literary phenomenon only; it is also observed in voluminous memoirs and testimonials of war experiences that have become available since the 1990s. In a personal chronicle of wartime Seoul, one author, a history professor, is at pains to describe the tumultuous situation in his neighborhood during the occupation of the city by the North Korean army. He writes about his neighbors, the Hong family.[36] Mr. Hong is active in the People's Committee, a local administration instituted by the occupation authority, and he is frustrated with the US military involvement in the war that resulted in the failure of the North Korean People's Army to liberate the southern half of the country. His wife is anxious, too, but about the future of her family and about the prospect that "the world will be turned upside down once again" if the town is overtaken by the US and Southern forces. She is also in agony in respect to her immediate family. Her brother was arrested by the city's revolutionary guards, accused of being a counterrevolutionary, but her husband is unresponsive to her desperate pleas that he should help save his brother-in-law's life.[37] Although the historian is sympathetic to the troubles the Hong family are going through, he and his wife are unable to console Hong's wife when she appeals to them: "Please help me. Please tell me what I should do." The couple cannot respond to Mrs. Hong's plea, lest they risk their own lives by doing so. She has been one of their closest and most trusted neighbors, but she is married to a rank-and-file member of the occupation authority, whose duty includes reporting to the authority what he hears in his neighborhood. Most of these testimonial accounts depict the lived reality of Korea's civil war as a series of tumultuous crises in the sphere of everyday life, in which people are torn between the existing norms of communal relations and the new rules of political order and loyalty.

These testimonial accounts of the social experiences of war have become available only recently as part of South Korea's political democratization since the early 1990s. Works on this development since the end of the 1980s highlight the politics of representation – the contest for power in the public political arena between organized civil actions and the state's formal bureaucratic and coercive power.[38] They vividly show the vigorous engagement of various sectors of society with the social ills of an authoritarian political system, from the perspectives of laborers, students, and intellectuals. Although most observers emphasize the vitality of informal civil associational activities in changing political systems, some take note of the fact that these citizens' activism took place within and against the strongly anti-communist political rule, and ask whether the shape of the public sphere that arises from this environment differs from the idea of civil society familiar in the Western context.[39] Reflecting on the ideological spectrum of left and right that is part of modern political debate and activism, for instance, Cumings asks whether these classificatory terms involve different moral imports between Korea and the United States.[40] He writes:

Since the collapse of the Berlin Wall and the fall of Western communism, a ubiquitous trope has emerged in American scholarship on the meaning of these critical events: civil society. This term, which was central to an older political sociology but had fallen into disuse, reappeared in two contexts: (1) what the former communist countries needed most was what the communists had respected least, namely civil society; and (2) what Americans needed was to repair and restore their own civil society.[41]

In debates on a broader terrain, the idea of civil society is closely associated with a hopeful vision for the social and international order after the Cold War. The sociologist, Anthony Giddens, characterizes the post-Cold War era's political development in terms of an imperative to further strengthen the vitality of civil society.[42] According to him, it means that the states, having long based their legitimacy in opposition to the political forces and state entities on the opposite side of the bipolar border, are no longer able to do so with the opening of the Iron Curtain. State entities in the post-Cold War era need to find a new rationale for political legitimacy, which should be found, according to Giddens, in their active role in empowering civil society. Mary Kaldor discusses a similar idea concerning the broader horizon of the post-Cold War world.[43] Her proposition centers on the idea of global civil society – the idea that the revitalization of civil society must take place on both sides of the former bipolar border, and that this development should involve a growing transnational network among various nationally based civil societies.[44] Kaldor presents global civil society as a principal instrument and forum for the making of international peace in the post-Cold War world. Notably, she bases her laudable vision on her experience during the Cold War as an activist who promoted an exchange network between critical thinkers in Western Europe and oppositional writers and activists in Eastern Europe. She introduces the significance of these informal non-state networks under the lens of E. P. Thompson's idea of the "détente of peoples rather than states."[45] In the post-Cold War world, according Kaldor, such cross-border networks of civil activists must expand into a wider transnational horizon in order to counter new threats of war that confront this world.

Kaldor's vision for "the transnational role of citizens" in the post-1989 world relates to her experience of "détente from below" in the 1980s, but it is also grounded in her general understanding of the Cold War as an imaginary war.[46] She writes: "I have used the term 'imaginary war' to describe the Cold War. It was a war sustained in our imaginations through the reproduction of an ever more fearsome military confrontation, through spying games and hostile rhetoric."[47] Her notion of imaginary war speaks to the widely held image of the Cold War as an unconventional war: the Cold War made no clear distinction between war and peace and no declaration of war or formal cessation of violence. Being neither a real war nor genuine peace, it was fought mainly with economic, ideological, and polemical means. The powerful actors of this war continued to build arsenals of weapons of mass destruction, hoping that they would not have to actually use them. The threat of mutually assured total destruction would help avert the risk of an actual armed conflict and, thus, resulted in one of the longest eras of international peace.

These renderings of the Cold War that prevail in the literature on modern European history, however, confront considerable conceptual obstacles if seen in a wider historical context. A history of the Cold War that is inclusive of the experience of decolonizing nations in Asia and elsewhere, rather than focused on Europe or the transatlantic, cannot be meaningfully addressed with the idioms of an imaginary war. The late historian of modern Europe, Tony Judt, raises the problem of parochialism in Cold War historical knowledge. In his critical response to John Lewis Gaddis's idea that the Cold War era constituted an extraordinarily durable time of peace, he writes that "this way of narrating cold war history reflects the same provincialism. John Lewis Gaddis has written a history of America's cold war. As a result, this is a book whose silences are especially suggestive. The 'third world' in particular comes up short."[48] In her more recent work, *New and Old Wars*, Kaldor does pay attention to these hitherto silent chapters of Cold War history.[49] She writes that the Cold War "kept alive the idea of war, while avoiding its reality. [No major conventional war] broke out on European soil. At the same time, many wars took place all over the world, including Europe, in which more people died than the Second World War. But because these wars did not fit our conception of war, they were discounted."[50] Kaldor calls these events of mass destruction that did not fit the dominant conception of the Cold War "irregular, informal wars of the second half of the twentieth century" that took place "as a peripheral part of the central conflict."[51] Following Kaldor, therefore, Cold War history appears to have a concentric form, consisting of a formal history of relative peace in the center and informal violence on the periphery. The Cold War was both an *idea* of war in the exemplary center and a *reality* of totalizing war and generalized violence in the peripheral terrains. In this view of the Cold War and what comes after it, the bipolar conflicts were not only an ambiguous phenomenon, being neither war nor peace, but also a contradictory phenomenon, experienced as an idea of war for some and as a reality of prolific organized violence for others. The end of the Cold War was a largely peaceful event and opened a constructive development of transnational integration in the conflict's central stage of Europe – a positive development that Kaldor envisions can be extended to other parts of the world to eventually transform into a global phenomenon. In this way, Kaldor extends the "détente from below" initiative from before 1989, based on dialogues among nonstate actors across the East and the West, to a vision for a global civil society in the post-Cold War world.

These laudable visions for social development in the post-1989 world need to be considered with caution, however. If the Cold War in the world at large was contrary to Europe's imaginary war, as Kaldor notes, it follows that we need to take into account these contradictory historical trajectories while contemplating the present and future of the post-1989 global world. In places where the Cold War was manifested as other than an imaginary war, the time was far from a long peace but rather a long-lasting unbridled reality involving catastrophic civil war and other exceptional forms of political violence and coercion.[52] Seen within such a milieu, it is impossible to envision the future of civil society without considering the legacies of civil war. Since the nature of modern civil war is that it tears apart the integrity of human communities by hammering into them the contending ideals of political society, any vision of new civil solidarity against this backdrop cannot be considered separately from the local community's efforts to confront the history of the civil war that has become part of itself. These efforts may be seen, moreover, as having relevance even in the sphere of global civil society. In stark contrast to Gaddis's idea of long peace, several prominent observers of contemporary history propose conceptualizing the Cold War as a global civil war. Notable is Reinhart Koselleck's idea of *Weltbürgerkrieg* – a "world civil war" in which "the historical philosophies of liberalism and communism provided the central and legitimizing weapons."[53] Also relevant are recent efforts among historians to highlight the place of the Third World in Cold War historical understanding – that is, the silent chapters in conventional Cold War historiography that Judt noted – and the related historical horizons where the advent of global bipolar confrontation met with the politics of decolonization.[54]

It is on this horizon that the bipolar conflicts of the second half of the past century took especially violent and tumultuous forms. If we bring Koselleck's global civil war idea to the space of the global Cold War, it is possible to place Kaldor's imaginary war idea in a new context. A civil war is an existential crisis for a society, whether it is a national or international society; yet, the violence of civil war can be felt more starkly in certain communities than others within society. This was the case with the American Civil War, and the same is true with Korea's civil war violence, which, as noted earlier, even neighboring communities experienced varyingly (see Chapter 1). In this light, we may conclude that the Cold War was indeed a global civil war, the intensity of whose violence, nevertheless, was manifested differently across regions and territories.

The important point is that in imagining the texture of global civil society in the post-Cold War world, we may not ignore the legacies of the Cold War as a *Weltbürgerkrieg*. This is especially the case when envisioning the future of a society that experienced the *Weltbürgerkrieg* in a localized civil war crisis. Since civil war tears apart communal lives as well as the life of society, any progression beyond the destruction of civil war must involve not only a recovery of civic sociality but also that of communal integrity. Contemporary attentions to civil society are based on the assumption that the road to democracy involves a contest of power between the top-down state machinery and the bottom-up social solidarity and mobilization. The principal subject of this solidarity movement is referred to as the citizen. In this discursive sphere, the quality of democracy is measured in proportion to the vitality of the public world that the rights-claiming citizens are to make up. Seen in this light, there is no doubt that the growth of civil society is one of the most prominent phenomena in South Korea's recent political history since the end of the Cold War as a geopolitical order in the early 1990s. The works that focus on this phenomenon commonly emphasize public events and actions of a national scale and significance, and, in doing so, view South Korean society and politics from an angle that may be called the perspective of *Gesellschaft*. Thus, the politically active civil associational activities addressed by these scholars mainly refer to distinct social groupings familiar to an urbanized, industrialized modern society based on class, gender, generation, and professional interests. Apart from some notable exceptions, such as Cumings's essay mentioned earlier, most existing attentions to South Korea's democratic transition tend to circumvent the fact that there are some unique, critical questions of citizenship involved in understanding Korea's modern history.

Enemies Within

For families related to the One Hundred Ancestors and One Single Descendant, there was a prevailing sense in their postwar lives that they were both national citizens (*kukmin*) and, at the same time, other than national citizens (*bikukmin*). This paradoxical condition of being both an insider and an outsider in relation to political society had many different ramifications for personal lives and interpersonal relations. These people were citizens: they paid taxes, took part in local and national elections, served in the military, and their names and genealogical identities were recorded in local registries. However, they were nevertheless considered less than legitimate members of the political community: for many years, they did not have the right to work in public offices or to enjoy mobility in general, including the right to travel overseas, and they were subjected to arbitrary political discrimination and violence without protection by law (see Chapter 4). Some of them experienced strict regular surveillance by the police, arrests without warrant or trial, and other forms of intimidation by the state's security agents. These experiences taught them that they were undesirable members of society with restricted civil rights, and that they could be stripped of basic civil and human rights on issues that the state considered to be matters of public and national security. The restriction of civil rights was unconstitutional, but it was nevertheless part of the order of law as it was experienced.

Similar situations are observed elsewhere. In her study of the detention camps in Greece during and after the country's civil war (1946–1949), Neni Panourgiá offers a history of "hyper-legality" – the 1871 law that permitted the prosecution of "everyone suspected of providing coverage for brigands," and how this measure was reinvented in the mid-twentieth century to serve the purpose of the authoritarian state in combating the challenges posed by communist insurgencies.[55] The civil war in Greece was intimately connected to the civil war in Korea in the international history of the Cold War. They were both "international civil wars," partly driven by the Truman Doctrine of 1947, and also grounded in the polarization of society into radical nationalist forces and anti-communist nationalist forces.[56] The Truman Doctrine announced the United States' active global leadership in the struggle against international communism, and the two civil wars marked the militarization and globalization of this struggle.[57] Truman, in fact, referred to Korea as "the Greece of the Far East" when war broke out in the peninsula, and said, "If we are tough enough now, if we stand up to [the communists] like we did in Greece three years ago, they won't take over the whole Middle East."[58] Panourgiá describes how the experience of civil war in Greece generated a class of citizens whose very existence was believed to be a danger to the political community, and how the situation resulted in "a political DNA of sorts, which organizes not only [the lives of these dangerous citizens] but also the lives of generations to come and has been organized by kinship lines that extend into the past."[59]

The politics of anti-communism in Korea invented similar techniques of social control, "punishing thoughts and beliefs rather than acts," and developing punitive measures against politically subversive individuals that criminalized the entire moral collectives to which these individuals belonged.[60] The generation of civil war Koreans is familiar with idioms such as "red blood line."[61] For people whose genealogical backgrounds include ancestors once classified as communist subversives, sympathizers of communism, or defectors to the communist North, the red blood line has been a terrifying idea, associated with the memory of summary killings and mass murders, experiences of social stigmatization for the surviving families, and the restriction of civil rights for their members. This politically non-normative status was enforced upon these families not because of what they had done (against the defined political and legal order), but primarily because of who they were, in terms of their given family relations. The restriction of civil rights for the families of the Jeju Sangmo-ri cemetery was caused by their genealogical ties to the dead buried there. For them, kinship relations were not merely a domain of amity and mutual support on which they could rely in moral and material terms. Nor was it a specific sphere of human relations, as dominant sociological theories claim, which is supposed to wither away in significance as society is modernized and urbanized. Instead, for these families, the domain of kinship increased in critical relevance along the progression of modern history, being a source of radical social stigma and existential burden, as well as becoming a site in which the relationship of political enmity prevailing in the wider world was actualized in microscopic form. The families coped with these imposed precarious life conditions in many improvised ways, sometimes relying on kinship networks for protection. This is evident in numerous testimonies that show how people tried to mobilize connections to relatives employed in the public sector while trying to protect themselves from shadowy political persecution and public discrimination (see Chapter 3). Yet, many of these families also encountered bitter experiences of undergoing discrimination and isolation even within relatively close circles of people, who refrained from being associated with a potentially dangerous political element even if this element meant their close relatives. Such discrimination sometimes existed even within the intimacy of a close family circle, and their politically non-normative status became a critical genealogical issue, as predicaments in one generation affected the life and career prospects of the following generation. For these *bikukmin* families in postwar Korea, therefore, the traditional world of kinship and the modern world of civic life became inexorably intertwined, and these two domains were inseparable no matter how hard they tried to pull them apart. If a person's political actions may have ramifications for the survival of his or her family, that person, in order to act politically in the public sphere, has to first find a way to break out of the logic of collective culpability. Traditional "community" and modern "society" coexist everywhere, and it is an illusion to believe that one form of human association can entirely replace the other.[62] This is particularly true in postwar Korean political life, and awareness of this truth must also be brought to the understanding of how, in certain conditions, aspirations toward democratic life can arise from the milieu of traditional communal relations as well as in the public space of civil and political society.

The Idea of "Bad Gemeinschaft"

In his foundational sociological text at the end of the nineteenth century, *Community and Society*, the German social philosopher, Ferdinand Tönnies, makes an interesting observation on the conceptual distinction between community and society in terms of moral judgment. Addressing family and kinship relations, which he defines as an ideal type of community, Tönnies observes that it is impossible to conceive of a "bad community." He argues that although one may speak of a society as a good or bad society (i.e., just or unjust society, or democratic or undemocratic society), this moral judgment cannot apply to community:

All intimate, private, and exclusive living together, so we discover, is understood as life in Gemeinschaft (community). Gesellschaft (society) is public life – it is the world itself. In Gemeinschaft with one's family, one lives from birth on, bound to it in weal and woe. One goes into Gesellschaft as one goes into a strange country. A young man is warned against bad Gesellschaft, but the expression bad Gemeinschaft violates the meaning of the word. [63]

Tönnies' point about the freedom of community from moral judgment speaks of the particular constitution of what he calls the "strange country" of modern society, in which members are to associate with each other, supposedly free from the dispositions of their familiar, rooted communal identities. Being strangers to each other, these newcomers to the "strange country," called individuals, invent new rules of mutual engagement and association. How they establish and agree upon these rules and what these rules may look like will speak volumes as to whether the strange, new country is to be deemed a good society or not. Once they start engaging in building this strange country's society, however, they are all equal to each other, no longer to be judged according to their place of origin.

Despite Tönnies' optimism, the ideal of freedom from "bad Gemeinschaft" has not come to fruition in the progression of modern political history – not only in terms of racial, ethnic, or sexual differences but also on political grounds. At the time of the civil war and afterward, South Korea was a political society on the frontier of the global Cold War that took anti-communism as one of its constitutional principles; the construction of national identity involved not only the creation of pure ideological selfhood on the frontier of anti-communism but also the containment of society from what the political authority defined as impure traditional communal ties. The construction of an ideologically cohesive and unitary society progressed, partly but crucially, through measures of control over traditional relations, including the punishment of what the state regarded as politically impure and subversive communal ties. In this milieu, the complexity of kinship ties was pitted against the simplicity and clarity of friends versus enemies, and communal ties were judged good or bad depending on whether or not they were contained within the projected space of political interiority and ideological purity. In order to come to terms with the human dimension of the Korean War and that of the wider global civil war environment called the Cold War that conditioned this brutal civil war, therefore, it is necessary to confront the way in which the making of a modern political society resulted in the moral classification and judgment of traditional communities and communal relations.

If the idea of bad Gemeinschaft has no place in modern life, yet nevertheless can exist as a formative element in the constitution of a modern political order, a progressive development away from this order must involve efforts to correct the disparity between the supposedly defunct conception of bad Gemeinschaft in modern society and the actuality of its proliferation in modern politics. Political democratization, in this developmental context, is not merely about a struggle in representation, more accountable governance, and the protection of individual liberty. It is also about the community's recovery of its freedom from moral judgment and its injurious and destructive consequences.

The human experience of Korea's civil war was densely communal and dense in its implications for communal life, and it needs to be untangled slowly and carefully in the same light. In order to come to terms with this history, it is first necessary to think of two forms of community as we proceed to think of the relationship between state and society. One form of community refers to the milieu of close interpersonal relations, having normative characters as well as practical implications, with the ties of kinship as an example. The reality of this community is densely present in the biographical and social-historical accounts of the civil war experience. Another form of community was as real as the first in the reality of the war, and this refers to the political community of the nation-state, which thrives on, according to Mosse, the myth of war experience. Numerous people sacrificed their lives and took others' lives in the hope of actualizing this envisioned community. In postcolonial Korea, the process of actualization involved two separate state institutions and powers, each of which was committed to building a single national community and to incorporating all traditional communities into that single unity. The two also regarded each other as an illegitimate political entity and identified the prospect of a meaningful national community with the elimination of the rogue state entity. The national community envisioned by each of these states was unitary and exclusive. In contrast, the communities that these states sought to bring to the mold of the envisioned political community were plural and inclusive, if seen in relative terms to the very sphere of absolute political cohesion and homogeneity coerced by the warring states. The story of two brothers walking along opposite pathways of war is lucid testimony to the point about the political plurality of community. The plural composition of these everyday communities was not their given trait; it existed in relation to the condition of political bipolarity and the related violent politics of ideological conformity. It goes without saying that it was this historically constituted, politically plural subjectivity of everyday communal relations that the politics of exclusive sovereignty were bent on destroying through coercive and violent means (see Chapter 3). Seen in this light, the Korean War as a war against society was, in principal, a war waged against the reality of plurality.

If an individual is less than a legitimate member in the public world due to his or her ties of kinship to a person that political society defines as an enemy of the state, a democratic life, for this individual, involves having his or her relationship to that person recover its normativity. In this context, moreover, the idea of bad Gemeinschaft loses its grip on society not merely when society recognizes that this concept has no place in modern political life, but also when the different communities that constitute political society come to recognize that, in their past, they all shared the politically mixed web of relationships – the recognition that against the backdrop of total civil war, no community may claim a pure political and ideological genealogy. The way toward a genuine democratic society, free from the radicalized ideologies of the Cold War, requires communities to think more truthfully about their genealogical past, and not merely strive to move out of this parochial realm in order to think in terms of a modern individual society. It is for this reason that, against the ruins of civil war, the moral and political actions of the community become as pivotal to the advancement of democracy, as those taking place within civil society.

Seen in this regard, "one hundred ancestors and one single descendant" is not only a language of kinship and genealogy. On the contrary, it addresses a sphere of politics that has life and death significance for communities, but which theories of modern politics and society, nevertheless, have no name for and thus fail to see. Then, the stone-inscribed national flag in the cemetery's epitaph begins to appear less strange than it did originally. Rather than an odd object in a communal graveyard, the carved image works as a protective charm – an object that is intended to protect the place and the dead buried in that place from the violence of the state by incorporating the state's sacred symbol into it. The cemetery's name also seems less mysterious. Rather than an anomalous, upside-down genealogical condition, the name of the place, One Hundred Ancestors and One Single Descendant, points to the norms of kinship to commemorate the dead and, when the commemoration concerns the reality of mass deaths, the imperative for the concerned families to create a bond beyond the narrow unity of genealogical relatedness.[64] Although 100 human remains were buried in the cemetery individually, these bodies were in actuality all intertwined, sharing the same fate and tragic circumstances of death. Likewise, the bereaved families are all interconnected, forming a single community of mourners, despite their differences in genealogical identity and separate blood ties to the dead. Today, indeed, these families gather to hold a joint commemorative death rite at the cemetery on the seventh day of the seventh lunar month each year – the day the victims were taken away from their homes in 1950. Also notable in the organization of the Sangmo-ri cemetery is the fact that the memorial stone standing at the center of this cemetery compound is not a solitary object. The stone does not merely represent the desire of the bereaved families to grieve for their tragically dead relatives. It also testifies to the fact that formidable obstacles exist against their commemorative effort. Standing next to the broken remains of the old memorial, the stone shows that it itself has a history of death and regeneration of life. It speaks of the fact that the rights of kinship to commemorate the dead can be negated by powerful political forces, and that the assertion of these rights is inseparable from the progression of a democratic political order. Seen from the vantage point of this cemetery, the history of Korea's political democracy is then about the right to grieve and remember the victims of the war's destruction without fear of retribution. This history is about creating a new public world in which people can disclose the conditions of their own private, yet highly politicized lives by speaking and acting on behalf of the dead. It is also about creating a bond of commemoration, illustrated by the idea of "one single descendant" among separate social entities of bereavement and beyond their separate ties of kinship.[65]

3   Peace in the Feud

Moscow holds a place of considerable authority in the history of international socialism. Its prominence is also evident in the history of intellectual and political movements against colonialism. In the second half of the twentieth century, throughout the Cold War, Moscow entertained a great concentration of geopolitical power within one side of a divided world. However, the power and authority that this city represented could also have relevance in a parochial local world, not merely in the sphere of international and world politics. In the turbulent reality of the early postcolonial Cold War, a local world could turn into a fractal image of the global political order.

Across rural South Korea are to be found villages once known as *moskoba* (Moscow). The name refers to somewhere the locals considered to be a communist stronghold in the area during the Korean War, although a place known as such may hold historical memories on a deeper temporal scale. In the latter context, a moskoba village may be where prominent nationalists of communist or socialist orientations were born and bred during colonial times.[1] In one such place in the southeast region of the peninsula, the village's moskoba historical identity involves the journey of a man originally from the village to Moscow in the 1930s as part of a delegation to the city's renowned University for the Toiling Masses in the East, a Soviet school for Asian revolutionaries. A moskoba village may also appear as a "red village" in the same conversational context, and local people might alternate between these two expressions when speaking of their Korean War experiences. For residents in the so-called red village, however, this expression is not at all interchangeable with that of moskoba. The reference to moskoba may invoke a sense of pride for people in such a village; albeit, a hidden and wounded pride relating to some of the village's prominent yet ill-fated ancestors. These ancestral figures are most often associated with the village's meritorious genealogical heritage of resistance against colonial politics and commitment to social justice. In contrast, the idea of a red village would typically provoke strongly indignant reactions from the people of such villages. Such a label turns the villagers' source of pride to that of stigma, as it pries open memories of hardships that they had to undergo due to their ancestral connections.

In one such village once known as the area's moskoba in the district of Andong in a southeastern region of the peninsula, disputes recently arose among the villagers about a village ancestral grave. Most people in this place share a common lineage identity, and they are intensely proud of their long, shared genealogical heritage, consisting of several locally eminent Confucian scholars and scholar-farmers dating back to the sixteenth century. Each year, one of the village's most important events occurs when relatives living elsewhere return to their homeland in order to join the ceremonies held on behalf of their lineage and village ancestors. On these occasions, the relatives arriving from distant cities are pleased to meet each other and exchange news – but not always so.

When a man cautiously suggested to his lineage elders that the family might consider repairing a neglected ancestral tomb, this broke the harmony of the family meal held after the ancestral rite. One elder left the room in a rage and other lineage elders remained silent throughout the ceremonial meal. The ancestor buried in the neglected tomb had been a prominent communist activist during the colonial era before he died at a young age in a colonial prison without a descendant; the offended elder's siblings were among the several dozen village youths who left the village together with the retreating North Korean army in October 1950. The elder believed that this catastrophe in village history and family continuity could have been avoided if the family ancestor buried in the neglected tomb had not brought the seeds of "red ideology" to the village in the first place.[2] Beautifying the ancestor's tomb was unacceptable to this elder, who believed that, because of this individual, many of his senior kinsmen had lost the social basis on which they could be properly remembered as family ancestors, within their immediate circle of relatives and descendants, after their death.

Histories of family dispersal and related ruptures in family genealogy are familiar in postwar Korean society. The condition of family separation between the North and the South has been one of the key contentious issues in the turbulent relationship between the two Koreas since the war ended. The plight of these separated families constitutes one of the most enduring human tragedies of the Korean War; however, the predicaments that these families faced in their postwar lives are also closely related to the vexing problems of Cold War political modernity that we discussed in the previous chapter with reference to Tönnies' idea of "bad Gemeinschaft." This chapter will explore the manifestation of this idea in postwar South Korean society in terms of red villages. The following chapter will narrow down our inquiry further and concentrate on the idea of the red bloodline.

Separation

The mid-twentieth century saw an unprecedented mass population displacement as a result of war, in both scale and intensity,[3] which, according to Peter Gatrell, was caused by "the collapse of multinational empires, the emergence of the modern state with a bounded citizenship, the spread of totalizing ideologies that hounded internal enemies, and the internationalization of responses to refugee crises."[4] The phenomenon of families divided between North Korea and South Korea is one of the most enduring consequences of the era's generalized population displacement. The painful circumstances of these families are forcefully demonstrated in the brief reunions held periodically near the border between the two Koreas; in recent years, this has been in the Hall of Family Reunions, prepared at the special zone of a mountain resort, Kŭmkang-san, north of the Demilitarized Zone. On these occasions, several dozen citizens from the two states are allowed to cross the otherwise impassable political border to enjoy a short encounter with their long-separated children, parents, spouses, and siblings, whom they had not seen since the time of the war or even before.[5] The visit usually lasts about three days, yet the actual time that families can spend together is limited to a half day. The moments of encounter are agonizingly dramatic, involving the eruption of intense emotions, and the South Korean media are eager to capture and disseminate these extraordinary moments. A truly painful moment comes, however, when the reunited families have to part again. When the time of their brief visit runs out and the participants are called upon to prepare for departure in separate directions, the agony of separation is hard to bear. For many elderly visitors, this new separation after their initial lengthy division means a truly permanent one, for they are aware that it is unlikely they will be selected again within their lifetime for the privileged experience of a family reunion. For this reason, a common farewell greeting exchanged at the moment of separation is: "So long, next time I will meet you in the world of the dead."[6]

The idea of the family reunion has been a central element in the turbulent historical process of rapprochement between the two Koreas. The first initiative took place at the beginning of the 1970s amid a tectonic shift in the structure of global power at the time. Notable in this regard is "the week that changed the world," referring to Richard Nixon's 1972 visit to China, and the subsequent "long 1970s," leading to the onset of economic reform in China in the late 1970s and the normalization of diplomatic ties between China and the United States in 1979 – a series of events that have received fresh attention in recent scholarship on East Asian and global history.[7] These studies typically view the rise of China to a global economic power (and its resurgence as a regional superpower) and the related tectonic shift in global power relations in the post-Cold War world as having originated in the momentous occurrence of bilateral détente between the United States and China from 1970 to 1972. The events of these years had quite different meanings for other Asian revolutionary socialist states, however. For Vietnam, they were devastating, close to an act of betrayal on the part of China. This time saw the apex of violence in Vietnam; communist North Vietnam was fighting the last stage of one of the longest wars in the twentieth century against the United States and its Southern ally. China's collusion with the Americans at this critical juncture deeply disappointed the Vietnamese leadership. China's reception of Nixon "caused serious apprehension in Pyongyang" as well, although China made a considerable effort to persuade North Korea to accept its change of course in foreign relations with the United States and provided substantial aid to North Korea for that purpose.[8] North Korea had a strong interest in the unfolding of the Vietnam War. It was also disturbed by South Korea's active participation in the war as a key military ally of South Vietnam and the United States from 1967 to 1973. This was manifested in the aborted attempt by the North to assassinate South Korea's head of state, Park Chung Hee, on January 21, 1968, by sending a group of commandos across the Armistice line. At the same time, North Korea captured the US Navy intelligence ship, USS *Pueblo*, from near its eastern coastal waters on January 23, 1968. As for South Korea, its participation in the Vietnam War proved to be a vital springboard for its speedy economic growth in the 1970s. However, Park was disturbed by the orientation of the Nixon administration, particularly by its lukewarm and increasingly apathetic attitude toward the security concerns of South Korea, despite having sent many tens of thousands of its soldiers to the most precarious combat zones in America's Vietnam War.

The détente between China and the United States, therefore, came as a stern warning to both North and South Korea. Leaders in each country felt that their powerful ally since the time of the Korean War, China or the United States, respectively, was becoming selfish and untrustworthy, forgetting the trust relations based on international revolutionary solidarity or the international solidarity of anti-communism. Many events of great importance followed "the week [in Peking] that changed the world" in and between the Koreas. Most notably, the disillusionment with great ally powers brought the two Koreas to a brief yet crucial period of rapprochement, the first of its kind since the partition of the nation in 1945. In his speech on August 15, 1970, marking the anniversary of national liberation from colonial occupation, South Korea's President Park proposed opening an era of peaceful coexistence between the two Koreas. A year later, the South Korean Red Cross met its North Korean counterpart to discuss, among other things, the humanitarian issue of helping the divided families of the two countries to resume contact. This was followed by a secret visit of the South Korean state security chief to Pyongyang, which eventually led to the historic joint statement about the prospects for reconciliation and national reunification on July 4, 1972.

While these initiatives were being taken across the Demilitarized Zone and the two states of Korea were coming to a reciprocal agreement on the imperative to resolve the national question by themselves, without big powers, important changes were also taking place in the domestic political order in both states. In South Korea, Park formally declared a political dictatorship in October 1972, through a constitutional change that enabled lifetime power for him, including the abolition of the direct ballot for presidential office. Two months later, North Korea undertook its own constitutional amendment, which established an absolutist political system (jusŏk system) and gave Kim Il Sung a position of power that transcended the power of the Party. By the end of 1972, therefore, a system of dictatorship was established in each of the two Koreas amid the first-ever initiative for dialogue with each other between the two national states and in reaction to the beginning of a détente between China and the United States.[9]

I describe the poignant moments of family reunions and their broad international ramifications in a rather detailed way to illustrate how in Cold War-era Korea, questions relating to the rights of human intimate relations have been interlocked with fluctuations in geopolitical relations. The history of Korea's separated families has frustrated hopes for familial reunions, relating to the failed political détente between its two polities at the beginning of the 1970s. The plight of these families has been intertwined with the international and national politics of détente, and has also been a prime symbol of the imperative to achieve reconciliation between the two nation-states. The South Korean media adds generous commentaries to family reunion events, describing them as being emblematic of the "sorrows of national partition." They also mention, as a matter of fact, "ten million [people in] separated families." A prominent dissident South Korean writer said during his visit to Pyongyang in 1990: "There are ten million [people in] separated families. If we count also their descendants, I believe that the entire seventy million people [of North and South] are suffering the pains of separation."[10] This figure of ten million people in separated families, which amounts to nearly a third of the entire Korean population during wartime, is probably exaggerated and has been contested accordingly.[11] The exact number of separated families remains unknown to date, partly due to the extremely chaotic conditions in which they were separated. However, the problem also relates to some definitional problems involving the notion of the family in contemporary Korean reckoning. Some formidable changes have taken place in this reckoning since wartime, resulting from the rapid urbanization and industrialization in South Korea since the 1960s, and in North Korea, not only from an equivalent postwar process of industrialization, but also from the country's revolutionary social transformation that began in the late 1940s. Both transformative processes involved, although clearly not in identical ways, the uprooting of the concept of the family from its traditional agrarian basis of wider descent grouping. The industrialization of South Korea generated the displacement of people from their traditional rural basis for a great part of the population, and this resulted in two separate conceptions of family relations coexisting today. One is the modern family – nowadays referred to as *gajok* (denoting primarily a nuclear family or a three-generation extended family), and the other has many references, including *ch'injok*, *ilga*, or *munnae* (the latter two meaning "people who belong to the same house" or "inside the door," expressions commonly referring to members of the family's agnatic descent group associated with a specific locality in origin). In North Korea, the country's post-Korean War revolutionary politics took the traditional system of patrilineal descent groupings and the idea of the family's root villages as one of the main targets of revolutionary social reform. The initiative was to sever the idea of kinship from its conceptual and practical basis in the feudal, agrarian society as well as its related patrilineal descent ideology. This reform resulted in a profound transformation in family and kinship relations in North Korea, if not necessarily in patriarchal ideology. These state constructions of modern family make it difficult for the postwar generations to share the conception of familial relatedness held by the war generation, for whom *gajok* and *ilga* were flexible and sometimes coterminous ideas.[12] Hence, what is clearly a condition of a divided family for people of one generation may not necessarily appear to be so for those of a later generation because of differences in how they conceptualize the boundary of close relations.[13]

This was made abundantly clear during my dialogues with such families about their war experiences, during which I sometimes misunderstood, earlier on in our conversation, the relationships between my interlocutors and their relatives missing from the war. On one such occasion my informant's accounts of his family's experiences centered on his elder brother, who had been a noted member of a communist youth movement in colonial Korea. His brother was in North Korea by the time the Korean War broke out and, during the war, came to visit his birth home once as a North Korean army officer. After his village area was liberated by the South Korean military forces and combat police, the police were informed of this visit, which then caused great suffering for a number of villagers. These included my informant's elder sister who was subjected to gruesome sexual violence perpetrated by a group of men and members of an anti-communist youth group, some of whom originated from the same village. Many years after the war, in 1972, the elder brother came back to his birthplace on a secret visit. He was on a proselytizing mission, sent from Pyongyang, and made an hour-long, late-night rendezvous with my informant's father. My informant does not understand how his elder brother's brief homecoming was later discovered by South Korea's security agents, but he recalls vividly what great calamities the incident caused to his entire extended family. The web of the state's surveillance had extended to some of his elder brother's old schoolmates. My informant's recollection introduced a large number of names and a complex network of what is referred to by an eminent Korean anthropologist as three principal relationalities of traditional Korea: "relations by blood," "relations by place [of birth or of upbringing]," and "relations of schooling."[14] Furthermore, it was only after several meetings, with many long conversations, that I discovered that his "elder brother," the memory of whom still haunts him, was actually the eldest son of his father's first cousin.

The plight of Korea's separated families was a critical issue during the war, especially in the long negotiations for an armistice agreement between the United Nations and the Chinese-North Korean counterparts, and it has been, as noted, one of the main issues in the turbulent process of mutual engagement between the two Koreas in subsequent eras. It has also been a major humanitarian issue involving the international and national Red Cross organizations. The problem of family separation across the bipolar political border goes well beyond the territorial boundary between the two Koreas.[15] Korean communities in Japan have numerous families who have close relatives in North Korea. Their relatives moved to North Korea in the 1960s and 1970s in the hope of escaping the ethnic discrimination and social disadvantages to which they were subject in Japan. The move was carefully orchestrated by the North Korean and Japanese administrations as well as Japan's Red Cross organization, according to Tessa Morris-Suzuki, who wrote a damning report on the collusion between the Red Cross's humanitarian concerns and the

Japanese administration's intention at the time, which was singularly interested in removing its former colonial subjects from its territory.[16] Nearly all of these "repatriates to the northern fatherland" were originally from Korea's southern regions, particularly from the Kyungsang province in the southeast where Andong is located, and many were also from the island of Jeju, some of whom, having escaped the island amid extremely violent counterinsurgency campaigns waged before the Korean War, were not able to return to their homeland, fearing persecution. Each time relations between North Korea and Japan worsened, these "repatriates" and their remaining families in Japan suffered from new deadlocks in communication, and the families in Japan, for many years until recently, were not able to communicate with their relatives back in South Korea either. These people had familial ties to residents in North Korea, which made them politically dangerous to associate with for people in postwar South Korea. Against this backdrop, when the North-South family reunions were on course in the early 2000s, a number of families in Jeju had the extraordinary experience of flying to the mainland, rather than to Japan, in order to meet their long-lost relatives at the Hall of Family Reunions prepared on the northern side of the Demilitarized Zone. The repatriates to North Korea also came from Soviet Russia in the 1960s and 1970s, from the island of Sakhalin in particular (the southern half of which was Japan's colony before 1945), who were also in origin mostly from southern parts of Korea. After the breakdown of the Soviet empire in the early 1990s, their families in Sakhalin slowly began to resume contact with their relatives in South Korea. For these families today, the result is dispersion of family ties on a transnational scale across several bipolar political borders, old or persisting.

Similar humanitarian crises of family separation existed elsewhere during the Cold War. Separated families constituted an important issue in the negotiations for rapprochement between the two Germanys in the 1970s as well as between the People's Republic of China and the Republic of China (Taiwan) in the 1990s. John Borneman speaks of the division of pre-1989 Berlin not merely with reference to the Berlin Wall that cut through the city but also in terms of the complications this partition created in many Berliner families' lives.[17] He highlights diverging notions of the modern family that emerged between the two German states during their different, competitive social developments, arguing that family relations were a main site of Cold War conflicts between Germany's two political systems. Charles Stafford argues that many Chinese understand the partition of their nation into mainland China and the island of Taiwan in terms of a family drama of separation and reunion, which is, according to him, a theme of traditional Chinese fascination rooted in their literary and oral cultures.[18] Similar points are raised with respect to the Korean context. It is argued that the representation of the Korean War, in contemporary South Korea, renders the war experience primarily as "a family tragedy to be followed by rites of reconciliation."[19] The negotiations between the two Koreas on family questions have been much more complicated compared to the German or Chinese cases, however, and the Korean discussions of families' rights to communicate with each other across the national border progressed far more slowly than in the other countries. The idea of freely visiting one's close kin living on the other side of the bipolar border, which was a major issue in the inter-German negotiations, remains a distant hope for most of Korea's separated families. The first historic meetings took place in Seoul and Pyongyang in September 1985, involving thirty separated families. The second meeting had to wait until 2000, and since then, there have been a dozen more encounters by the end of 2007, each involving about 100 families, when the humanitarian initiative was again discontinued amid the worsening relations between the two Korean governments.[20] As I am completing this book, new hopes have emerged on this humanitarian front, following the inter-Korean summit on April 27, 2018, and the ensuing meeting in Singapore on June 12, 2018, between US President Donald Trump and North Korea's current paramount leader, Kim Jong-un. In reaction to the sluggish progress of formal negotiations at the governmental level, various informal ways to make family contact developed in the 1990s through northeast China and other overseas routes. Quite a few families made contact with their long-lost relatives through these informal routes. Recently, the two governments introduced digital technology to the family reunion project. This was presented as an alternative to the program of physical reunion, which is limited in numbers and mired with political and diplomatic disputes. I am not sure if the virtual space is an appropriate arena for human encounters in this context, and doubt whether this measure alone will have any substantive effect on alleviating the agony of divided families or improving their rights. For most separated families in Korea, the best they can hope for at the moment is to be able to see their loved ones at least once before death. This means having the luck to be selected to join the occasional spectacle of reunion organized by the two states and their Red Cross representatives. It also relies on North Korea's relations with South Korea (and those with the United States and Japan) not deteriorating in the future, which is a prospect yet uncertain today. Here too, as is the case with Koreans in Japan, interstate and geopolitical relations have direct relevance for familial relations, and small changes in the diplomatic terrain may be experienced in the domestic arena as a world-transforming event, either in terms of rekindled hope or in that of renewed loss of hope.

Choon Soon Kim calls this state of being, which he himself has experienced, "faithful endurance."[21] The "endurance" is manifested in myriad forms. Mr. Koh lives in the old quarter of Seoul, on the hillside a short distance from the bustling commercial and tourist areas. His modest three-room house stands out as the only authentic traditional house in his neighborhood, where practically everyone else undertook major home renovations during the economic and housing boom of the 1980s. Although the district office today praises Koh as a man with a taste for traditional architecture, his neighbors are aware that he has other reasons for keeping his house unchanged – how his parents, together with his three older siblings, evacuated to North Korea during the war, leaving behind them their youngest child and his grandparents, and how he has been faithful to the wishes of his grandparents, who believed that their house should stay identical to how it was in 1950 so that should any of their lost family return home, even as a communist spy, he or she could find it again without difficulty. Madame Yang has the portraits of leaders of North Korea prominently displayed in the living room of her modest house in Osaka. Underneath these portraits is a picture of her late husband, who, throughout his adult life, had actively served the North Korea-affiliated association of Koreans in Japan. Upstairs are parcels that she has prepared to post to her two children in North Korea as well as her other children living elsewhere in Japan. She is saving money for her children in North Korea, while also hoping to make a small contribution to the ancestral rite organized by her relatives in Jeju with whom she recently resumed contact. Most important in her daily life is to make small offerings to the humble shrine in the corner of her kitchen dedicated to the household Kitchen God, a practice that she has carried from her birth village in Jeju, to whom she entrusts the protection of her dispersed, transnational household.[22]

A prominent public figure in South Korea recently said, reflecting on his experience of inter-Korean negotiations on family reunion during the first half of the 2000s, that the main obstacle on this front is the disagreement between the two Korean governments in defining the nature of the problem. South Korea sees separated families as a humanitarian issue that is, in principle, independent from the politics of inter-Korean relations, he said, whereas for North Korea, they are a political question through and through, inseparable from other foreign policy agendas. If we look at the problem of separated families in the contemporary context, indeed, the lack of progress in dealing with this problem may be primarily blamed on the reluctance of the North Korean political administration and the way in which this administration approaches the question of separated families: as an extension of politics, as part of the negotiations for security guarantees and economic aid with the United States and South Korea, rather than an independent humanitarian issue. Seen historically, however, the issue is more complicated. After the war, the two states of Korea continued to be in a state of war against each other, thereby domestically maintaining a system of governance akin to a perpetual state of siege. This system imposed on the postwar society a radically clear distinction of friends versus enemies and, accordingly, criminalized any type of unauthorized contact, real or hypothetical, with the elements of the enemy state, including through family and kinship ties. The empowerment of a radical friend/enemy contrast induced the divided families of Korea into a highly precarious position of being a potential or latent enemy of the state simply by having blood ties with those who inhabit the enemy state. The domain of kinship became a principal site and object of the state's containment and deterrence policies against society in postwar Korea, and many separated families from the war consequently fell into the status of ideologically impure, politically undesirable, and morally non-normative citizens by virtue of their kinship ties.

Notable in Korea's wartime human displacement is the direction that the movement took. The frontier of the 1950 war moved first southward in July to September 1950, pushed by the triumphant North Korean forces, and then in the following few months in the reverse direction, before the Chinese forces intervened in aid of their fragmenting ally and began to push the frontier back again toward the south. Each military movement resulted in an exodus of civilian refugees. Whether the refugees left for the South or the North in this situation is, from their family's perspective, of marginal importance compared to the common critical fact that people were displaced from their homes, and they had to leave home to survive. In the public discourse, however, the exodus to the North and that to the South were not treated in the same way, and whether an individual took one direction or the other mattered greatly.

A man recently posted a note about his missing father to the South Korean government's official family search website:

My father led the People's Committee in Banwŏl District, Hwasŏng County during the war. During the retreat of the People's Army, he brought my mother and his three children to Dolma District, Gwangju, Kyunggi Province, so that we could take refuge with my maternal family. He visited us briefly for a night immediately before September 28 (the day of liberation of Seoul by South

Korean and United Nations forces), said farewells, and went away, over to north, together with my mother's brother.[23]

He used the word *wŏlbuk* to describe the departure of his father and his maternal uncle. In the previous decades, it would have been unthinkable to encounter such sensitive accounts of family histories in the public media. Postwar Korean society developed a complex set of classificatory terms with reference to the displaced population of the Korean War. In the South, these included *wŏlbuk gajok*, a highly stigmatizing term in the postwar era. It literally means "families who crossed to the North," but actually refers to the families who are related to an individual believed to have moved to the northern part of Korea during the war. The meaning of this term is in contrast to other categories of separated families; *wŏlnam gajok* ("families who crossed to the South") and *napbukja gajok* ("families related to a person who is forcibly taken to the North"). All these categories are part of the broader generic category of Korean War separated families, *isan gajok*; each subcategory not only indicates a physical orientation but also assumes a particular political orientation. The category of "crossing to the North" was nearly equivalent to being a "sympathizer with the North," especially when seen in relation to the category of being "forced to cross to the North." The term *napbuk* ("taken to the North") indicates that the individual's northward movement was a coerced one, which, by extension, means that the person's conscious choice of loyalty was with the Southern polity. Set in contrast to this term, the expression *wŏlbuk* ("crossing to the North") carries the sense that the crossing was a willing and willful act, which then becomes a determining statement for the actor's political identity.

The history of the Korean War's human displacement and family separation is imbued with these classificatory terms and the critical, often life-determining consequences of these arbitrary categories. One observer argues that the classification is a reflection of the binary logic that prevailed in postwar society, which set the "red" families (who moved to North Korea during the war) against the patriotic "anti-communist" families (who left North Korea during the war).[24] Another commentator writes that, consequently, the lives of the war-displaced families became a field of conflict between "family feelings" and "political ideologies" and that, as such, the plight of these families crystallize "fundamental contradictions in postwar Korean society."[25] Although all these families experienced the pain of being separated from their loved ones, according to these observers, their public identities were not the same. Certain family feelings were considered a public enemy, as evidenced in the many handbooks about the citizen's everyday vigilance against communist infiltration published in South Korea in the late 1960s and 1970s. The anti-communist public education material published in 1967, titled *Readings in Anticommunist Enlightenment*, for instance, warns that citizens of South Korea might fall for a seditious network to the benefit of the communist North through contact with their relatives in the North.[26] It highlights, among other risks, the danger for people of failing to overcome their family feelings (which it calls "innocent corporeal emotions") when the enemy seeks to appropriate these emotions.[27] Although both the South-crossing families and the families tied to an individual who went over to the North may encounter infiltration attempts, the manual postulates that the latter are especially vulnerable to such attempts for the reason that these people's familial feelings are less disciplined concerning what it calls the ethics of anti-communism.

The actual circumstances in which people left home were much more complex, however, than the binary scheme of southward anti-communist versus northward pro-communist movement can explain.[28] Nor is it correct to assume that the individual decisions to leave were mainly due to that individual's specific ideological commitment or orientation. Earlier in this chapter, I mentioned a controversy over a neglected ancestral grave. The difficulty was that the village ancestor buried in that tomb was a prominent communist activist during the colonial era, a legacy that the villagers found hard to carry on after the war. The village's dispute over the tomb, however, had another hidden history – an event that the people of this village now remember as one of the most catastrophic events in their community's history. In this incident, a majority of the village youths left home northward, a few days after the occupying North Korean troops had evacuated the area and shortly before the South Korean troops came to take control of it. Some village elders today believe that this decision by the village youths related to the legacy of several of the village's colonial-era ancestors having been active in communist and socialist movements. They recall how the residents of this village, the youths in particular, were encouraged by the wartime communist authority to play an active role in their occupation politics and took the view that this demand fell upon their village more strongly than other villages because of the village's ancestral legacy.

Exodus

This impression concerning the community's fate is widespread in the broader area around this village, which I will call Flying Heron with reference to the nearby mountain range. From July to September 1950, the people of the Flying Heron area, apart from those who had relocated to other areas that were still defended by the South Korean and US forces, had a brief experience of a political world that the locals refer to as the time of the People's Republic (an abbreviated reference to the Democratic People's Republic of Korea, that is, North Korea). As elsewhere, this political world not only came with a new state power but also changes in relations among the villagers and between village communities. In certain areas, especially where the residents had suffered greatly from South Korea's prewar counterinsurgency violence, the arrival of the People's Republic was a welcome and liberating experience. For other local communities, the same event was a confusing experience, involving great anxieties about what the future had in store for them and what life would be like in the new world. Beyond these differences, for all local communities, the change involved an exodus of the local population and consequent dispersion of families into separate, contending political worlds, at the outset of the communist occupation and especially at the end of it. In some places, however, the arrival of the People's Republic meant a reunion of separated family members.

   This happened in one settlement west of the Flying Heron mountain range. Occupation politics in this village were initially focused on mobilizing the locals for war-support activities. The village notables and the village youths were encouraged by the occupying forces to join the local county-level People's Committee and youth organizations. One of these village notables was a close relative of a prominent communist activist during the colonial era, which made the elder's family and his lineage group stand out in local politics under the occupation. Another village elder was even more closely tied to the occupation authority. His youngest son, who had left the village in 1948, returned home together with a unit of North Korea's People's Army as the political officer for this unit. Although this elder personally refused to play any public role in the revolutionary mass-mobilization (it is known among the locals that he even refused to welcome his son into his home), his family was given a prominent profile in the local political arena during the occupation. The returnees, such as this elder's youngest son, were expected by North Korea's higher authority to renew their ties of kinship and friendship with the locals and to mobilize these connections in order to facilitate the war effort. It also happened that some of these returnees had been actively involved in grassroots mobilization in the locale prior to their leaving home before the war. Their prewar organizational activities relied on ties of kinship as well as other close interpersonal relations based on a common place of origin and common educational backgrounds. They often had a deeper historical background from the colonial era, during which progressive intellectuals advocated reforms to agrarian relations in their birth villages, especially those between landowning families and landless peasants, as well as, via informal schooling, familiarity with modern knowledge for the village youths and women. Interestingly, some of these activists were also deeply engaged in issues of social reform within their familial milieus – notably, issues of women's rights and of equal rights between the so-called primary and secondary line of descent, the latter often meaning children of a concubine who were typically unable to join the ancestral rites. Against this backdrop, a historian familiar with the local political situation under the People's Republic found that "once someone was taken out [to join the politics of the People's Republic], the entire lineage group of this individual came out along with the latter like a fishnet. This solidarity was the norm and the rule that shaped orientations in the wider social arena."[29] The occupation force's politics brought these existing local networks of historically constituted close interpersonal ties into its service, which became the source of profound instability for the locals when the tide of war changed and these ties subsequently became a liability for them in relation to the political authority on the opposite side of the conflict.

North Korea's occupation politics focused on mobilizing local resources, both human and material, in support of their war effort. The obligation for local support activities fell initially heavily on the youths and the women, whom the occupation authority was particularly intent on organizing. The occupation force's politics initially put great emphasis on earning the sympathy of the locals through various study and cultural performance meetings (such as the teaching of North Korea's revolutionary songs to local children). As the battles intensified, however, North Korea's war effort became increasingly dependent on the provision of food and labor from the occupied localities. Villagers were required to contribute a large proportion of their agricultural produce (25–30 percent) to the North Korean army; the army also needed labor to transport provisions to the front and, increasingly, more labor for their fighting forces. The last started as the mobilization of volunteers from the local population but later became more one of forced conscription.[30]

In Flying Heron, when the Northern troops were preparing for evacuation and the arrival of the Southern forces was imminent in mid-September 1950, anxiety about the uncertain future brought life in the village to the brink of collapse. One villager, the eldest descendant of one of the area's main lineage groups, vividly recalled the strange quietness of his village at that time, in which neighbors suddenly stopped paying visits and speaking to each other. He also recalled the heavy silence of his uncles and aunts when his grandfather reproached them for having committed, in his words, rash and thoughtless deeds under the People's Republic. He

later learned that his grandfather had been concerned about the consequences of the village youths, including his own children, taking part in
the revolutionary youths' and women's organization activities. His grandfather's consistent opinion throughout the occupation period was that
any involvement in politics in the conditions of war ran the risk of
jeopardizing the family's prospects for survival, and that anyone's involvement in the politics of the People's Republic threatened the safety of all
others in the family. He was not alone in his opinion. The returning
political officer of a North Korean army unit, mentioned earlier, joined
a welcoming gathering for his homecoming organized by the youths of his
lineage group. In response to the questions from his young relatives about
the outside world and his experience in North Korea, the cadre told them
instead that it was not the time for them to get too heavily involved with
the outside world, and that they should refrain from being too visible in
the world outside of the village. According to a villager who was present at
that reception, the cadre was not impressed when he told him that he was
hoping to join the youth theater troupe that was being organized by the
local People's Committee. The cadre remained unresponsive to his
enthusiasm throughout the meeting. When he was about to leave and
was putting on his shoes, the cadre made a remark to him in a quiet voice
that left a great impression on him: "It would be better if you stayed in the
village. Your responsibility is to keep this village safe. I say this to you as
your elder brother."

When these youths later heard the rumor that the Southern army was
closing in on the area, they and their families were greatly concerned.
They knew that some of the other village youths had left home, heading
toward the North, and were not sure whether they should follow. They
feared the uncertain immediate future and were unsure as to what punish-
ments would ensue from the approaching army against people like themselves who had taken part in the youth activities of the People's Republic.
However, none of them was able to make a decision between the two
equally undesirable choices available to them: stay home and face the
retribution or leave home and face the uncertainty of an exodus and the
possibility of a permanent displacement from home. The youths tried to
solicit advice from their family elders. They divided the group into two;
one group went to speak to the cadre and the other group to the village's
most prominent elder and scholar of Confucian classics. When the group
met again to discuss the results of their consultations in an isolated,
abandoned house on the outskirts of the village one quiet evening, the
young villagers were disappointed. It transpired that neither the village
Confucian scholar nor their communist cadre relative had any concrete
advice to offer. I cite from my fieldwork diary:

Sŏrŭng ajae [the Confucian scholar] was silent for a long while. So were we. Then, at last, he put aside his smoking pipe and let out a deep sigh. He said that on this matter, he had no advice to give to us. He said, "This time, you have to find your own way." We were shocked to hear that, for he had been always prepared to give clear answers to everything. Bŭmgol ajae [the cadre relative] was no different. We asked him whether we should follow him or stay at home. He responded that he was not able to help us on this matter. He said, "Only you can judge what you will do with your life." We were shocked to hear this from him, because we believed that he knew the world.

The above incident left a profound impression on my informant, which meant, for him, a collapse of the authority of seniority. It meant that the situation was so unintelligibly chaotic that any traditional intuition and any amount of knowledge of current affairs could not lead to a meaningful conclusion from which people could make their decision. A testimonial account of this confusing moment from another villager says: "Some of us went with the retreating People's Army, but most stayed on. How could we know how far and widely they [the South Korean forces] would draw the circle of the reds?" The survivor who provided this testimony had been in fear due to his work during the North Korean army's retreat, which was to help carry the army's wounded soldiers to the village north of his.[31]

Despite their confusion and difficulty in deciding, however, a decision had to be made and made quickly. The eight youths made their choices during the weeklong political vacuum after the cadre and his unit had left the area, leaving the administration of the district's People's Committee to a few local recruits. Five of these youths left the village for the North. The rest remained in the village area, two of them taking shelter in the homes of their maternal relatives in other villages nearby. Of the five who left the village, two eventually came back after encountering South Korean troops on their northward journey and, therefore, found that there was no escape route. Another village youth returned home because he ran out of food provisions. Although these young people had diverse backgrounds, their decisions to return were all influenced by the perceived roles that they had played in occupation politics, on the one hand, and, on the other, by their positions in the family. Those who played a relatively more visible public role in occupation politics were more inclined to leave their homeland. These included the villagers who took up a leadership role in the revolutionary youths' and women's organizations. In evacuating the village, some of these youths were accompanied by their siblings, cousins, and other close relatives, who, although having played only a marginal or no role in occupation politics, chose to put their fate with their siblings or cousins whom they trusted or had strong ties of affinity with.

The strong bond that existed among these young villagers was not reducible to a common political commitment. The villager whom I cited above left the village together with his half-brother and cousin. He said that he could not let go of them as he had a strong attachment to them, and they had always been protective of him. He recalled how in the prewar conflicts between the youths of his village and those in a neighboring village, which he called a "right-wing village," his two relatives had tried to shield him at school from intimidation by students from the other village. If ties of kinship and interpersonal affinity were a source of collective action and decision, the contrary was also true, and kinship status and family connections sometimes made it difficult to undertake such an action. Even for a family that played a visible and prominent role in occupation politics, it was difficult to envisage that the family as a whole could abandon their ancestral land, even if they were in fear of the consequence of not doing so in a changed political situation. There were elders to be cared for, and married women with children were generally reluctant to undertake such an uncertain and dangerous journey away from home in the continuing fog of war. Whereas the fear of retribution was strong among the villagers, equally strong was the ethos that someone in the family should remain in the ancestral land in order to keep the house safe and to attend to ancestral graves. This was the case even with the family of the cadre mentioned earlier. Some of the cadre's relatives urged him to bring all his siblings and close cousins with him, fearing that the latter might face immediate danger to their lives when, as one villager who knew the family well told me, "the national flag on the flagpole of the district office changed from one kind to another." The cadre apparently contested their opinion and insisted that his youngest cousin should remain in the village and keep the ancestral home. Other families also tried to keep at least one child or grandchild away from the exodus to the North.

For these families, the term *wŏlbukja gajok*, families whose close relations crossed to the North, was a highly stigmatizing concept for much of their postwar lives. This category implies that certain connections existed between separated families across the bipolar border, and that these connections were intrinsic to their kinship ties. Grounded on a seemingly innocent idea of the amity of kinship, the category, nevertheless, is a profoundly political and politicized concept. It assumes certain authenticity of family feelings and their relative autonomy from prevailing political forces and imperatives. However, this category also distorts the meaning of family feelings by appropriating them as a political instrument for an ideologically pure and disciplined society (see Chapter 4). In this context, the amity of kinship comes to have two related, yet radically different meanings. On the one hand, it shows that a certain domain of human relations cannot be entirely subjugated to the grid of modern political forces no matter how ferocious these forces may be. The projected relative autonomy of this communal domain from modern politics, on the other hand, makes such a domain an important object of political intervention and control. The ideal citizen of the anti-communist polity is, then, an individual who, like the state, is devoted to the principle of freedom from communism as the first principle of political existence. The political principle, for the ideal citizen, should come before the amity of kinship and should override the latter if necessary. The paradox is, however, that in order for it to stay meaningful, this principle requires the continuous existence of objects to discipline, which means that the citizens of this polity cannot possibly ever entirely sever their ties from the politically tainted domain of kinship. In other words, the ideal citizen of this polity is not a truly modern individual subject, supposedly free from communal bonds. Instead, they are a communal being in a double sense of the term, who, being related to both the traditional community of kinship and the modern community of national society, is committed to making and keeping the former in the image of the latter.

Crosscutting Ties

The idea that a kin-based social order is woven by relations of amity but is also rife with structural conditions of enmity and possible sources of conflict was what the South African-born anthropologist Max Gluckman was mainly concerned with in his 1955 BBC lectures.[32] In these lectures, Gluckman spoke about the dynamic nature of the Nuer political system in southern Sudan, in which people aggregate to form a large collective in the dry season near the scarce sources of water, and disperse in small, largely autonomous units to an extensive terrain during the rainy season. Because of this seasonal variation in the ecological and social patterns of dwelling and grouping, Gluckman argued, following Evans-Pritchard whose ethnography of the Nuer he drew upon, that the Nuer had developed not only the solidarity and autonomy of a descent-based small territorial group but also complex interlocking ties between different territorial groups. When groups are in dispute involving the risk of an armed confrontation, therefore, the Nuer not only unite along their separate group loyalties, but they may also mobilize the crosscutting ties that exist between discrete groupings. Hence, people may try, particularly those who have marriage ties with people in the opposite group, to moderate the escalating hostility between the two groups. Calling this condition "peace in the feud," Gluckman defined the crosscutting social ties existing between territorial descent groups as the principal buffer against the prevailing condition of conflict and war in the Nuer tribal system. Gluckman delivered these ideas in 1955. In doing so, he was clearly conscious of the polarizing situation of the international community at the time, although his effort fell short of bringing elements of existing ethnographic knowledge about tribal politics to a novel perspective on global politics. However, the message he tried to get across in his lectures on crosscutting ties can throw light on understanding the human experience of the violent politics of the postcolonial Cold War.

In Flying Heron, as in many other places in South Korea, the occupation by the Northern forces involved the incorporation of local communities into the occupying power's war efforts. When the tide of war turned and control over the village transferred to the opposite state power, these communities faced a life-threatening situation. A number of villagers were arrested and subsequently underwent intense interrogation at the district office, which had changed from the North Korea-run People's Committee to the headquarters of the South Korean military police. These included all adult members of the cadre's family. His father was accused of having collaborated with the enemy in the capacity of village representative to the local People's Committee, and he did not survive the wounds that he received during the weeklong interrogation. Other family members survived, although not all, thanks in part to the long friendship between the cadre's father, who was a respected scholar of Confucian classics, and one of his distant relatives, the former principal of a local secondary school. In their youth, these two men studied in the same traditional school that taught Confucian texts. The school principal was a senior advisor to the local anti-communist youth organization, and his younger brother was a relatively high-ranking civil servant in the wartime South Korean administration. The schoolmaster played a critical role in protecting the cadre's family from the retributive violence committed by the South Korean military and police authority. His intervention on behalf of the cadre's family was partly in return for the debt that his family owed them. During the early days of North Korean occupation, the schoolmaster's family had received threats from the occupying power while he himself was away in hiding. It is known among the residents of Flying Heron that these threats were neutralized by the intervention of the cadre's father, the village Confucian scholar, through his family connections to the communist occupying authority. Although these reciprocal actions did not entirely protect the schoolmaster's, or the Confucian scholar's families from physical losses and hardships, they nevertheless provided crucial niches of survival for both. Furthermore, these stories of common survival remain in Flying Heron today as a pivotal episode of the war, repeatedly told among the war-generation village elders and trans-mitted to the postwar generations.

In other hamlets nearby, ties of marriage proved vital for survival. In a village south of the Flying Heron mountain range, introduced earlier as a moskoba village, the chaotic politics of occupation and liberation had particularly dire consequences. This largely single-lineage village had sev-eral prominent ancestral figures relating to the nationalist-communist intellectual and political movements of the colonial era. Some of their colonial-era ancestors had a distinct history of initiating education and social reform movements based in their birthplace. Their locally grounded anti-colonial activism involved youth educational activities and the con-solidation of peasant cooperatives, and this legacy left a profound impact on the village's fate during the war. The local youth educational movement contributed to bringing about strong solidarity among the village youths, adding to their existing ties of descent and locality the new ties resulting from a common educational background. The strength of these combined ties of solidarity was forcefully manifested in the village's response to the political reality of the Korean War. The village's reputation in the area as the birthplace of the area's prominent radical nationalist activists contributed to attracting attention from the North Korean occupying authority, which subsequently encouraged the residents of this "patriotic village" to play an exemplary role in the social mobilization for the revolutionary war. This pressure was particularly strong on the families of the village's anti-colonial activists. When the North Korean occupation was over, the elders of this village were gravely concerned about the possibility that in the new situation, the village as a whole might be judged to be a large, single collective of collaborators with the enemy. Their fears were not unwarranted.

A number of youths left their village amid the chaos of September 1950. Then, one day, a large group of youths arrived in the village, armed with clubs and sickles. These young men from a nearby village began searching the houses, looking for their targets, who they believed had caused hardship and suffering to their own village during the communist occupation. An unpublished village chronicle speaks of the moment when the people of the moskoba village faced the threshold of life and death. While the youths were rounding up the villagers, an elderly man hastily arrived from the youths' own village. Related to some of the youths in ties of kinship, the man had also held a senior position at the local anti-communist youth organization before the war. According to the chronicle of the era kept by a local villager, the elder confronted the mob:

This village and your village have a long history of friendship. Your grandmothers came from this village, and your fathers' sisters were married to this village. That makes you all of having mixed blood, the same mixed blood that people here have. You destroyed the earthenware pots kept in your grandfather's sister's home and now intend to use those clubs against the children of your great grandmothers. How dare you! Do you know what ignorant people you are and what an act of utter ignorance this is![33]

The mention of "mixed blood" remains in the moskoba village as one of the most cherished memories of this otherwise painful and chaotic time that the end of 1950 was for the village, when young men and women from practically every household had to leave home and have never been heard from since.[34] Their remaining families had to endure the consequences of their exodus to the North for many years after the war ended; not only the pain of missing their loved ones but also the troubles resulting from the public label of their home as a red village and red lineage group. The time remains a dark hole in the village's history, which local people find difficult to recall even today. The act of intervention by the elder and the magical power of his words, "mixed blood," however, stand out in the village's otherwise deep silence about the time as one bright shining episode that is still being talked about.

These acts of mutual assistance for survival actually abound in the lived history of the Korean War, even though their stories seldom appear in the existing historiography. Such actions also continued after the war, offering vital niches of survival for many in Flying Heron. One villager in the north of the mountain range survived the punitive violence against collaborators, despite the fact that he had held a position of moderate importance during the North Korean occupation. This was largely thanks to the efforts of his relatives who mobilized on his behalf their wide kin and marriage networks, which included people who held positions on the opposite side in the war. Even after the war, this kin and friendship network had to be remobilized occasionally. In the early 1960s, with the help of some of his old school friends, this same man managed to find a job in a local school as a teacher of mathematics. His friends put their names forward as guarantors of his ideological health when the latter made an appeal to the police. When the mathematics teacher was later refused a promotion and, subsequently, forced to take early retirement (it is known that this was caused by a jealous colleague in his school who wrote a letter to the local education board denouncing his past history), he was heartbroken. After this incident, every now and then, the teacher's relatives were faced with new heart-stopping situations. On one occasion, the teacher was found in front of the district office (that was the office of the People's Committee during the North Korean occupation), after spending an evening in a bar with friends, saying in loud voice, "Long live the People's Republic!" Then, the lineage elders of his birth village had to gather at an emergency meeting to find a way to counter this new crisis facing the extended family as a whole. By that time, fortunately for the people of this village, several members of the lineage group held positions of some influence in the local administration and economy.

The Ethics of the Heavens

These episodes are a source of dignity for the people of Flying Heron, whereas their most bitter memories of war relate not merely to the experience of violence and loss but also to failures in mutual caring, which typically involved someone's indifference to his or her close relations who were at the threshold of life and death. Although we may say that the history of these inactions is about failures in the moral life of kinship, the people of Flying Heron do not express their past experiences in such a way. For them, the history is unspeakable as it concerns violating "the ethics of the heavens," the most elementary ethical rules that govern human relations and which make the relations human.

On a closing note, a few more words are due regarding the controversy over the renovation of the ancestral grave mentioned at the outset. The man who proposed the idea of renovation was the only descendant of the person buried in the neglected tomb, having been adopted by the latter in his childhood for a ritual purpose. He was nine years old at the time of his adoption. The ancestor at issue was his birth father's elder brother. His adopted father died in 1939, and his biological father moved to North Korea during the Korean War and has not been heard from since. The adoptee also spent a brief period of his childhood in North Korea together with his younger brother and his birth parents. After staying a few months in Northern Korea, his birth father sent him back to their home in Andong. The returnee now believes that his birth father brought his family to North Korea in the hope of finding a safe place for his family during the war, and that his father sent him back home hoping that his son would carry on family duties in their native homeland. These duties were principally caring for his grandfather, who had been left behind in their home village, and later, taking charge of the death-day rites for family ancestors. He has duly performed this duty for the past six decades, first together with his grandfather. Since his grandfather passed away in the early 1960s, he has been holding death-day rites for both of his adopted parents, his grandparents, and his great-grandparents in his modest home in the suburb of Daegu, where he has been settled since 1969.

Performing these rites has placed a tremendous burden on him. This was not merely because of the care that he and his family had to invest in these rites despite their meager earnings in the city. The ritual obligation came with an unwanted, stigmatizing affiliation, which he was not able to undo. Until very recently, he was not able to tell his children who their grandfather (his adopted father) really was. Each time he held an ancestral death-commemoration rite, it brought back the memory of discrimination and fear that he had endured in his home village and elsewhere as a descendant of "a red family line." He was aware that people in his home village complained about the way their village as a whole was viewed as a subversive place by others. Although he was sympathetic to their indignation, it was hard for him to come to terms with the accusations made by some of these villagers against his family. He was indignant at the fact that a history that had nothing to do with him was weighing on his life and his children's lives. His frustration was also set against his own inability to free himself from the burden of his genealogical history. Recently, he finally found the courage to tell his children about their grandfather. He has also taken the initiative to speak to the elders of his ancestral village about his long-held desire, which was to improve the tomb of his adopted parents. He has had new worries since then, however. When he prepares death-day rites for his adopted parents nowadays, he is anxious with thoughts about his birth parents whom he last saw in North Korea more than sixty years ago. He is sure that they are no longer alive, and the uncertainty that bothers him is about his younger brother and whether he survived the war. He is anxious with the thoughts of whether his brother in the North, or anyone else in the world, is offering commemorative meals to his birth parents. He is also struggling with the irony of history: his adopted father has recently been reinstated as a contributor to the national independence movement by the South Korean government as part of the government's initiative to accept the history of Korea's communist and socialist resistance to colonialism as a meaningful national heritage. The initiative was welcomed by many residents in Flying Heron, and it was, indeed, as a result of this background that the adopted son of the communist ancestor found the courage to speak to his village elders. The beneficiaries of the government policy were restricted, however, to historical actors of the colonial era – that is, those who had nothing to do with the struggle of the Korean War. They excluded people like the man's birth parents who moved to North Korea during the Korean War. Because of this, the adopted son now feels that in the end, it worked for him that he had been severed from his birth family who, unlike his adopted family, have no prospect of being freed from the iron cage of history and the scarlet letters of a red bloodline.

4   Guilt by Association

When we become strangers to society, due to our family ties to an individual whom the state deems its enemy, how do we then find a space in that society for a livable existence? Is it possible to cut ourselves off from the crushing ties of kinship? Or is there a place in the world where we might be free from the burden of genealogy? And what is to be blamed for our precarious life – the weight of kinship relations or the reality of the political world? Questions such as these appear prominently in testimonial accounts of the rule of associative guilt – the shadowy instrument of societal control that was in operation throughout the postwar years and for the duration of the Cold War. What is striking about the system of associative liability is that the disciplinary power of this political practice, while working against the organization of kinship, nevertheless aims to work from within it as well. It is an effective disciplinary technology of the state over society. However, the efficacy of this modern disciplinary mechanism necessitates relational and mutually constitutive persons, rather than individuated and autonomous subjects; that is, what is often referred to as "the moral person" in the existing sociological and anthropological literature in distinction to the philosophical idea of the modern individual.

One established way to clarify this distinction between the moral person and the "natural person" (as the modern individual is sometimes referred to in the philosophical literature), within the discipline of modern sociocultural anthropology, is through recourse to two different classes of things exchanged among people, which are gifts and commodities. It is assumed that people who exchange gifts with each other do so as moral beings: the things given contain parts of the donor's moral self and are, thus, inalienable from the latter even if these objects physically depart from the donor's immediate milieu. Each time this moral self gives something to another person, what is given is not merely a thing but also a part of that self. The exchange of gifts, therefore, represents the history of the moral relationship between the donor and the receiver and contributes to reproducing this given relationship. In contrast, commodities are alienable from those who produce and exchange them, and they exist in the realm of quantifiable exchange values, rather than unquantifiable social norms and cultural values. Commodities contain no property of moral selfhood and are defined as such by this absence.

The underlying ideas of the political and penal institution of associative guilt are not, therefore, unfamiliar in the tradition of modern social thought. The institution projects the objects of its disciplinary power as social, nonindividuated, and "gift-like" beings whose selfhood is not conceptually independent from the webs of intimate moral relations surrounding it. The self faces the state not as a singular and philosophically sovereign being but as a relational and socially embedded one. However, crucial differences also exist between the idea of the moral person familiar from the sociology of personhood and that of the moral subject caught within the system of associative culpability. The institutional practice of associative guilt is an appropriation of moral personhood by the state in a modern constitutional society, which is founded upon the banishment of such practices from the sphere of penal law and practice. The politics of associative culpability flourished within the environment of modern law and irrespective of the latter, whose guiding principle is the rule of individual responsibility. If the object of the state's disciplinary order is both an individual (in formality) and a moral person (in practice), it follows that the actions intended to challenge this order may also have a duplex character, not reducible either to the political realm of *civitas* or to the interpersonal sphere of *societas* (see the Introduction to this volume). In this context, the moral person's struggle to exist autonomously as such can turn out to be a powerful public political action in the recovery of individual liberty and the rule of law.

The Roots of Communism

Korea was not the only place where family and communal relations became the object of political control and punitive actions during the era of the global Cold War. Discussing the impact of the anti-communist terror unleashed in Java and Bali in 1965–1966, the historian Geoffrey Robinson describes how the generalized terror campaign distorted the moral fabric of Balinese communities.[1] He observes that the widespread practice of punishing the chosen victims together with their families and close relatives left deep scars in the affected communities. The tragedy was triggered by an alleged coup attempt by a group of army officers sympathetic to the Indonesian Communist Party, which provided the pretext for the anti-communist army leaders, led by General Suharto, to step in to obstruct the coup and, subsequently, launch an offensive against the left. The offensive against the Communist Party quickly evolved into a widespread death campaign against segments of the population believed to be harboring communist sympathizers, as a means of purifying the Indonesian nation and ridding it of the pollutants of alien ideology and beliefs. The state's violence against society was based partly on "the logic of associative guilt and the need for collective retribution," which aimed to destroy the ideological enemies within society "down to the roots."[2] In these historical contexts, it was possible for individuals to be labeled "red" just because they belonged to a specific social group, and to experience accordingly something akin to extreme racial discrimination in society even if they had the same skin color as everyone else.

The anthropologist Robert Lemelson's documentary, *40 Years of Silence: An Indonesian Tragedy* (2009) movingly shows how the Balinese landscape is indeed soaked in the unresolved memories of 1965. The film follows several individuals and their post-1965 lives. One of them is a daughter of an ethnic Chinese family, whose father was involved in a radical democratic political movement during the Sukarno era. The brutal death of her father in 1965 led to social stigmatization and economic hardship for the surviving family after the massacre. In the subsequent era of democratization leading to the fall of Suharto's rule in 1998, the family's daughter turned into a locally prominent human rights activist. She struggled to put to rest and move beyond the painful memory of the family's past sufferings; her efforts included the moving scene of her mobilizing aid and charities for the victims of a recent natural disaster in her old birth home. Some of these victims were the perpetrators of the violence in 1965 that killed the woman's father. The film also features a man who returns to his home village after being absent since childhood. The village is silently yet bitterly divided in its memory of the chaos of 1965, and the returnee has to face neighbors who were directly responsible for the death of his father. His attempt to make peace with one culpable individual fails, and instead, he faces bitter disapproval from his surviving relatives. He is also trying to reconcile with the memory of his mother, who he long believed had abandoned him. The man learns slowly and painfully how his mother's decision to marry one of the killers of her late husband was her only option to save her child, forcing her to leave her son behind.

During the Vietnam War, people in the southern and central regions of Vietnam were familiar with the expression *hat giang do*. This idiom, meaning literally "red plant [from red seeds]" referred to people who were believed to be "communists born and bred." Widely used in the former South Vietnam during the political campaigns to uproot communism from Vietnamese society, the idiom implies that doing so requires eliminating not only the "plants" of individual suspects but also the "seeds" of their social, genealogical origins.[3] Stephan Feuchtwang investigated the incidents of anti-communist state terror in Taiwan in the early 1950s (which were, together with the politically opposite but structurally similar terror events in mainland China at the same time, closely related to the outbreak of war in the Korean peninsula), with the focus on how the experience of state violence is transmitted within families and across generations.[4] In a broadly similar context, Greg Grandin investigated the alleged "susceptibility of Mayans to communism" during the 1981–1983 terror campaigns in Guatemala against indigenous communities.[5]

During the Greek civil war (1946–1949), according to Polymeris Voglis, "the line between legality and illegality was drawn along the lines of nationalism versus communism. Ideas, intentions, and even family relations during the Civil War were labelled as 'antinational' and thus became new forms of illegality."[6] Voglis describes how family relations became "new objects of punitive practices" and how the terrifying label "antinational" exerted enormous pressure on the prisoners and their families. He reconstructs the intimate experiences of these people, drawing upon their diaries and memoirs, and situating their experiences in the broad historical context of post-Second World War Europe. In doing so, he raises objections to Michel Foucault's seminal thesis on the birth of the modern prison.[7]

Voglis's objections to Foucault are broadly based on two grounds. One of them concerns Foucault's differentiation of modern from premodern penal practices in the context of European history. Under this distinction, premodern practices consist primarily of introducing physical pain to the prisoner's body in a spectacular way, while modern penal technology is focused on disciplining the body within a system of surveillance, as Foucault illustrates with Bentham's panoptical structure.[8] According to Foucault, "In a society in which the principal elements are no longer the community and public life, but, on the one hand, private individuals and, on the other, the state, relations can be regulated only in a form that is the exact the reverse of the spectacle ... Our society is one not of spectacle, but of surveillance."[9] Voglis argues that this sharp contrast between the premodern spectacle of physical punishment and the modern disciplinary surveillance regime does not fit with the actual penal history of modern Europe, especially in the punishment of political crimes in which torture and surveillance were both liberally used. Voglis highlights measures such as the forced removal of children from female inmates who refused to make a confession, which was widely practiced against Greek political prisoners during and after the civil war. He questions whether such measures should be considered corporal or noncorporal punishment, considering that the inmates who underwent this harrowing experience regarded the coerced separation from their children as something akin to an experience of torture. Voglis questions whether Foucault's thoughts on the evolution of penal technology, which is grounded in the idea of the modern individual human subject, can apply to the condition and subjectivity of Greek political prisoners, which were, according to him, fundamentally social and political.

The punitive, disciplinary power of the Greek penal camps was concentrated on punishing the anti-national ideas and ideals believed to be held by inmates, which was crystallized in the extraction of confessions from these inmates in the form of their renouncing such ideals. Coerced confessions were also liberally practiced in postwar Korea against political and ideological prisoners. In regard to this history, a South Korean historian recently protested that "Human thoughts and minds must not be the object of law for control. The freedom of conscience is an absolute [human] right."[10] These inmates were exposed to a variety of intense physical abuses and torture, as recent inquiries and testimonies have shown.[11] However, the pain that they experienced within the system of confession was not merely corporal (bodily pain inflicted for refusing to make confessions). For the Greek political prisoners, the form of punishment was inseparable from the contradictions existing between the inmates' obligations to their families outside the prison on the one hand and, on the other, their loyalties to other inmates and comrades – contradictions that the politics of conversion and confession systematically exploited. In the Korean context, the historian mentioned above notes the gruesome practice of punishing prisoners who refused to denounce communism (for those who had families in the South) with punitive measures, sometimes including physical punishment directed against their parents or siblings instead.[12]

What follows in this chapter supports Voglis's observation that the body as the object of punitive actions can be a social body located in a web of social and moral ties, rather than the docile body of an isolated individual located within a "minute web of panoptic techniques," as it appears in Foucault's work.[13] In an ideologically charged conflict, such as the Greek civil war or the Korean War, the weight of political punishment often fell on people who were suspected of harboring subversive ideas, rather than those who had actually committed a political crime. If the object of disciplinary penal actions is a body of ideas and ideals that the state hopes to eradicate from the space under its rule, where would it find the targets to discipline and punish in the first place? What are the ways to materialize the condemned body of ideas (what George Orwell called *thoughtcrimes*) so that political and administrative resources can be invested against the condemned? The history of punishment can take a radically different route from that described by Foucault in places where the technology of power had to first invent the materiality of the condemned body before it could set out to punish and discipline it.

Collective Culpability

One of the most distinctive penal systems in postwar Korea was a set of rules and practices classed as the *yŏnjwaje*. The broad purpose of this system, according to the definition provided in the 1980 Basic Laws of the Republic of Korea, which banned the practices, was for a person to experience disadvantages due to actions committed not by him or her but by someone related to the person. In a narrower definition, which is how the term has been used in postwar Korea, the rule of *yŏnjwaje* refers to the specific domain of civic life in which the culpability for an individual's criminal actions, if these are judged to threaten national security, may be shared by the culpable individual's close relations. The rule was in practice in both Koreas during and after the war, although the specific ways in which it was implemented differ between the two societies. This is due to, above all, North Korea's liberal use of labor camps for containing politically subversive individuals and their families, an institution that North Korea borrowed from Soviet Russia. This is unlike South Korea where containment took a relatively more socially diffused technical form.[14] In postwar South Korea, *yŏnjwaje* is popularly understood, according to one observer, primarily as "a type of guilt-by-association in which one leftist in a family could subject all relatives to surveillance."[15] In North Korea, a systematic compiling of information on *yosiin* ("people who require inspection") – individuals over the age of fourteen who are deemed impure social elements (and whose lives, therefore, require careful inspection by the revolutionary state's security agencies) – was put in place before the war and further empowered after 1950. Controls deployed against these individuals included surveillance of their family ties, which sometimes included even affinal relatives and maternal relations.[16]

In the literature of law and ethics, similar institutional or customary practices appear under the rubric of collective responsibility and collective punishment, contrasting with the principle of individual rights and responsibility sanctified in modern society and law.[17] A distant example would be frankpledge, which was widely in place in England during the Early Middle Ages, a system of mutual accountability and compulsory sharing of responsibility in legal matters among members of a group.[18]

More recent and directly relevant ones would be reprisal killings and mass retribution for resistance activity during the First World War (as in some villages in Belgium and France under German occupation) and the Second World War (in German- or Japanese-occupied territories), against which the 1949 Geneva Conventions ruled that "no persons may be punished for an offense he or she has not personally committed" in Article 33. These practices appear in the literature of legal history under the general idiom, "guilt by association," "a deplorable ethical concept, a carry-over from our barbaric, tribal past," according to legal theorist Larry May.[19] Such deeds are a violation of the "sacred ethical principle" in the modern world that "one bears responsibility only to the degree that one has taken part and acted."[20] They also go against the grain of modern social theory. In Durkheim's theory of penal evolution, for instance, individualization is central to the understanding of modern law and society. In premodern societies, responsibility may be shared collectively, with kinsmen being held liable for transgressions committed by individuals. In modern society, however, Durkheim states that "these elementary groups lose their autonomy and become merged with the total mass, and responsibility becomes individual."[21]

Yŏnjwaje has been a familiar term for Koreans, especially those of the war generation. It is associated most prominently with the prevailing wartime and postwar conditions, in which the punishment of an individual whom the state has defined as an enemy of the political community might fall on the individual's family and kindred. The presence of this individual within the family could be a postmortem condition, or it could take on other forms of physical absence, such as someone who went missing during the war or one who is believed to have joined the opposite side in the war. The criminalization of the family was nominally against the law: the practice of collective responsibility was unconstitutional, banned as early as 1894 when the first modern constitutional rule was established in Korea. Nevertheless, it was an integral element of the state's penal practice throughout much of the twentieth century. Although there have been several attempts to eradicate the practice of collective culpability, which includes the 1980 Basic Law mentioned earlier, this draconian practice actually lasted until very recently.[22]

The existence of *yŏnjwaje* goes a long way back in the history of Korea. In premodern times, collective culpability was an explicit, legitimate element of the penal institution of feudal dynastic rule, in which those who were judged to have challenged the authority of the sovereign were punished not only with their death but also with the death (or enslavement or banishment to remote areas) of their entire family. The term *yŏnjwa*, meaning literally "relations seated together," refers to the structure of the feudal court where the judgment against the accused was pronounced in the presence of his dependents and descendants gathered at his back. Although the *yŏnjwa* system has a long history in Korea, its modern ramifications, however, are not to be considered merely in terms of historical continuity or deplorable cultural survival, as the legal historian cited earlier argues. The "barbaric" institution of collective punishment existed in twentieth-century Korea not merely as a remnant of the backward past but, as I will argue shortly, more because the institution was a highly effective instrument of social control in a particular condition of political modernity and crisis. Moreover, the institutional practice of collective culpability proliferated in Cold War-era Korean politics and society, despite the clear public awareness that the practice was unwarranted in modern life.

The persistence of this practice is evident in the continual attempts by South Korean lawmakers to annihilate the *yŏnjwa* system. The leader of the 1961 military coup promised to abolish the system during his presidential campaign in 1963, and this was followed by the announcement from the South Korean interior ministry in 1966 that the system no longer existed. However, when a new group of military-political elite subsequently took power, a new promise was made to abolish the *yŏnjwa* system. This happened in 1980 and again in 1987, and each time, the decision was supposed to be a real and final abolition. The *yŏnjwa* system was, therefore, in Korea's Cold War modernity, both a conceptually defunct penal institution in modern society and, in practice, a useful and indispensable instrument in modern politics. The important point about the *yŏnjwa* system is, therefore, that it existed both outside the rule of law and inside the legal order in practice. It was in part a feudal legacy outlawed in Korea's modern constitutional history; nevertheless, this punitive system has had a powerful shadowy presence in the country's modern political and legal history. Its existence in modern life became a source of suffering and bitterness for numerous families and individuals, and it continued to exist until the geopolitical structures of the Cold War began to crumble in the late 1980s. Hence, it is possible to imagine that the system of collective culpability has both premodern and modern origins. The fact that the institution was in practice in modern Korea in spite of the general public awareness of its unlawful status within modern politics shows the limits and distortion of political modernity at the outposts of the global Cold War.

The "survival" of the feudal penal system in modern political life may, therefore, be seen as an invention of tradition, relating to the critical questions of sovereignty and citizenship arising from the particularly volatile condition of the Cold War that societies faced in the second half of the twentieth century. Alternatively, the phenomenon can be considered, rather than as an expression of a specific social order and historical tradition, more squarely as an integral element of the global political ordering of the time. The validity of this second view becomes apparent if we pay attention to how widespread and generalized the politics of collective culpability was in the mid-twentieth century. We focus in this book on the systems of associative guilt as these were manifested in the global South and amid the postcolonial Cold War. However, we know that collective punishment was liberally practiced in the process of state-building in the socialist revolutionary world. We also know that in the United States, during the drive to cleanse society of so-called un-American activities, "guilt or innocence has turned upon charges of association with other persons or with organizations tainted with suspicion."[23] The system of associative guilt, therefore, bespeaks not only the predicaments of sovereignty and citizenship in the decolonizing world but also the limits of the Cold War's political modernity more broadly and globally. What was this system that shaped modern politics outside modern law? Why did kinship become the principal site of contradiction between law and politics in Korea's Cold War?

Two-Colored Family Genealogy

In November 1978, the eldest descendant of the Anh lineage group, in a village north of Andong, in northern Kyungsang Province, had an unforgettable encounter with the history of his lineage. Arrested at home on the previous evening, Anh was brought to the basement interrogation room of what he later found out was the office of the province's state security agency. In this room, the then 45-year-old rice farmer was made to face a large wall-mounted drawing. Trembling in extreme fear, Anh recognized that the drawing depicted a family genealogical chart. The drawing listed a number of names branching out from left to right, connected by a gradually expanding set of horizontal and vertical lines. Being the eldest descendant of his lineage group, Anh kept a collection of records in his home that had similar genealogical drawings. It took time, however, before Anh realized that the two dozen names written on the wall-mounted paper were those of his family. It was much later that he also noticed that the names were written in two different colors – most in black and a few in bright red. Eventually, Anh recognized the red-colored names introduced at the center of the genealogical chart as those of his two paternal uncles, who had been leading members of Korea's communist movement during the colonial era.

During the next five days, Anh was supposed to assist his interrogators with putting his family's genealogical history in order. What the investigators wanted from him was not clear to Anh at the outset. Anh was repeatedly told that he had to say truthfully and without concealing anything, everything he knew about his family's past and present in full detail. However, he was confused as to what he could do to meet this request since the interrogators did not tell him what they were looking for in his family history. He received beatings, sometimes severe ones, each time he failed to relate "everything." After each beating, he was commanded to look again and examine the drawing on the wall. This went on, and as the hours passed in that dreadful basement room, Anh said that things started to become clearer to him. He slowly began to understand what his interrogators expected from him, what the drawing on the wall meant to him, and why he had been brought to the room in the first place: his job was to explain the relationship between the two red-colored names and the genealogical lines presented on the drawing.

The objective of the interrogation was to superimpose a structure of political and ideological ties onto the structure of blood relations depicted on the wall-mounted drawing. It aimed to establish a web of collaborative political relations between the red-colored names on the chart, on the one hand, and, on the other, the rest of the names, which were connected to the red-colored names by lines that indicated descent and collateral ties. Anh's duty was to provide detailed information about the extent to which his descent group harbored the "red ideology" (i.e., communism) beyond the two red-colored individuals, his two paternal uncles. The interrogators also wanted him to provide detailed biographical and historical information about the way in which the commitment to red ideology was allegedly diffused from his paternal uncles to those in other collateral lines within his lineage. Each time an interrogation session was over and Anh was given a few moments to gather his thoughts, he noticed that more red lines had been added to the genealogical diagram. And each time Anh protested the spread of the red-colored lines to his close and distant relatives, he experienced another round of physical abuse. By the time the interrogation was over, the genealogical chart had changed color. The red-colored elements on the chart had grown from a small to a large proportion, and many new red lines had been added to the black-colored lines. Looking at it, Anh said that he felt that nearly the entirety of his lineage group was drenched in the bright-red color of communism.

Anh's experience speaks of the broadly held understanding in postwar South Korean society that the family genealogical record, being an important symbol of communal integrity and continuity, could turn into a weapon against the community's welfare and survival. The cultural and moral importance of the genealogical record is well illustrated in an episode featured in a biographical account of the Korean War: when a house was set on fire in the midst of a counterinsurgency action, the family's grandfather tried to rescue household treasures from the burning thatched-roofed house. When the old man narrowly escaped a collapsing beam and was carried out to safety by his neighbors, people were surprised to see that the treasure for which the family's grandfather had risked his life was an old faded book – the family's *jokbo* or book of genealogy.[24] The significance of the book of genealogy has another dimension, however. In this story, the counterinsurgency group set the family's home on fire as a punishment in relation to the old man's eldest son, whom they suspected of being a left-wing intellectual. After the son was later arrested and executed, the book, which the grandfather treated as the family's most treasured object, became the source of a nightmare for the family, especially the grandfather's eldest and only grandson, who was the narrator of this story. The grandson, as a child, endured the stigmatizing experience of hearing the villagers whisper about him and his family as "a family that has red lines in the genealogical record."

"Red lines in the genealogical record" was a powerful idiom in postwar South Korea. The lines indicated, in popular understanding, that there was a family member whose loyalty to the current political society was in doubt. Having these lines in the family record meant that the family as a whole had a politically dubious background. The family record in this context does not refer to the privately possessed documents of genealogical history, such as that which appears in the story just related, but the family genealogical registers (*hojŏk*) kept in the public office.

The latter was invented in the 1920s by the Japanese colonial administration and has since been a primary public source of personal and collective identification in Korea. Recorded information included the person's name and place and date of birth in the context of his or her family relations, as well as the identity of the family group as a whole in terms of its place of origin. "Place of origin" typically refers to the family's "root," the place where the family's original patrilineal group is believed to have been based. In this system, a person may be considered to be rooted in a place that is other than the person's place of birth and where he or she never lived. In today's context, therefore, someone's "root" identity signifies more a place of the dead rather than that of the living: it is where the graves of family ancestors are located and where individual families, while living separately from each other and many in urban areas, gather periodically to visit these ancestral graves, thereby renewing a sense of togetherness through ancestor worship. The public genealogical documents are associated with this "root" identity and are usually kept in the registry office of the district where the place of root identity belongs. It is, then, clearly understandable why the thought of a "red line" introduced to this document provokes such strong fear and indignation in the popular imagination. The red line is not merely an element of personal identification; it is an indicator of collective identity, such that the family as a whole may have a questionable public and political identity.

In actuality, lines of this kind were not often applied to the public family records in physical terms, and, although the fear of them was real for many postwar families, they mostly referred to more implicit indicators of politically non-normative identity. These traces could take the form of a simple handwritten comment on the record – for instance, a note saying, "The aforementioned has been missing since July 1950," as was the case with one of my interviewees. This apparently innocent information turned into a powerful threat to my interviewee's personal safety when the information was passed down, through a chain of command, to the security department of the army unit in which he was serving. One of his superior officers later told him that on his family record, which was seen by the officer, someone had written next to the note in red-colored pen that the "aforementioned person" (the soldier's father, who had disappeared from home during the Korean War), was a "security suspect demanding attention." With reference to the postwar experience of separated families who had relatives in North Korea, it is observed:

The surveillance against these families, apart from occasions of direct control by the police's security personnel, was on an everyday basis. Most other people encounter the state power when they have broken the law, whereas these families encountered the state's power of exclusion in their everyday life and in a diffused way, on occasions as diverse as when applying for jobs or schools, choosing a spouse, or obtaining a permit to travel overseas. Since their experience of exclusion and discrimination took place in the space of everyday life, such as at school, rather than necessarily in the appropriate designated public space, such as in the police station or in the court, these families tend to speak of these experiences as private affairs [rather than a public, systemic phenomenon].[25]

Indeed, the recent testimonial histories of the Korean War compiled by South Korean historians and anthropologists amply show that the *yŏnjwaje* was a widely applied punitive and disciplinary technique.[26] For people who experienced this particular, extraordinary disciplinary system, it is said that the experience was akin to being placed in "a prison without bars."[27] A family related to people buried in the cemetery in Jeju introduced earlier, One Hundred Ancestors and One Single Descendant (see Chapter 2), speaks of their encounter with the penal system: "What was harder to stomach than the desecration of family graves and the destruction of ancestral stones was the so-called *yŏnjwaje*, which stroked our lives like a menacing specter."[28] *Yŏnjwaje* applied to diverse aspects of postwar civic life, but was nevertheless without clearly specified rules. One broadly held view understood the rule of collective responsibility in terms of a concentric circle. In this view, as illustrated by many stories told by people who claim to have been victimized by the rule, the *yŏnjwaje* draws a circle around the vital public institutions that constitute state power, and those social groups, whose political loyalty the state doubts, are not given the right to join the space within the concentric circle. The many episodes of failing to enter the civil service, legal profession, national police, or the military officer corps in the case of children from families with "red lines" illustrate the existence of the *yŏnjwaje* rule in this political concentric form.[29]

A number of instances have also been reported in which children from these families were forced to choose alternative careers in the so-called outer circle of public service, such as in the teaching profession within the national educational system, where the imposition of security rules was relatively less severe. Some of these episodes also feature differences between public schools (state-directed schools) and private schools (i.e., run by Christian or Buddhist religious groups or by other private sectors) in relation to the career prospects of people who have politically non-normative family backgrounds. Furthermore, it is suggested that this aspect of the *yŏnjwaje* rule explains the relatively high proportion of such people in South Korea's literary world, who, in turn, played a pivotal role in the 1990s in exposing the hitherto unseen history of the Korean War in fictional and semi-fictional forms, departing radically from the existing dominant national narrative (see Chapter 5).

The predicament of Anh was mainly related to the historical fact that his paternal uncles had been active in Korea's communist movement during the colonial period in the 1930s. His father was the eldest son of a large landowning family, who supported the Korean nationalist movements in China, the provisional Korean government based in Shanghai in particular, by opening a rice-trading business in Daegu in 1921. He also supported his younger brothers while they were in hiding and, later, in the colonial prison. His family was related to the family of Kim Jae-bong, a prominent figure in the Korean communist movement in the 1920s, through ties of marriage. Following the death of this man, the responsibility to keep the ancestral farmland, family tombs, and the genealogical record of the lineage fell on Anh's shoulders. As the eldest descendant of his lineage, he is nominally in charge of their lineage affairs and regarded as such by his kin. The gruesome experience he endured at the security office was primarily because of his status as the eldest descendant, who is supposed to have a broad knowledge of the lineage's genealogical history and family affairs.

However, after he was released, Anh discovered that he was not the only one from the family who had been arrested. While he was held in a room in the basement of the security agency, his cousin, who was the descendant of one of Anh's paternal uncles, was undergoing a similar ordeal in another room. Although Anh still does not understand what the interrogators wanted from him in concrete terms and why they were interested in his family's genealogical order and history, he said that he understood at least why he had been brought to them: "For my cousin, it is obvious. He is a man with a communist father. That makes him a red. For me, it is equally obvious. I am the eldest descendant of what they see as a red [communist] bloodline. That makes me a red who carries on his back the heritage of a red family." Another victim of collective culpability, the son of an active organizer of the Korean War bereaved families' movement in 1960 introduced earlier (see Chapter 2), recently said of his past experience:

My grandmother and other relatives indoctrinated me not to take any visible roles in public affairs. The *yŏnjwa* system of the time was such that even for a young student like myself, travelling was restricted. I had to report to the police if I had an occasion to join a meeting or group that involved more than five people. Naturally, I had no close school friends and no close teachers, who were all reluctant to get to know me. In the end, even my relatives began to distance themselves from me. I turned into a living corpse.[30]

These experiences were hardly isolated incidents in postwar South Korea, and their hidden stories continue to be uncovered today.[31] In the winter of 2005, I met a man from the east of Incheon (close to the Incheon International Airport terminal where overseas visitors to Korea first arrive today), who underwent a similar ordeal as Anh in the late 1970s. His father was a fisherman and was held captive in North Korea after his fishing boat was captured by North Korea's naval ship in the disputed western coastal waters between the two Koreas. The incident not only shocked his family and caused them economic hardship but, later, also an unimaginable existential crisis. Accused of having had covert communication with his missing father, who had allegedly become a North Korean agent, the man's entire family had to undergo a harrowing interrogation at the hands of a state security agency. These devastating accusations of treason could fall upon fishing families far away from the disputed sea frontier. In November 2009, South Korea's High Court held a hearing about the "family agent for North Korea in Jindo" incident in 1981.[32] The incident refers to the alleged North Korea-orchestrated revolutionary cell-operating group, consisting of seven members and relatives of a fishing family on the island of Jindo on the peninsula's far-southern coast. The family's father had been missing since the Korean War; the accusation was about the remaining family's alleged illicit contacts with the missing man on behalf of the North Korean regime. Those arrested included the missing man's two children, his wife, his younger brother and his wife, and his sister and her spouse. In the following year, another family-based proselyting group on an even larger scale was reported to have been uncovered. Called the "Song family spy ring" incident, this alleged anti-state family-based political group involved more than two dozen agnatic and affinal relatives of the group's central figure, a schoolteacher and daughter of a man missing from home since the Korean War.

Returning to the Jindo case in 1981, members of this alleged spy ring received a severe verdict, including life imprisonment for the missing man's eldest son, which was later reduced to seventeen years. Released in 1998, he was not able to return to his home village. The villagers did not welcome him and shunned his family in fear of appearing to be associated with them. After the court hearing in 2009 cleared their names, the son recalled how the incident had broken his extended family morally as well as physically. Not only were they isolated from the community, but the violence and stigma broke relationships within the family: his wife divorced him in a desperate attempt to protect her children from the stigma of their paternal family line; and the man's mother took refuge in a reclusive life in a Buddhist pagoda, never entirely recovering from the effects of torture as well as, in the mind of her son, from the crushing burden on her soul of having had no means, unlike her daughter-in-law, by which she could protect her children. In a poem titled "Flowers in the Other World," an ailing woman speaks to her husband missing from the war:

> I do not know whether I will be going there first,
> Or if you're already there waiting for me.
> Our child who is, like you, so intelligent,
> He is now tilling the soil in the countryside, having been chased away
>   from the city.
> No news of you yet, after so many years,
> That makes it hard for me to leave this world.
> I wonder if you've already moved to the other world, the world of the
>   dead,
> For I have been less harassed recently by those who always had
>   watched over us.
> I haven't had the chance to see you again in this world.
> Now I hope I will be able to see you – as flowers in the other world.

But how in the name of the heavens will I be able find to you without
  knowing your day of death?
For all those numerous days, I lived as the woman of a red and your
  child as the child of a red,
Under the *yŏnjwaje*.
Leaving behind our child who has never had a chance to live a decent
  life,
I guess the time has come for me to leave for the other world. [33]

Surveiller et punir

Foucault's account of the origin of the modern prison draws upon
Bentham's panoptic techniques. These techniques are emblematic of
Bentham's general utilitarian approach to modern society and governance, which is focused on the economic efficacy of institutional forms.
Foucault allocates another dimension of efficacy to the techniques –
namely, that in the system of surveillance, the object of the disciplinary
action (the isolated docile body) participates in the system quasi-willingly
(rather than necessarily being forced into it) on the basis of its adaptation
to the system's "mechanics of power" (thereby becoming what Foucault
calls "the practiced body").[34] The panoptic techniques are portable to
other institutional contexts, such as schools, the army, and hospitals,
according to Foucault and, therefore, generate a higher efficacy (the
body trained in one specific institutional disciplinary context is already
made ready for adjusting to another, thus becoming "useful individuals"
for society).[35] The portability (or what Foucault calls "the art of distribu-
tions"), in turn, generates the benefit of an economy of knowledge, in that
the knowledge of control obtained and accumulated in one institutional
setting can apply to controlling activities in another setting since, according to Foucault, "each provides a model for the other."[36]

  This depiction of the origin of modern penality is so widely known and
cited that I will not go into more detail here. Instead, I will limit the
discussion to two specific issues concerning the relational human body
mentioned at the start of this chapter. Firstly, the premise of the docile
body is predicated on the modality of the individual subject and the
related assumption that, in modern societies, the relationship between
the person and the community is replaced by that between the individual
and the state. Before becoming docile within the structure of power, the
human subjects need to be isolated from one another, and, for this, it is
required that the subject becomes a modern self, freed from traditional
communal bonds. Only this radically free self, or, in Alasdair MacIntyre's
words, the individual separated artificially from the roles that he or she

plays, such as that which appears in existentialism, may join the modern disciplinary regime as a meaningful participant in the way described by Foucault.[37] In other words, the docile body is the body of an autonomous individual in action, and not that of a human actor who is yet unacquainted with the modern ontology of individualism.[38] Of course, this individual that appears in Foucault's work is different from the image of the individual that appears in classical liberal theories of the individual – for the former, freedom and autonomy are ultimately illusive ideas, being instruments of power rather than an authentic, inalienable property of the self. It is also true that Foucault framed his study of the modern being caught in the web of modern disciplinary technology partly as a critique of the free or singularly freedom-seeking human subject as this appears in the work of Sartre.[39] The docile individual, or the human being in the modern biopolitical order as this appears in Foucault's later works, is an illusionary autonomous subject in that the sense of autonomy is viable to the extent that the subject is oblivious to its actual, helpless subjugation to the vectors of the state's life-determining, life-deciding biopolitical power. His primary interest is how this illusive human subjectivity took shape and in what historical and social conditions. For this reason, as one observer argues, Foucault's insights have been taken up by many groups of social scientists, including anthropologists who investigate modern Western medicine and biotechnology, as an inspirational guide for the critical examination of modern biopolitics and a powerful critique of modern individualism.[40] In my reading, however, Foucault's critique of the sanctity of the modern individual subject, in terms of his exposition of this subject's docility to the technological system of modern power, should not be confused with the fact that he advanced this critique on the basis of the notion that a decisive rupture took place between the premodern and modern disciplinary systems. Following Foucault, it is not really that we are taught to be individuals within modern social systems; at least in his early work, it is rather the case that we need to be individuals, illusive or otherwise, prior to being meaningful subjects in the modern disciplinary system. What emerges from this exercise is, as mentioned, an image of the individual quite different from those that appear in classical theories of the individual. Nevertheless, for Foucault, the modern penal and disciplinary system is meant for individuals freed from their traditional bonds, not for people who are trapped in traditional communal relations or those who have not yet had the chance to replace this life in a relational world with one in the web of vectors of state power. This is to say, perhaps, that Foucault had a theory of the modern institution but not necessarily a theory of the modern person. He took the idea of an autonomous human subject as a historical construction and social fiction, and sought to render how this illusive idea was brought forward. At the same time, however, he took for granted the pervasiveness of this idea in modern politics and approached the latter's institutional order assuming that the constitutive element in this order's disciplinary regime is the body of an isolated individual.

Secondly, the human body that inhabits a modern disciplinary regime is primarily a physical body. Thomas Flynn observes:

> Although a history of the modern "soul," *Discipline and Punish* is primarily about the *body*. First of all, it is about that physical body which can be trained, whipped into shape, rendered a docile, productive tool of society. But it is about the "body politic" as well, a term which gains new meaning at Foucault's hands, namely, "a set of material elements and techniques which serve as weapons, relays, communication routes and supports for the *power and knowledge* relations that invest human bodies and subjugate them by turning them into objects of knowledge" (original emphasis).[41]

If the regime controls the body, it can control the individual (and, therefore, society) through it, for, by controlling the body, the regime can control the person's soul. In this way, Foucault shares one of the central tenets of the early French sociological school: "the soul is the prison of the body."[42] This maxim was a prominent constitutive element in Durkheim's sociology of religion and, as such, represents a break of modern knowledge practices from the previous theology-dominated era. In the premodern era, the focus of knowledge was on the question of soul because the idea that a soul brings man to existence prevailed at the time; modern knowledge turns away from this tradition, shifting its focus to observable facts and phenomena, such as the body.[43] Thus, the human subject as the object of knowledge is not what it thinks and believes but, rather, what it does and how it does it. Likewise, according to Foucault, it is this "very materiality as an instrument and vector of power" on which the political investments of modern times focus.[44]

Foucault's erudition is, therefore, based on the idea that a radical break – from the control of soul to that of body, on the one hand, and, on the other, from the person-community nexus to the individual-state axis – took place in European penal practices in the transition to modernity. In his work on the history of prisons, Foucault associates this rupture with the rise of the panoptical surveillance system as the dominant technology of control in place of the spectacle of punishment. The change in penal system is closely related, in his understanding, to the rise of the autonomous, isolated individual in place of the community-bound moral person as the new object of social control. Thus, in his account, the invention of the modern prison corresponds closely to the invention of modern society and modern individuality – that is, the transition from *Gemeinschaft* to *Gesellschaft* (see Chapter 2). Foucault illustrates this historical rupture in a plague-stricken French town in the late-seventeenth century, from which he derives the idea that the origin of modern disciplinary society is a mechanism of disease control – the invention of "the seeing machine," as he calls it:

The town was a quarantined space against the spread of the plague that it was suffering from. The residents were locked up inside their houses, allowed to communicate with the outside world only through the syndic who keeps the street under surveillance, and they were forbidden from leaving the street, the violation of which constituted a condemnation to death. The syndic kept an eye on the houses of the street he was in charge of and was to report to the intendant responsible for quarantining the wider residential area. At the end of each street was a sentinel where guards stood on alert, and all the gates to the town were also guarded by the militia and at each of them stood a tall observation tower. Each household was compelled to report everything about its activity to the chain of the quarantine authority – "to speak the truth under pain of death"; the authority was to observe all actions and events taking place within the regimented city's space through its agents of surveillance entrenched in the regimented spatial order. [45]

Foucault presents the structure of the quarantined city as a "political dream" of the modern disciplinary society – "the utopia of the perfectly governed city" – an ideal exemplar of Bentham's panoptical technology of control, in which "each actor is alone, perfectly individualized and constantly visible," and "he is seen, but he does not see; he is the object of information, never a subject in communication."[46] As such, he contrasts the city's spatial structure with what he sees as the quintessential modality of disease control in premodern times: the exiled community of the leper:

The leper was caught up in a practice of rejection, of exile-enclosure; he was left to his doom in a mass among which it was useless to differentiate; those sick with the plague were caught up in a meticulous tactical partitioning in which individual differentiations were the constricting effects of a power that multiplied, articulated and subdivided itself; the great confinement on the one hand; the correct training on the other. The leper and his separation; the plague and its segmentations. The first is marked; the second analyzed and distributed. The exile of the leper and the arrest of the plague do not bring with them the same political dream. The first is that of a pure community, the second that of a disciplined society. Two ways of exercising power over men, of controlling their relations, of separating out their dangerous mixtures.[47]

An epidemiological model of society as a vulnerable organism was familiar to the politics of anti-communism in the early Cold War.[48] For Arthur Schlesinger, communism is a phenomenon of the transition from stagnation to development, a "disease" of the modernization process (citing Walt Rostow), which explains why it appeals to nations in the early phases of development such as Russia, China, and the underdeveloped nations of the global South that see it "as the means of rapid and effective modernization."[49] Edgar Hoover saw communism as "a condition akin to disease that spreads like an epidemic, and like an epidemic, a quarantine is necessary to keep it from infecting the nation."[50] In early 1950, an important report from the US National Security Council described the Soviet Union as aiming to "contaminate" the Western world with their preferred technique of infiltrating "labor unions, civic enterprises, schools, churches, and all media for influencing opinion." This report known as NSC-68 is considered to be one of the most formative documents of the early Cold War that paved the way for the transformation of the United States into a global military empire in the second half of the twentieth century. In parallel with the urgency to stop domestic contagion, the document argues that, internationally, there is a need "to quarantine a growing number of infected [by the disease of communism] states."[51] NSC-68 asserts that the enemies of the liberal world are shadowy and entrenched within society as well as embodied by radical political movements and states out there on the distant geographical horizons. These assertions materialized with public policy initiatives in the United States in the mid-century, as seen in Harry S. Truman's 1947 speech, "Disloyal and Subversive Elements Must Be Removed from the Employ of the Government," concerning the establishment of the Disloyalty Review Board – a dragnet persecution of enemies within – which was to take on a more radical tone and form with the outbreak of the Korean War.[52] Considering this development, Ron Robin writes: "American society of the 1950s was increasingly fascinated by the threat of a foreign presence within the American body politic. The political, social, and intellectual atmosphere of the period reflected concern for, and fascination with, the enemy within."[53] The resulting persecution or "a wholesale inquisition" as one critic calls it, advanced the "doctrine of guilt imputed by association" by which the effect of the acts of one person was attributed to another.[54]

The anti-communist politics of postwar South Korea were at the front line of the global "quarantining" and also advanced an epidemiological view of social and political relations. Syngman Rhee once said, "Communism is like cholera. One cannot make compromise with cholera [virus]."[55] These politics also advanced the metaphoric color classification of the Cold War (red versus non-red) to a literal, corporeal phenomenon. An important South Korean government document from the late 1960s argues: "In closed communities, once a leading member of a village community was reddened, due to the importance of consanguine and local ties in these communities, it was unavoidable that people of the entire lineage group or those of the entire village community turned into members of the communist party."[56] The politics aimed to build an ideologically pure, morally disciplined society that stood meaningfully on the global front line, and it sought to deal with "the threat of a foreign presence" within the body politic accordingly. The enemy within and the carrier of infectious foreign ideology that was given concrete form in this political process was not an individual. The object of discipline and punishment was not necessarily the individual's isolated body, but the rich web of relationships that makes the individual a moral person. Because the focus of punishment was on relations and the body in relation, the body of the accused was never isolated in the first place. Thus, the accused was not able to prove his or her innocence unless he or she was able to pull him- or herself out of the condemned relational body or make the relational body as a whole innocent.

The disciplinary society invented in the age of the Cold War and at the front line of the global ideological struggle was neither merely in the image of the pure community of lepers nor solely according to the segmentary structure of the plague control. Rather, the political dream of this society was close to a creative combination of these two modalities of control, thereby making a polity of docile subjects based on the isolation from society of contaminated relations. The structure of this disciplinary society is unintelligible if we take for granted what Foucault says about these docile subjects as being "alone, perfectly individualized and constantly visible." On the contrary, the ideal subjects, in the political dream of the frontline Cold War society, were those who were never alone and never free from the liabilities of communal relations and who were constantly vigilant against the contamination of these relations by alien thoughts and beliefs. The fact that this political dream was pursued more vigorously in the Cold War's frontline societies, however, does not mean that the pursuit of this dream was a local phenomenon, confined to societies treading between the traditional and modern forms of human association. As we will see in the next chapter, the high politics of the Cold War were, crucially, also grounded in the pursuit of a dream for a clean community and an immunized family of nations on a global scale.

5   Morality and Ideology

State-building in postcolonial Korea was based on a radical negation of each other's legitimate existence by the two state systems that emerged in the era, in close collusion with the bifurcating political dynamics in the broader global political landscape. The explosion of this reciprocal negation, in the form of a mass-mobilized civil war, drove the lives of a great part of the population caught in the middle into an extremely precarious situation. In the South, the civil war generated a host of outlawed individuals, politically damned consanguine relations, and ideologically impure and undesirable families. For individuals who had fallen victim to the anti-communist state terror, their historical traces became an ominous threat to their surviving families, who faced the hazard of turning into enemies of the state by the mere fact that they were related to the victims through kinship. For those who had gone missing in the chaotic reality of the war, their absence ran the risk of being considered a result of defection to the communist-controlled territory, thereby making the relatives left behind "families whose members crossed to the North," a highly stigmatic and, at times, life-threatening status in the postwar era.

In the short story *Soji* (a traditional custom of burning paper to deliver a message to the dead) by the South Korean writer Lee Chang-dong, a man is enraged by his younger brother's involvement in a resistance activity against political dictatorship in the postwar era and speaks to him cynically about their missing father: "We both are children of a red [i.e., communist]. You sure have inherited the blood of a red."[1] The man's anger is not necessarily about his brother's political commitment but rather about possible calamitous consequences that such activity may cause to the family's survival. It is also directed against his brother's ignorance of the fact that his family is not an ordinary family but one consisting of people who have less civil and human rights than ordinary South Koreans due to their ties to the absent father. After the war, many of these politically non-normative families were exposed to intimidating surveillance by the state security apparatus as well as systematic discrimination in their public lives. Life was hard for these postwar Korean

111

families who failed to demonstrate that they had maintained a clear, untainted identity throughout the chaotic war – proof that they had stayed within the imaginary circle of absolute political and ideological purity as defined and drawn by the state hierarchy. It was practically impossible for numerous families and communities to stay within the circle amid the war's changing tides and frontiers; the reality of the Korean War, in the lived experiences of these communities, was principally about having to accommodate the demands for total loyalty coming from both of the mutually negating forces of war. In popular knowledge, the last situation is often expressed with the traditional idiom for an extreme state of confusion that says poignantly: *uwang jwawang*, "Move to the right and then to the left [and then again to the opposite direction without knowing where to go and what to do]."

Lee Chang-dong is not alone in depicting the legacies of the Korean War as questions of family genealogy and as part of the conflicts arising within the domestic sphere. The narrative strategy is found widely in contemporary South Korean literature on the Korean War. The same is true with literary renderings of war experiences in the earlier postwar years, before the 1990s, when the ideology of anti-communism was much more strongly entrenched within society than today. The representation of the civil war experience as a familial crisis is a strongly consistent theme, therefore, despite the fact that, as we will see, remarkable changes have taken place in the public understanding of the meaning of the Korean War since roughly the end of the Cold War in the early 1990s. This chapter examines elements of continuity and discontinuity in Korean War narratives in South Korea, told across the threshold of the decade of the 1990s. In doing so, however, it is necessary to broaden the horizon of investigation to the realm of global politics. Recent studies of Cold War cultural history show that idioms of family feelings were far from unfamiliar in the era's international politics of containment and alliance-building. This entails that questions about the morality of kinship run through different layers of Cold War historical reality, locally and internationally, albeit with divergent ramifications. Notable among these questions are those concerned with conflicts between siblings and the fate of orphans.

Masterwork of Civil War

Civil war is often referred to as a war that pits brother against brother. Writing of family life in the Border States during the American Civil War, and the way in which this is represented in the literature, Amy Murrell Taylor observes that "tales of warring kinsmen appeared throughout the war in both sections of the country and dramatized the problem of dividing one nation into two. The authors may have been influenced, in part, by a sentimental literary tradition in which the family was central, but their focus on kinship relations also reflected a reality of the Civil War."[2] These tales depict the political urgency of a nation divided in a domestic crisis of escalating tensions as to how to respond to the war – arising between generations and siblings and between spouses or lovers.[3] They include the tragedy that occurred at Perryville, Kentucky, in October 1862. In this incident, a soldier named Hopkins took a shot at an enemy soldier some twenty feet away who the shooter knew was his own blood. After wounding him, Hopkins approached his brother and gave him water and a blanket. Later, he returned to the scene and stayed with his dying brother through the night. Citing a newspaper report that presents the last action as proof that Hopkins was "a man of family," Taylor asks, "How could a man simultaneously shoot and embrace his own brother?"[4]

Such masterwork of civil war, as Ambrose Bierce once called it, exists elsewhere. The literary and musical tradition of Vietnam, particularly that which advanced in South Vietnam during the Vietnam War, abounds with tales of two brothers being brought to confront each other lethally.[5] The celebrated songwriter Pham Duy's powerful lyrics from "Brothers" say: "There were two soldiers, both of one family. There were two soldiers who lay upon a field, both clasping rifles and waiting. There were two soldiers who one rosy dawn killed each other – for Vietnam." It is reported that the continuing crisis in Afghanistan is pulling apart Afghan families. In the Zabul province along the southeastern border with Pakistan, a man recently dropped out of his school to join the ranks of the local Taliban. Razziq, his younger brother, also left home but went down a different path to join the country's national police supported by the United States. Razziq said, "I don't know when I will face my brother on the battlefield, but it's only a matter of time." When this happens, he believes that he will have no choice but to fight back.[6] Gul, the elder brother, sees Razziq as a traitor and apostate, whereas Razziq believes that Gul, by joining the Taliban, abandoned his role as the eldest son and put his entire family in danger. Such a situation is hardly unfamiliar in other parts of the country; in the northern province of Faryab along the border with the former Soviet republic of Turkmenistan, bitter divisions within the same family were already widespread during the 1980s, when the region witnessed violent clashes between the Soviet-supported communist government in Kabul and the mujahideen guerrillas receiving support from the United States.[7]

The literature on the Korean War also abounds with similar stories of siblings going down different roads. As in the case of Gul and Razziq, these stories are as much about the morality of kinship relations as about the politics of war. They demonstrate two separate notions of betrayal; one according to how this is defined by the specific political reality and the other in relation to how the historical actors understood the imperative of familial survival. The "masterwork of civil war" in this context is not necessarily a question of morality focused on an individual actor, as implicated in the question, "How could a man simultaneously shoot and embrace his own brother?" Rather, it engages with the vexing relational arena of moral judgment in which taking a specific political position in the spectrum of war is equal in meaning to violating the morality of kinship relations.

Two Soldiers

South Korea's National War Museum, located at the heart of Seoul near a large US military base, which is now being relocated elsewhere, has a prominent memorial that depicts two men in a passionate embrace, depicting "an extraordinary encounter of two brothers in the battlefield," according to a museum booklet. Based on "a real wartime story," this Statue of Brothers expresses "the nation's will to transcend the national partition and confrontation between South Korea and North Korea." The booklet continues: "One would normally expect these two soldiers to point their muzzles at each other with wide-opened, disapproving eyes. The fact that they are embracing each other in such a vigorous gesture makes us rethink the meaning of the Korean War."

The elder brother depicted in this statue is an officer of South Korea's National Army. He is taller and better built than the relatively diminutive younger brother, an infantryman of North Korea's People's Army. The officer is also the only one carrying arms. The embrace appears to be quite paternalistic, showing the burly officer holding the fragile infantryman in a dominating gesture of fraternal embrace. Several critics consequently raised objections to the statue's form, pointing out that the memorial projects a hierarchy of status and power between the two soldiers and, hence, between the two protagonists of the civil war that they are meant to represent.[8] Another criticism I encountered pointed to the claimed historical realism of the brotherly encounter. A military historian and the curator of a military museum situated along the Nakdong River, one of the fiercest battlefields of the Korean War, agreed that the statue of the brothers in the Seoul museum was based on a true wartime story. However, he raised a strong objection to the way in which the National Museum appropriated the story. According to him, the true story was a pure tragedy with no element of redemptive encounter as depicted in the statue: a South Korean soldier, after having survived a chaotic hand-to-hand hill fight in the thick of night, felt that one of the enemy soldiers he had slaughtered during the fight seemed familiar to him. He went back to the trenches the next morning to take a look. He found in the field of the dead the body of his younger brother. The museum historian argued that the story originated from the Nakdong battlefield where his museum was located. Saying that the story was a tragic episode of the Korean War, and true to the tragic nature of that war, he disapproved of what he believed was a distortion of the war's reality, even if the intention was for the good cause of national reconciliation.

Sheila Miyoshi Jager and Jiyul Kim note, in their reading of the displays in Seoul's National War Museum, that the dominant representation of the Korean War in contemporary South Korea renders the war experience as "a family tragedy to be followed by rites of reconciliation."[9] Reflecting on the Statue of Brothers in this context, they argue that it depicts the tragedy of the civil war as the tragedy of a family: the nation is like a single family unfortunately divided into two; the war was a brutal conflict within the family in which brothers were called to kill each other; after being made blind to the fact that the enemy in view is in actuality a blood brother, the two soldiers recover the truth of their consanguine ties and make a passionate gesture of reconciliation. The Statue of Brothers speaks of the moral imperative that the divided nation's separate halves should recover their common origin, according to Jager and Kim, and this objective of national reunification is expressed in the form of a brotherly reunion.[10] Other commentators in South Korea observe that family separation has been a prime symbol of the partition of the nation into two mutually hostile polities, and that the aspiration to change the historical condition has been expressed in postwar decades in a related language as the imperative to bring the dislocated, dispersed families back together (see Chapter 3).[11] The National War Museum depicts the coterminous relationship between the fate of the nation and the condition of the family in various ways, not only with material objects, such as the Statue of Brothers, but also with statements, such as "blood is thicker than ideology," which features prominently in one of its main exhibition halls.

Such metaphoric fusion between the familial and the national is far from exceptional. In her reading of war films in both South and North Korea, Hyangjin Lee observes "familialism as the moral foundation for restoring a unified nation in the future. In this sense, the representation of nationhood in South and North Korean films can be seen as an extension or variation of familyhood. In other words, nationhood is simply a form of familyhood amplified to a societal level."[12] The very concept of the modern state in East Asia, which was invented in late Meiji Japan and later disseminated to other parts of Asia, in fact, conjoins the Chinese character of the polity with that of the household, thereby enforcing an understanding of the modern state as a household writ large (with the emperor as the head of the political household in the case of imperial Japan). It is observed that the political system of North Korea constitutes a "family state," in which the country's founding leader stands as the political father to the people as a whole within the so-called great socialist family.[13] The history of modern nationalism abounds with other examples in which the idioms of familial, household, or consanguine integrity are extended to become forceful symbols of national unity and state sovereignty.[14] In this regard, Ernest Gellner comments on the unique place of nationalism in the tradition of modern social philosophy. He argues that early social theorists (in the latter half of the nineteenth century and the early twentieth century) took for granted the evolutionary scheme of the *Gemeinschaft* and *Gesellschaft* contrast (see Chapter 2), which permeated both the libertarian and critical intellectual currents of the time. These thinkers envisaged varying ways in which human beings can liberate themselves from the traditional communal bond and imagined different forms of new human sociality. Despite their differences, according to Gellner, all of them commonly took for granted the validity of the contrast and the inevitability of the historical transition from an enclosed holistic community to an open civil society. Gellner reflects on how this philosophical orientation missed out on one crucial phenomenon in modern political history: the power of nationalism to make a community out of a society; that is, the power to generate thick, imaginary relations of shared origin and destiny from thin relations among strangers.[15] A similar idea is proposed by Benedict Anderson, who sees the modern nation-state as a society that is nevertheless construed and imagined as a community.[16] Anderson highlights the pivotal role of universal literacy and literature in generating and disseminating a sense of common origins and shared destiny in the transformation of an aggregate of strangers to a community of thick, imaginary memories.[17] That the thin relations of a society may be subjectively experienced as thick relations of a community in modern politics is a much discussed topic in modern social thought, and recent scholarship has added to the debate the important issue that the fusion of community and society may take diverse forms against different historical and cultural backgrounds. These studies of modern nationalism commonly show that the rise of modern society is not a one-way progression from place-bound "mechanical" solidarity to associational, modern "organic" solidarity. They argue that these two ideal types of human sociality, rather than replacing one another, actually reinforce each other and are intertwined in the unfolding of modern history. Recent studies of nationalism extend this perspective to a more refined comparative historical perspective that pays attention to the plurality of the nation-building process across the European and postcolonial historical contexts. Here too, strong reservations are expressed against the social evolutionary assumptions in modern European social thought.

In his celebrated book, *Provincializing Europe*, Dipesh Chakrabarty discusses the Bengali ideas of kinship and nationhood, contrasting them with the formulations of national identity developed in early European political thought of the eighteenth and nineteenth centuries. The latter was grounded in the rise of the bourgeoisie as a distinctive social category, from which came John Locke's idea of fraternity among property-holding individuals as the foundation of modern democratic polity. According to Chakrabarty, the Lockean notion of national brotherhood as a contractual relationship among autonomous, self-interested individuals does not extend to the ideal of brotherhood advanced by the early Bengali nationalist intellectuals under British rule. He describes how the Bengali understanding of political brotherhood is anchored in *kula*, their traditional patrilineal kinship system, which situates a person's identity in a vertical line of male descent and under the unchallenged sanctity of patriarchal authority. The Lockean idea of the nation as a brotherhood of men assumes that the constitutive elements of this fraternity, which are men, are freed from paternal authority through their possession of private property.[18] By contrast, according to Chakrabarty, private property

was never stipulated as a requirement in Bengali nationalist thought that the political authority of the father be destroyed before the brothers' compact could come into being ... Fraternity in Bengali nationalism was thought of as representing a natural rather than contractual solidarity of brotherhood. European bourgeois assumptions regarding autonomous personhood based on self-interest, contract, and private property were subordinated in Bengal to this idea of "natural" brotherhood.[19]

Chakrabarty's critique is more than a project of history. It is also part of a broader project of postcolonial criticism intended to confront the problematic process of decolonization: postcolonial modernity was envisioned in the colonies in terms of the model of political modernity learned from Europe; this makes resistance to colonial domination an act of emulating the dominator rather than an authentic, creative act. He proposes that the project to "provincialize" the European heritage of political modernity is a necessary step for pluralizing modernity, which is, in turn, an indispensable step for the decolonization of the imagination. Making one's own political history distinct from the theoretical premises of historical development in European thought, in other words, is an act of obtaining freedom from colonialism in thought.

Considering this broad objective, it is understandable that Chakrabarty presents the idea of traditional Bengali brotherhood in sharp contrast to the Lockean idea of political brotherhood. Upon further examination, however, we notice that there is something not quite viable in this project to provincialize the Western representation of political modernity. The idea of the postcolonial experience proposed by Chakrabarty is based on a conceptual separation of colonialism into two domains, an institutional order and a cultural schema, and the related premise that the latter, colonialism as culture, continues after the achievement of political self-rule, that is, the end of colonialism as an institutional order. He conceptualizes the predicate "post" in *postcolonial* as potent symbolic vitality in the present of the past experience of the actual existence of colonialism. In this rendering of historically spectral but experientially real continuity of colonial imaginaries, however, it is surprising to see that the project of postcolonial criticism makes no analytical associations with the political history of the Cold War, which apparently coincides with the historical change of colonialism from an institutional structure to a cultural form. The idea of postcolonial culture tends to project the historical epoch from the end of the Second World War to the present as an uninterrupted struggle to be free from the cultural and mental effects of colonialism, after this world is freed from the formal institutional grid of colonial subjugation from the 1950s to the 1960s. This conceptual scheme does not consider the momentous shift in global power relations during this period, from colonial to bipolar in nature, or the resultant complication for nation-building in the postcolonial world. Most of all, the scheme is oblivious to the radical political bipolarization of postcolonial processes and the consequent complications in human communal life.

What is distinctive about societies that experienced the postcolonial Cold War in the form of a civil war is the fact that the rendering of this symbolic analogy between family and nation takes on, rather than a positive fusion, a negative condition of partition and distortion – a condition that needs to be overcome in the future with appropriate actions.[20] In these contexts, it is difficult to conceive of a "natural" or prepolitical brotherhood as a discreet indigenous entity, which then can be conceptually pitted against the idea of political brotherhood appearing in Western political thought. Such an idealized image of indigenous kinship as existing seemingly autonomously from the political reality does not apply to the fate of human kinship struggling with the crisis of postcolonial civil war. In order to understand this struggle, we need to find a way to think of the two ideas of brotherhood, political and "natural" – and the normative and political dimensions of human solidarity that they represent – in less dualistic terms than how these are rendered by both the liberal theories and their postcolonial critique.

Family Feelings

The political system of postcolonial Korea is often referred to as "one nation and two states." Although this reference does capture the basic structural condition of Korea's modern experience, it is, nevertheless, not entirely correct if seen from a historical perspective. The postcolonial process of state-building in Korea was coeval with the advent of the early Cold War, of which Korea became a main site where the global battle was fought within national politics. Accordingly, the process was based on a radical negation of each other's political legitimacy by the two postcolonial state entities that emerged after 1945. Each state claimed to be the sole legitimate nation-state, encompassing the entire territory of the peninsula and the population within it.[21] The basic law of South Korea claims that the territory it represents consists of the whole peninsula of Korea and all of the islands surrounding it. For quite some time, the country also enshrined anti-communism as "the first principle of the existence of the state,"[22] and "patriotism based on anticommunist democratic spirit" as the principal, sacred civic ethic.[23] The civic duty included recognizing the idea that "communism is the enemy of humanity" and, based on this recognition, "to grow the strength to defend the homeland from communism and to win over communism."[24] In this scheme of exclusive sovereignty, each postcolonial state of Korea considered the other state entity existing in the peninsula as a rogue state, or even as an unlawful political group close to the status of illegitimate political rebels and insurgents, which must be eventually dealt with by the state's solely sovereign, coercive power.

The situation changed when North Korea and South Korea were admitted jointly into the United Nations in 1979. The two states of Korea were then both formally recognized as sovereign bodies by the international community, which implies that the two states also recognized each other as such. This was made explicit in 2000 when the heads of the two states met in their first ever summit meeting in Pyongyang. This historic meeting followed South Korea's opening of diplomatic ties with the countries of the former Eastern Bloc, and it also raised the expectation that North Korea would do the same with regard to the opposite bloc, particularly with the United States and Japan. Although the expectation was not realized then, it is nevertheless now taken for granted in the international community, through the series of events since 1979, that two sovereign states exist on the Korean peninsula. In the two Koreas, however, the idea of "one nation and two states" has not entirely dispelled the old, opposite idea of exclusive sovereignty, and the related understanding that one or the other solely legitimate state is in a perpetual state of siege, facing an insurgent political group that unlawfully occupies a part of its sovereign territory, posing a threat of aggression to its singular sovereign power.

In today's Korea, therefore, the historical reality of "one nation, two states" exists together with its historical negation, "one nation and one state." The negation is deeply entrenched in the history of the Korean War, and in the fact that this war still remains an unfinished, unending war. The negation of the other existing state as a rogue entity, enshrined separately but commonly in the foundation of the two postcolonial Koreas, constitutes the origin of the Korean War. It was also the primary cause of the suffering that the war enforced upon the population. Another related contradiction is found in the literature. The Korean War is often referred to as a "war between peoples of common blood" in South Korea's literary tradition. As is the case with the incongruous conceptual relationship between nation and state noted earlier, here too, two mutually contradictory ideas about human solidarity are found to coexist. The literary history of the Korean War is in great measure about how to reconcile the contradictions between the perceived common origin and the reality of ideological incompatibility. In this context, the experience of civil war came to be expressed in different forms of family conflicts in the postwar era, as we will see shortly.

Familial metaphors played a formative role in the wider theater of the early Cold War, which the Korean War played a major part in radicalizing and militarizing. The US military budget quadrupled during and after the Korean War, which historians define as the critical moment when the United States assumed global military supremacy in the post-Second World War era. In the US domestic landscape, the militant anti-communist public campaigns, known as McCarthyism, gained force after the outbreak of war in Korea, thereby influencing the course of action taken by the Truman administration. In addition to these widely mentioned historical facts about the early Cold War, recent studies show how the idioms of kinship also played a formative role in shaping the broad political culture of the early Cold War.

Particularly notable in this matter is the politics of international adoption. Christina Klein argues that the history of transnational migration in the twentieth century was intimately connected to the Cold War geopolitics of containment and shows how their connectedness originally took the form of transcending racial and cultural differences through some particular kinship practices.[25] Focusing on the policy documents and the middlebrow mass-educational material of mid-century America, Klein traces how the adoption of children from troubled regions of Asia developed into a powerful geopolitical practice during the 1950s. Advancing the political objective of the global containment of communism, Klein argues, US policymakers were worried that America's leadership in the free world lacked a positive substantive quality. Anti-communism was not an authentic but a reactive ideology; liberal individualism or benevolent capitalism were hard to sell to the Asian populations who associated such ideologies with Western colonialism. With this background of needing to persuade Asians wary of Western imperialism as well as Americans wary of expensive overseas commitments, according to Klein, a new rhetorical form was invented that rendered the problem of the US political obligation to Asia as a problem of family.[26]

Hence, the prominent educational media of the 1950s disseminated the extension of kinship as a prime strategy for fighting Asian communism. American families were encouraged to adopt the homeless children of Calcutta and Bombay, the abandoned "GI babies" in Japan, and the war orphans in Korea. They propagated that these "hungry children of the world are more dangerous to us than the atom bomb"; these downtrodden children, unless they were brought into the paternalistic care of benign American power, would transform into "the most powerful weapon in the hands of the communists."[27] Klein's persuasive analysis presents how the practice of adoptive kinship was a two-way process of learning: the American "parents" learned about the misery and inhumanity caused by communism, and the adopted Asian "children" learned about "the material abundance and personal generosity that the free world offered."[28] This ideology of paternalistic love, according to Klein, was meant to distinguish America's Cold War civilizing mission from the imperial practice of European nations, on the one hand, and, on the other, to mobilize the US public in the aggressive battle against communism by letting them participate in this geopolitical act through their intimate domains of family norms and religious charity. Consequently, the horizon of transnational ties and mass immigration began to change considerably in American society, which had restricted immigration from Asia since 1875 on racial grounds.[29]

Klein claims that the construction of America's "Cold War orientalism," as she calls it, and its related advocacy of "benevolent supremacy" in the decolonizing world, was about encountering alien cultural worlds, while at the same time inventing a new way to assimilate these alien worlds into the context of a global ideological struggle against communism: "The United States [after the Second World War] became the only Western nation that sought to legitimate its world-ordering ambitions by championing the idea (if not always in practice) of racial equality. In contrast to nineteenth-century European imperial powers, the captains of America's postwar expansion explicitly denounced the idea of essential racial differences and hierarchies."[30] She argues that in the cultural sphere, the US postwar imperial expansion was based on exclusionist rhetoric against communism (as a mode of life incompatible with the American way of life) on the one hand and, on the other, on ideas and ideals about tolerance (of cultural differences) and inclusion (as cultural progress). She illustrates this changing horizon and texture of orientalism with the phrase "Getting to Know You" – the theme song of the important and hugely popular musical and motion picture in postwar America, *The King and I*.[31] In her meticulous study of the history of transnational adoption, Eleana Kim similarly concludes that the Korean children adopted by US families functioned as "tranquilizing conventions" during and after the Korean War by enabling the American soldiers in Korea and the American families back home to interpret their country's intervention in a war in a distant and unknown place as a meaningful humanitarian intervention.[32] Kim approaches international adoption as a preeminent case of intimate diplomacy during the Cold War era.[33]

The adoption of war orphans was also a notable element in the politics of state-building and war in Korea. The North Korean leadership made a notable effort to shelter their orphaned children from the violence of war, in part by sending a large number of them, particularly those of revolutionary war-martyr parents, to ally countries in Eastern Europe. Kim Il Sung, the supreme commander of North Korea's war efforts, argued during his 1956 visit to Eastern Europe that the international history of fostering Korean War orphans helped to forge strong solidarity among the socialist countries across Eurasia. These orphaned children were brought back to their homeland in the late 1950s. Some experienced great hardship in readjusting back home, and others grew up to become elite cadres in postwar North Korea, thus playing a pivotal role in the consolidation and sublimation of Kim Il Sung's unchallenged political power. North Korea established several special schools for these war orphans, called schools of children of revolutionary martyrs, which trained the future elite party cadres and army officers. Meanwhile, North Korea unleashed a concerted campaign against its antagonist South Korea, propagating the superiority of their paternalistic political system in comparison to conditions in South Korea, in which war-orphaned children allegedly drew no sympathy from the state administration. At the same time, these campaigns emphasized the proliferation of racially mixed children during the war, who, fathered by ally soldiers, were left abandoned both by their motherland and the imperialist paternal authority.

The embrace of war orphans by the polity's benevolent, paternalistic leaders was a prominent theme in postwar North Korea; in South Korea, in contrast, the plight of war orphans was a relatively less prominent public issue. It was certainly not an issue that attracted concerted interest from the state power as was the case in North Korea. However, as Klein shows, it was a highly meaningful issue in the broad structure of Cold War power politics, especially in relation to the US approach to emerging postcolonial nation-states in Asia and the Pacific. Nevertheless, stories of war orphans did appear in the representation of war experiences produced in postwar South Korea, although in strikingly different ways from how the issue was dealt with in North Korea. Notable in this matter is the story of a group of marines involved in the Incheon landing, an event sometimes called the Normandy of the Korean War, which contributed to changing the tide of the war and was featured in the important 1963 motion picture, *The Marines Who Never Returned* (henceforth, *The Marines*; in Korean, *Dolaoji atnŭn haebyŭng*).

The Fraternal Conflict

On their advance into Seoul, while fighting their way along the streets against the remaining communist forces, a group of South Korean marines discover a girl caught up in the cross fire, lost next to her dead mother. The marines rescue her, risking the sniper fire, and later decide to keep the young girl, Young-ju, knowing that she has no place else to go and has no surviving relatives who can care for her. Young-ju stays with her marine "uncles" all the way to Korea's border with China, and later back to Seoul, when her uncles are forced to retreat after the intervention of China in the Korean War. Her presence in the unit contributes to strengthening the comradeship among the battle-hardened soldiers by adding a sense of family feeling. Her uncles begin to feel differently about the war. In place of the earlier structure of feelings anchored in a vague notion of patriotic anti-communism, the soldiers now define the objective of the war for which they were called to fight in terms of the imperative to build a decent future for their collectively adopted little sister, Young-ju. They share the determination that at least one of them must survive the war in order to properly care for the girl when the war is over.

Young-ju develops a particularly strong affective relationship with two of her uncles, who are initially hostile to each other. Their hostility originates from the two soldiers' hidden, interwoven family histories.

After the marines had rescued Young-ju and annihilated the enemy snipers, they discovered a pile of dead bodies in the building where the snipers had been hiding. The victims were townspeople of Seoul, families of South Korean officials and army personnel, who had been executed by the city's communist sympathizers before they evacuated together with the retreating North Korean army. These victims included the younger sister, who was about Young-ju's age, of one of the marines. This man learns from Young-ju that one of the perpetrators of this crime was the younger brother of one of his comrades in the unit. The victim's brother and the perpetrator's brother are old school friends; however, the incident fractures their friendship, and the grieving soldier can no longer accept the perpetrator's brother as his comrade-in-arms. Young-ju's presence in the unit interacts with the old friendship and the new enmity between these two men: she becomes a substitute sister for the grieving man and, for the other soldier, a poignant reminder of the despicable crime he feels responsible for as the elder brother of the perpetrator. Both men suffer from guilt: one from having failed to protect his sister and the other from having failed to help his younger sibling follow the right path. Young-ju tries to ease these two men's separate but intertwined guilty feelings. Later in the story, the two soldiers slowly manage to restore their companionship through their new role as the guardians of the orphaned child, before they both fall in an outnumbered and outgunned fight with the Chinese forces, along with all the other members of their unit, once again leaving Young-ju a displaced orphan and a lonely soul.

The Marines was released in 1963. Throughout the story, the adopted orphan girl is a constant reminder of family tragedies and failed family responsibilities. The story unfolds from the two men's separate yet common family-related feelings of guilt. Similar emotive and moral predicaments continued to be a prime element in the narrative of war in subsequent years.

In postwar South Korea, fictional and semi-fictional accounts of the country's civil war experience dramatized how the war consumed the family, dividing it into opposing political pathways. One well-known war fiction, Kim Dong-li's *The Brothers* (Hyŭngje), depicts the political crisis in a southern coastal town in 1948 in terms of "a broken familial amity and a crisis in the ethics of kinship."[34] One of the most dramatic episodes of the story is when the family's elder brother – who is named tellingly "believer in humanity" and is pitted against his antagonist, his younger brother called "believer in spirits [or superstition]" – rescues a child, the only child of the younger brother, from the threatening hands of a mob. The younger brother is a member of a local communist organization and, when an uprising orchestrated by the organization takes over the town, he turns into a trigger-happy hit man against "the reactionary families." His elder brother is a member of an anti-communist youth organization and feels distressed by his brother's behavior, particularly when he hears that his brother has even attacked the family's close relatives as part of his cleanup action against reactionary families. After the communist uprising fails, an angry mob gathers at the younger brother's house. Having lost their relatives to the violence of the communist insurgents, the mob calls for revenge and is about to release their anger against the man's child after failing to capture the culpable man. Someone in the crowd yells, "The reds must be terminated by their roots!" The elder brother intervenes at this critical moment, rescues the child, and escapes the town through its narrow, dark alleys.

This story, according to a South Korean literary critic, adopts a plot that is typical of South Korea's war narratives: rendering the left and right ideological confrontation as a family affair and, more broadly, the tumultuous reality of war as a crisis in family relations.[35] According to the critic, this narrative strategy has an ethical as well as a political dimension. An individual's affiliation with the wrong political ideology (according to how this was defined by the given political community) is manifested in the individual's committing immoral acts in the domain of kinship (i.e., the communist younger brother does not see a moral dilemma in punishing his close relations deemed to be counterrevolutionaries). Thus, the wrongness of an ideology is judged on the basis of what the ideology does to people who make a commitment to it, turning them into a nonperson from the perspective of kinship and family morality. The righteousness of the opposite political position (anti-communism in this case) is, in turn, manifested by the position's association with an ethical subjectivity in the world of kinship. Therefore, in the story, the elder brother, although he shares the anger of the mob, cannot let this anger (and the clash of modern ideologies that generates it) overpower his primary commitment to his blood relations (hence, he defies the mob and rescues the child).

Indeed, the depiction of political identity in terms of ethical subjectivity in the domain of kinship relations has been a prominent theme in South Korea's postwar cultural productions.[36] This is according to the broader ethos of South Korea's postwar politics of anti-communism that highlighted the moral dispositions of opposing social systems, rather than differences in economic and political ideologies, as was the case in Cold War politics in the wider world. According to the interestingly named South Korean official publication, *Readings in Anticommunist Enlightenment*, produced in 1967, what is wrong with communism is the way in which this ideology distorts the fundamental "morality and ethics of the human social order."[37] As an illustration of these distortions, the book introduces the story of a covert proselytizer sent from North Korea shortly after the end of the Korean War, who approaches his elder brother in South Korea in the hope of turning the latter's home into a base for his covert actions.[38] The story has a telling title, "The case of deceiving the elder brother to coerce him into *buyŏk*."[39] The term *buyŏk* was a frightening word during the war, referring to all manner of acts that are believed to benefit the enemy. The book ends with a stern warning: "If ever your families decide to conceal these elements following the principle of the amity of kinship [*hyŏlyukŭi jŏng*; literally, "the amity of blood and flesh"], think again. You will be committing irrevocable, grave errors."[40] *Readings in Anticommunist Enlightenment* asserts that the immoral nature of communism is found above all in the ideology's propensity and willingness to appropriate even the most intimate dimension of human relations for political purposes. It also makes it clear that one of the most important aspects of general societal resistance to communist infiltration is the civic duty to go beyond kinship ties, if necessary, and to overcome the amity of kinship in the struggle against communism.

Morality of Ideology

The literary world in South Korea has recently moved a considerable distance away from conforming to the state's dominant anti-communist doctrines that prevailed in the immediate postwar decades and which continued to exert power until the 1980s. However, it is interesting to find that the tendency to represent ideological differences in terms of normative positions in kinship relations still continues today.

Particularly revealing in this regard is the epic account of the Korean conflict by the celebrated South Korean writer Cho Jungrae, *Taebaek Mountains* (Taebaek Sanmaek). Cho's story draws upon Yeosu, the same local context as Kim Dong-li's *The Brothers*. This southern coastal area underwent a whirlwind of violence in October 1948 and, again, during the early days of the Korean War. Among the story's protagonists are the Yŏm brothers. The elder Yŏm is an intellectual who, after the failed communist uprising in 1948, joins a mountain-based partisan group, which is at war with the South Korean counterinsurgency police and military forces. His younger brother is recruited into a local anti-communist youth organization and, later, into counterinsurgency activity. Based on his meticulous research of historical facts, Cho's epic accounts deal with actual events, and they depict the precarious life in the coastal community partly in terms of an increasingly radicalized confrontation between the two brothers of the Yŏm family.

Taebaek Mountains was published in the latter part of the 1980s in a literary journal, and it provoked huge public controversy. Some critics argue that it was one of the first truthful accounts of ordinary people's experiences of Korea's violent ideological conflicts, parting decisively with the prevailing ideology of anti-communism. Sympathetic readers appreciate how the story depicts the communist partisans as moral subjects as well as how the work took on the difficult task of exposing the brutality of the government's counterinsurgency measures not only against the partisan groups but also against numerous innocent civilians in Yeosu and elsewhere nearby. Despite its popularity and widely recognized literary merit, the publication of *Taebaek Mountains* also attracted angry reactions from some public sectors, and Cho was subsequently brought to court on the charge that his book violated the country's National Security Law. The negative reactions to the story pointed, among other things, to the way in which it depicts the moral character of the younger Yŏm, a member of an anti-communist youth group, as an uneducated and trigger-happy hooligan in stark contrast to his main political antagonist, his elder brother, who is depicted in the story as a learned and disciplined man.

Taebaek Mountains is considered one of the most important epic narratives of the Korean conflict to have emerged in recent decades and a game-changer in the politics of war representation. Its scale is much wider than that of *The Brothers*, published in the immediate postwar years, and its plot is much more complex. Nevertheless, the two stories commonly depict the political crisis of civil war primarily as radical moral and ethical crises in family relations. The last installment of *Taebaek Mountains* appeared in 1989, the year when the sudden collapse of the Berlin Wall shook the world. Since then, a flood of new works has appeared in South Korea on the theme of Korean War memories. This new post-Cold War Korean War literature since the end of the 1980s, of which *Taebaek Mountains* stands as one of the first and most emblematic examples, attempts to break with the previous literary tradition of the Korean War. Its most distinctive feature is the conscious attempt to be free from the ideology of anti-communism that prevailed in the old narrative tradition. The end of the 1980s was a time of radical transformation for South Korea, characterized not only by the end of the Cold War as a prevailing geopolitical order of the twentieth century but also by the eruption of forceful mass protests against the then military-dominated domestic political regime. It was also when South Korea pursued the so-called Northern Policy, equivalent to West Germany's earlier *Ostpolitik*, aimed at opening up diplomatic and trade relations with countries in the Socialist Bloc. In this atmosphere of general thawing, there also arose strong public interest in telling the history of the Korean War differently and more truthfully, moving away from the hitherto dominant theme of a heroic, united national struggle against aggression by an illegitimate communist regime.

Another important fiction appeared in 1988: *Southern Guerrilla Forces*. Dealing with the same historical period and similar historical events as *Taebaek Mountains*, *Southern Guerrilla Forces* provides a sympathetic picture of the communist partisans – as human beings who love life as well as cherish their ideals, rather than as terror-prone traitors of the nation and blind, emotionless followers of an alien ideology, as these people were typically portrayed in the previous postwar years.[41] These two fictional accounts of the Korean War were subsequently made into films, thereby contributing even more forcefully to the momentous changes of the 1990s in how the public related to the legacy of the Korean War and understood its meanings. The year 1990 also saw the publication of an important Korean War history, volume two of *The Origins of the Korean War* by the historian Bruce Cumings. Like Cumings's first volume on the subject published in 1981, this book was hugely influential among Korean intellectuals and students as well as in shaping public opinion in South Korea about the most important and catastrophic event in their nation's modern history. That *Southern Guerrilla Forces* was released around the same time as *The Origins of the Korean War* was more than a coincidence. In *The Origins*, Cumings traces the root causes of the Korean conflict to the alienation of Korea's anti-colonial nationalist forces from the US-supported anti-communist regime of South Korea, and the manifestation of this alienation in 1947–1948 in the form of the rising armed partisan resistance activities in South Korea's mountain regions, which in fact constitutes the historical background for *Southern Guerrilla Forces* and *Taebaek Mountains*. These new accounts of war in both historical scholarship and cultural productions challenged the hitherto dominant conception in South Korea, according to which the Southern partisans were the puppets of the North Korean and, ultimately, the Soviet communists. They contributed to reconsidering the crucial historical transitional period from 1945 until the outbreak of the war in 1950, thereby revising the temporality of the Korean War to one that is inclusive of the earlier political and military crises in postcolonial Korea.

In short, it may be said that the 1990s was an era in which a new "revisionist" historical and literary scholarship of the Korean War took root in South Korea, in part according to the idea of revisionism familiar in the historiography of the Cold War. The revisionist scholarship in Cold War history sought to challenge the previously dominant trend in this research area that placed the blame for the constitution of the global bipolar order and the escalation of related political and military tensions primarily on the shoulders of the Soviet power. The challenge consisted of, among other things, eliciting the active part played by the American power in the making of Cold War global politics. The changes in the interpretation of the origin and reality of the Korean War that swept the South Korean public world in the 1990s largely followed the pattern of changes that occurred in the interpretation of the broader international politics of the Cold War era. In this development, South Korea was no longer the passive victim of aggression from international communism but increasingly became an active player in the origins of the Korean War. Accordingly, the United States became relatively less a savior of the Korean nation from the menace of communism but instead, increasingly, a powerful actor who, by dividing the postcolonial nation into two and by occupying the country's Southern half, was culpable for sowing the seeds of the fratricidal war in the peninsula.

Subsequently, in the latter part of the 1990s and into the 2000s, a number of other new investigations of the turbulent political reality of early postcolonial Korea from international, national, and local perspectives came to light. These works raise questions not only of the legitimacy of the violent terror perpetrated by the South Korean regime at the time against radical nationalist groups but also the regime's reliance on the colonial-era administrative machinery to do so. These questions were already raised in Cumings's *The Origins*, which presented the rise of radical insurgency in prewar South Korea in a scheme of historical continuity, as a phenomenon that inherits the colonial-era nationalist resistance movement and as an expression of indigenous revolutionary aspiration, thereby challenging the position of the post-Second World War US administration that viewed the phenomenon in the prism of the Soviet-US contest for power and, therefore, as evidence of the expansion of Soviet ambition for global dominance to northeast Asia.

Cumings's investigation of the origins of the Korean War is centered on the postcolonial process of state-building, focusing on how the process was distorted by the rise of the Cold War and the related intervention in the process by the era's new superpowers. It takes Korea's nationhood as a fundamental and unquestionable category, being sympathetic to how this ethnically homogeneous and historically rooted nation had to endure division into two mutually hostile political entities, having just recovered from the Japanese colonial conquest. The modern tragedy of Korea, for Cumings, started when "Dean Rusk first etched a line at the 38th parallel in August 1945."[42] In this historical perspective, the historical nation stands as a primal category in the unfolding of Korea's modern political history, although in a negative sense related to the radical incongruence in postcolonial Korea between state and nation due to the partition of an ancient nation into two artificial Cold War polities. Cumings is critical of US policy on the Korea question as much as he is sympathetic to the sorry fate of postcolonial Korea. Gregory Henderson also wrote in 1974 that "there is no division for which the U.S. government bears so heavy a share of the responsibility as it bears for the division of Korea."[43] In these accounts, the seeds of Korea's civil war were sown when the US administration attempted to establish a separate anti-communist regime in the Southern half, ignoring the strong desire of Koreans for a united, genuine nation-state. Thus, he concludes that Korea had been already in a state of civil war before the Korean War broke out, between the US-backed South Korean state apparatus on the one hand and, on the other, the increasingly cornered radical nationalists, which, as depicted in *Southern Guerrilla Forces*, had taken to armed insurgency activities many months before June 1950.

Questioning the origin of the Korean War in this way was taboo in South Korea under the previous postwar authoritarian, military rule until the late 1980s. The public appearance of stories such as *Southern Guerrilla Forces* was emblematic of the weakening of this political taboo. Changing interpretations of the origins of the Korean War also affected how war experiences were represented. The 2000s saw a flood of memoirs and new literary accounts of the Korean War experience in South Korea. Notable in this development was, as mentioned earlier, the retreat of anti-communist slogans and sentiments and, in their place, a growing emphasis on the brutal nature of the civil war particularly in regard to civilian lives. The war stories of this decade parted, in a significant way, both from the form of *The Marines* and from that of *Southern Guerrilla Forces*. Instead of the experience of combatants – be they freedom fighters against communist aggression or revolutionary fighters against US imperialism – these works typically choose to portray the fate of ordinary people torn by forces of war and between clashing assertions of state sovereignty. They depict how the lives of ordinary people were pulled apart, toward the two sides in the politico-military conflict, and then shattered by the forces of both sides as the tides of war turned.

The writer Park Wan-suh's autobiographical account of her family's life in wartime Seoul is an exemplary case of this new literature of the Korean War (see Chapter 2), although many other equally moving and poignant stories came to light during the second half of the 1990s and the 2000s. The novelist Lee Chang-dong, for instance, tells a gripping story of his childhood experience of witnessing his family's disintegration after his father fell victim to summary execution at the hands of South Korean combat police. Kim felt hostile toward his "communist father" each time

he was ridiculed at school as the "child of a left-handed [leftist] man."[44]
He offers a moving account of his memory of his widowed mother, who
delves, in his words, "ever more deeply into the authority of Jesus Christ
in her desperate attempt to find a minimal order and grace in her life after
the war."

Fraternity

The fate of wartime family life then became the motif of the hugely
influential film, *The Brotherhood of War*. Released in 2004 and hailed as
Korea's *Saving Private Ryan*,[45] the film was an instant success, known to
have attracted more than ten million viewers within two years of its
release. The analogy with Spielberg's *Saving Private Ryan* refers partly
to the scene of an elderly Private Ryan visiting the graves of those who
died during their mission to bring him home from behind German lines.
He was the last remaining brother of four; the rest had perished in the
theater of the Second World War. The story of *Brotherhood of War* also
begins and ends with an elderly veteran visiting the shallow grave of a man
who later turns out to be his missing elder brother, killed in action as
a soldier in North Korea's People's Army. Both films place the political
brotherhood of war and related concept of fraternity in contradiction to
the pre-political kinship idea of brotherhood. Despite these superficial
similarities, the two war films portray very different dramas of brotherhood, and these differences bring us back to the question of civil war and
its specific impact on the fabric of family lives.

The story of brothers in *The Brotherhood of War* depicts the dramatic
fate of a family caught in a civil war. The drama begins when the teenage
younger brother, Jin-seok, is literally snatched from the street (the public
square of Daegu's railway station) by overzealous South Korean army
recruiters. His elder brother, Jin-tae, tries to rescue him and, when this
fails, he signs up for the war himself in the hope of staying close to and
protecting his bookish younger brother. The brothers survive the ordeal
of the hill fights along the Nakdong River, which is the background of the
brotherly reunion depicted in the Statue of Brothers, and join the liberation
of Seoul as well as the ensuing advance of the South Korean and UN
forces to North Korea's border with China. Throughout this perilous
time, Jin-tae is dedicated to carrying out good fights, not because he
believes in "the ideal of patriotism or the ideology of democracy" but
mainly to keep his younger brother safe. In an earlier scene, before the
war breaks out, the viewer is given a glimpse of Jin-tae's normative world.
During a death-day anniversary ceremony for their late father, Jin-tae
recalls his father's last words that entrusted him, the eldest son, with the

roles of breadwinner for the family and a father figure for the young Jin-seok in his absence.[46] Then, he speaks to his father's ancestral tablet, "Father, you should not worry. I am here to protect Jin-seok, and Mother, too."[47]

The single-minded dedication of the paternalistic Jin-tae to his roles as the protective elder brother and the family's responsible eldest son faces a whirlwind of crises during the withdrawal from the Chinese border following the intervention of the Chinese forces in the Korean conflict. Forced to trace their way back to Seoul and preparing for a further southward retreat, the brothers discover that their family is facing a gruesome reality that they did not imagine. Jin-tae's fiancée had been arrested by the paramilitary forces of South Korea, accused of having collaborated with the communist occupiers, and was in imminent danger of summary execution together with another group of townspeople. In a desperate and unsuccessful attempt to rescue her, the two brothers are embroiled in a confrontation with the anti-communist paramilitary and are consequently jailed by the military police. In the ensuing chaos in the city, Jin-tae believes that he has lost his brother to a fire in the jail, which had been deliberately set by the commanding officer of the defending South Korean forces in order to eliminate the prisoners before the communists took over his position. Jin-tae is shattered beyond belief by the vicious violence that befell his fiancée and then his brother – violence against his family committed by those whom he previously believed belonged to the same side. Taken as a prisoner of war by the Chinese, in the file of prisoners, Jin-tae spots the officer who ordered the setting fire to the jail. In a feat of vengeful fury, Jin-tae picks up a stone and savagely bashes the man's skull. With this action, the story of brotherhood develops into a powerful, poignant commentary on the brutal reality of civil war.

After what he believes to be the death of his brother, Jin-tae transforms from a decorated war hero in the battle against the communist invasion to a fearsome warrior of the communist shock troops that terrorize the South Korean and UN forces during the stalemated trench warfare along the 38th parallel. His public status as a war hero is intertwined with Jin-tae's private family feelings, because he earned this status while trying to shield his brother from dangerous combat duties. Therefore, he fights the war more vigorously than other soldiers and as if his soldiering also included his brother's. His notoriety (to the Southern forces) as a leader in the vanguard of North Korean shock troops arises from the violent loss of the foundation of his identity, as a protector of the family, and the subsequent breakdown of his moral selfhood. At first, Jin-tae joined the war without any self-conscious commitment to a specific political cause. Likewise, we may say that his change of position and dedication to the opposite side in the war is a moral rather than a political action. His actions are portrayed as being driven by the norms of kinship rather than according to the claims of the political authority. Jin-tae associates with such political claims from the state only because he recognizes that this is unavoidable for the survival and sustenance of kinship. The imperative of family survival and the morality of kinship constitute the supreme and only meaningful value and *telos* for this war hero. Thus, the experience of war is more about the continuity of family responsibility in a time of public crisis than transcending this private domain to assume the role of a dutiful, patriotic citizen soldier at a time of crisis in the political community.

In *The Brotherhood of War*, brotherhood is portrayed as a primary and pre-political relationship, swept into a turbulent history but nevertheless maintaining its integrity despite that history's bifurcating, destructive force. The elder Jin-tae is an uncompromising follower of the norms of kinship and acts as such in the wider sociopolitical sphere characterized by patriotism and radical friends/enemies contrast. In the philosophical literature, patriotism is defined as "a unity and identification of individual interest with the universal public interest" and "a form of mutual recognition that suspends and transcends the opposition and contrast between universal and particular."[48] The phenomenal existence of patriotism is often employed to invalidate the theory of social contract, for in patriotism, atomistic individuals and "such distrustful individuality, difference, and otherness are transcended in a higher form of self-recognition in and union with other."[49] In patriotism, according to Hegel,

the other ceases to be other, and there is an identification of the individual with the whole in which the individual's private interests, property, and life itself are secured. Yet such securing does not return to atomic individualism, because the patriotic individual is willing to subordinate and sacrifice his interests, property, and life itself for the sake and defense of the whole.[50]

The whole, in the Hegelian philosophy of politics, is distinct from the mode of interhuman relationships, such as in the family where love is a natural and immediate property. It is a higher form of solidarity that is at once beyond "the particular altruism" of the family and "the universal egoism" of the individuals or the civil society constituted by them.[51] The morality of brotherhood portrayed in *The Brotherhood of War* is at odds with such a philosophical ideal of human solidarity based on a dialectical resolution between the particular and the universal. Unlike *The Marines* or *Southern Guerrilla Forces* where the brotherhood of war is the preeminent subject in terms of a shared sense of a common collective fate, brotherhood depicted in *The Brotherhood of War* is presented rather as an expression of indomitable family feelings – the "particular altruism" of a pre-political, ethical life of kinship relations in Hegelian terms. In this narrative, the pre-political ethical life is shown to be fundamentally at odds with modern political brotherhood based on a shared sense of collective good and destiny. This is particularly evident in the rendering of Jin-tae's persona, for whom the survival of family from the destruction of war provides the will to fight the war.

Notice also that there is an episode of tragic civilian killing in both *The Brotherhood of War* and *The Marines*. In *The Marines*, the killing was committed by the communists against the families of the enemy officials and combatants, whereas in *The Brotherhood of War*, the victims were accused of having collaborated with the communists and the violence against them was committed by anti-communist paramilitary forces. Historical records show that the occupation and liberation of Seoul resulted in atrocities against civilians on both sides of the conflict, whereas the crimes committed against the so-called collaborators with the communists have long been a taboo subject in South Korea. In this sense, *The Brotherhood of War* represents a new era in South Korea, in which society can express its collective memory of the Korean War's violence against civilians in more historically truthful ways, departing from the era represented by the story of *The Marines*, where the subject remained strongly censured. Another important difference exists between these two stories. The incident of civilian killing in *The Marines* involved the younger brother of one of the marines, and the moral and ideological conflict between these two brothers looms large throughout the story and behind the unfolding of another brotherhood founded on common, patriotic spirit. The soldier whose brother is responsible for the atrocity and his comrade whose sister fell victim to the atrocious killing both suffer from guilt. However, they overcome their separate feelings of guilt eventually through a new sense of brotherhood as comrades-in-arms. *The Marines* celebrates the latter, the political form of brotherhood and, in doing so, presents political conflicts between consanguine brothers as irreconcilable moral contradictions. Since the 1990s, by contrast, the new narratives of war sought to challenge the existing moral hierarchy between the two forms of political brotherhood, anti-communist and revolutionary, and also to present a more accountable history of the Korean War's violence against civilian lives. Through these efforts, the idea of the Korean War as a family crisis and a brotherly conflict continued to evolve.

Pre-Political Brotherhood

Contradictions between two claims of loyalty, political and familial, have long been part of Korea's literary and cultural tradition. Cumings observes,

"Loyalty and filial piety form the deepest wellsprings of Korean virtue, nurtured over thousands of years."[52] However, the virtue of *ch'ung* (loyalty to the sovereign) and that of *hyo* (filial piety) are separate principles. Although it is true that in traditional Confucian societies, the two virtues conceptually formed an ethical, ideological whole, it is important to recognize that filial piety, unlike loyalty to the sovereign, constituted an absolute ethical principle. The South Korean anthropologist Lee Mun-Woong notes that "In traditional Korean society, the filial relations were considered to be the primary backbone of all human relations; by comparison, the relations between the ruler and the ruled were secondary in significance and were not an all-encompassing, powerful element."[53] Even in a highly dogmatic Confucian society as in pre-eighteenth-century Korea, the subjects of the sovereign, be they indignant mandarin scholars or angry peasant rebels, had the right to withhold their loyalty to a particular sovereign order if they felt that the order violated the virtue of politics (e.g., the heavenly mandate or the principle of filial continuity within the dynastic succession of power). Another telling example is a famous story of a peasant soldier, told by Kim Si-sup, the eminent scholar and literary giant of fifteenth-century Korea: a young soldier joins the army not out of loyalty to the sovereign but because of his filial obligation to his conscripted father, in the hope of staying close to the latter to protect his life. *The Brotherhood of War* draws upon this traditional idea of moral hierarchy between the amity of kinship and loyalty to the sovereign order, and between the domestic and the political, to express the moral triumph of kinship ties over the ties of modern political brotherhood.

The representation of the Korean War in postwar South Korea took the contradiction between the amity of kinship and the condition of enmity in the political sphere as a key constitutive element. Sometimes the amity of kinship stood for an autonomous domain that, although swayed by the polarizing politics of the wider world, may survive the bipolarizing force and recover its normative integrity. Yet, at other times, the life of kinship was rendered as the very field in which the violent bipolar history plays out with its full weight and shatters the normative fabric of intimate human relations. In the latter context, political history unfolds as a series of crises within the relational world of kinship rather than being an external condition against which the autonomy of kinship exists. Although the representation of the Korean War experience has changed remarkably in recent decades, becoming less constrained by Cold War-era anti-communist ideology and increasingly open to the hitherto untold aspects of the war's reality, the newly emerging accounts continue to be told within the framework of family history and as moral crises in kinship relations. One of the eminent South Korean writers of war epics, Kim Won-il, ends his 1997 *Feast of Fire* with a scene of cockfighting, in which one spectator remarks to another villager: "Do you know those two cocks are actually two brothers? One is older than the other by one year, and they both originate from a seed cock in Masan that has a distinguished blood genealogy." The villager replies, "Is that right? How is it that two brothers are after each other's blood? Good genealogy or not, they are certainly true beasts!" The spectator adds: "Humans do the same, you know. These cocks are fighting for death and are ready to shed blood merely because they belong to different masters. They must show loyalty to their masters."[54] In this development, the idea of brotherhood is not reducible to the ideal of modern political brotherhood, as defined in the Western philosophical tradition. Nor is it the same as the unproblematic notion of natural brotherhood, as rendered in the critique of the Western idea of political brotherhood. The experience of a mass-mobilized and ideologically charged modern civil war can turn the realm of human kinship inside out, thereby making the idea of natural brotherhood painfully unreal.[55]

On a closing note, let us go back to *The Marines* to illustrate a historical reality that this drama fails to touch upon. The backdrop to the story of *The Marines* is the liberation of Seoul from communist occupation after the successful amphibious assault by UN forces on North Korean positions in Incheon that began on September 15, 1950. The island of Jeju provided many men for this important military action that turned the tide of war from a defensive to an offensive position for South Korea and keeps a compelling history of how these men came to join the liberation of Seoul in the first place. Villages in Jeju are dotted with memorials dedicated to the fallen marines from the Korean conflict, and the island's provincial capital has a prominent monument dedicated to "The Spirit of Jeju Marines," located at the center of the town's commercial and administrative area. These material objects are intended to commemorate the island's youths who sacrificed their lives to the national cause and to demonstrate the community's tribute of honor to them. In each of these local memorials, however, there are hidden, yet untold histories of sacrifice.

Before the outbreak of the Korean War, the island of Jeju suffered an extreme crisis related to a failed communist-led uprising in April 1948. Brutal counterinsurgency campaigns followed the uprising, which terrorized the entire island until the end of the Korean War in 1953. Many innocent civilians were lost, accused of collaborating with the rebels or their sympathizers, and the punishment for collaboration frequently fell on the families and relatives of the defined enemies of the state. In this extreme situation, one way to preserve life, both for the individual and the family, was to join the army and to leave home to fight the war on the mainland.[56]

Similar complications were witnessed in the very city that these mobilized young men from Jeju were trying to liberate. While the UN forces were advancing on Seoul followed by a successful landing in Incheon, a revamped campaign for war mobilization was unleashed in the city by the occupying authority. A historian and resident of Seoul describes the situation in his diary entry on September 17, 1950.[57] He heard the appeal from his neighbor, Dokhwa's mother, to her absent husband:

Dokhwa's Mother's appeal to her husband was particularly painful. She said: "We are deeply ashamed that you became the enemy of the people, standing on the side of the US imperialist buglers and Rhee Syng Man puppet cliques. Our daughter Dokhwa volunteered for the People's Army in the hope to repent your crimes on your behalf. I spend sleepless nights, haunted by dreams in which you and Dokhwa are poised to kill each other with rifles and bayonets. Please come back. Please come back to the side of the people."

Hearing this, the historian laments what the war is doing to the ordinary townspeople of Seoul, and how Dokhwa was forced to join the North Korean army, which he knew was probably the only way for her family to survive the occupation – the family of an officer of the South Korean army.

The Jeju-based scholar, Gwon Gwi-sook, has investigated the life histories of some of the Jeju veterans who took part in the liberation of Seoul.[58] These veterans are proud of their achievements in the Incheon landing, which the military history of the Korean War highlights as one of the war's most significant battles. Most of them are active members of the island's veterans' association and join the periodic commemorative events for the fallen of the Korean War organized in the province's capital. At the local village level, however, some of these veterans have recently been active in different communal commemorative initiatives, relating to the village's victims of the 1948–1953 state terror. In a number of villages in Jeju, it was in fact these veterans who initially raised voices, against many odds, in favor of these memorial projects. Many of these veterans of the Korean War originate from the bereaved families of the civilian massacres of 1948–1949, and they had the strength that other villagers did not – the moral authority of having fought on the patriotic front against communism. This moral authority proved vital for breaking the coerced silence about the brutal terror of 1948–1953 that the villages of Jeju had undergone during the postwar decades. One veteran remembers what his grandfather told him in 1950 – that he would have to join the war and fight hard against the communists if he wished to survive in the world, and that this was the only way for him to shake off the stigma of a red family that was weighing on him. He said that for him, the question was not whether to fight for the country to protect his family from the enemy; the real question was to fight for the country to help his family survive in that country.

Is blood thicker than ideology? The answer to this question depends on the possibility of separating the sphere of consanguinity from that of ideology in the first place. In order to imagine this possibility, it is necessary to set aside the milieu of consanguinity and give it a normative life of its own that is independent from the forces of modern ideology. Important narrators of the Korean War have all struggled with this possibility. Cumings's *The Origins of the Korean War* assumes a primordial domain in the form of a historic nation and contrasts it with the artificial division of this entity by modern geopolitics. Another acute observer of modern Korean political history speaks of "a substantial disparity between the primordial unity of the nation and people of Korea and its more recent divided status as two incomplete states."[59] *The Brotherhood of War* explores a related possibility, by pitting the life of consanguine brotherhood against the reality and myth of the political brotherhood of war and the nation-state. In both types of narrative, despite their differences in genre and scope, the modern experience of ideological polarization and political division is commonly pitted against forms of traditional unity, real or imaginary.

The experience of the Jeju veterans complicates this narrative order, however. The milieu of kinship from which these men were brought to the fog of war was not an entity that could be set discreetly aside from the forces of modern politics. Rather, it was a world that had been already brutally torn apart by those very forces. The pre-political image of familial unity emerging from the narratives of the Koreas' civil war is an important means by which the narrator can maintain some distance from the crushing politics of state sovereignty. It is also an important means for expressing a hope for the possibility of a form of reconciliation between community and state. However, this should not obscure the fact that kinship, in the history of the Korean War, is a profoundly wounded entity that struggled with a tumultuous existence during the entire period of the long Cold War, and even before the full-scale civil war started.

6 The Quiet Revolution

Earlier we briefly discussed George Mosse's "the myth of war experience" idea.[1] The idea refers to the ways in which, after the First World War, certain types of stories were publicly and prolifically recycled in societies that had been major parties to the war. More specifically, it addresses how these public representations of trench warfare systematically concealed the painful, soul-shattering experiences of those who fought in it, instead highlighting tales of romantic heroism. Notable in the era's "mythmaking" was the sublimation of camaraderie, the comfort and beauty of solidarity among otherwise unrelated individuals who were brought together for a higher purpose that transcended the narrow world of these actors' separate individual interests and preoccupations. The myth-making was principally about freedom and its intimate ties to violence – as Friedrich Schiller propagated in his *Reiterlied*, "Only the soldier was free."[2] War experience as the object of mythmaking created rare and sublime occasions, in which modern beings became free from the banality of their everyday lives and the constraints of inequality in bourgeois society. In Hegel's discussion of patriotism in his *Philosophy of Right*, such war experience as an expression of the virtue of patriotism is a supreme symbol of modern freedom.[3] It constitutes the modern individual's fullest freedom, which elevates their particularistic interests to the sphere of a universal spirit. We also discussed critical responses to this rendering of modern war experience. These critical interventions aim to do justice to the aspects of the war-experiencing self that refuse to fall within Schiller's notion of freedom and, in doing so, bring to the fore the authenticity of the historical self – the human self that struggles with captivating memories of the war's brutality and which, in doing so, seeks freedom from the myth of war experience itself.

The encounter of the mobilized youths of Jeju Island with the Korean War, mentioned briefly at the end of the previous chapter, calls for another, alternative way of thinking about the subjectivity of war experience. Recall that these humble actors of history joined the armed struggle against communism in the hope of saving their families from the terror of anti-communist violence. Their Korean War experience was not a shedding of their privatized and isolated selfhood for the enchanting existence in what Schiller called a single land of brothers. Nor was it merely a historical subject whose sovereign individual selfhood is in critical dialogue with the intoxicating force of mythmaking. The subjectivity of war experience, in this historical milieu, was fundamentally relational in that the idea of freedom involved in it meant, rather than an escape from the burdens of everyday life, this lifeworld's freedom from threats to its very existence. Likewise, an understanding of this historical subjectivity requires a conceptualization of community in a way that parts with the concept of community familiar to our received wisdom. The latter places community as an a priori reality and as a given condition of human being-in-common that is, in the words of Roberto Esposito, closed off from the constitution of modern political society.[4] The making of modernity, according to Esposito, has at its core "the sacrifice of community" and the immunization of the concept of the political from the life of community. He calls this process of immunization "the myth of community" in modern political thought. What he means is, in my interpretation, that the concept of the political, in the tradition of modern liberal political thought, is squarely anchored in the idea of the individual and in that of society composed by these philosophical individuals. The life of this concept, therefore, implicates the death of community as a political concept and the relegation of community to a pre-political existence – the theoretical problem that Esposito refers to as the sacrifice of community in modern politics. An understanding of the war experience of the Jeju veterans of the Korean War calls for a confrontation with both streams of mythmaking in modern politics – the myth of war experience based on a romantic, ultimately apocalyptic idea of freedom, on the one hand, and, on the other, the myth of community in which the life of human community is stripped of a meaningful political existence in modern society and modern political thought. The idea of *communitas*, if understood in this way as a political concept rather than a pre-political entity, comes close in meaning to that of *societas* (defined in distinction to *civitas*) that we discussed earlier with reference to Lewis Henry Morgan's understanding of kinship and politics (see the Introduction to this volume).

The important point is that (traditional) community does not need to be understood merely as other than (modern) society when the question is about political life. On the contrary, in the actual empirical reality of modern times, we all carry out our lives as moderns and as less than (or more than) modern individuals. Community can be different from society, but this does not mean that the former has no political life in the space of modernity. Society may exist as an external environment of community and, at once, shape community's life from within. Seen against the background of a civil war, this question of society within community speaks of the fact that ordinary lives in a community are far from ordinary, keeping in them memories and traces of the extraordinary time in the past – the time when the community was turned inside out and made into a mirror image of the larger political society in a state of siege and exception.[5] It is this particular destiny of community during and after civil war that this book has focused on – an entity that is relegated to a pre-political status by modern ideology despite its historical experience in a supremely political way and as a microcosmic society at war. If the history of a society at war affects lives in a community in the present, it follows that the community has to come to terms with this history in order to obtain a condition of social peace in its own way, both communally and politically. In this final chapter, we will explore how a community takes the initiative to make peace with itself and, in doing so, sets out to undo the "myth of community." We will see how closely intertwined this process of demystification is, against the background of civil war, with efforts to undo the myth of war experience.

1989

In November 1989, the world was riveted by the powerful drama unfolding in Berlin. While the wall that had divided the city since 1961 was crumbling in the hands of ordinary Berliners, an event that subsequently became the shining marker of the end of the Cold War, the island of Jeju was witnessing its own era-ending drama. This drama also involved opening a wall, although in this case, the wall was a less materially tangible one compared to that in Berlin – the wall of silence that had enveloped the islanders' everyday lives for the past four decades. The opening began with an act of speaking out, which entered the public sphere in 1989.

Entitled *Now We Speak Out* in the islanders' distinct indigenous language (*Ijesa malhaemsuda*), this act consisted of twenty eyewitness accounts of the violence of 1948–1953, the time that is typically referred to as the "April Third Incident" or simply 4/3. The "incident" refers to an armed uprising by a small group of local communists on April 3, 1948, first directed against several police outposts across the island. However, the incident also includes numerous atrocities of civilian killings that devastated the island communities following the uprising, caused principally by brutal counterinsurgency military campaigns and, in part, by counteractions by the communist partisans. The counterinsurgency campaign had been initially launched by the US Military Government of Korea before it was taken over by the nascent government of South Korea after the latter was sworn in, in August 1948. The communist insurrection was, in part, in protest at the US Military Government's move to install a separate state in the southern half of Korea under its occupation. A more immediate background was the Military Government's drive to revive the colonial-era state bureaucracy, especially its repressive police forces, as part of its preparation for a southern Korean state; a move that provoked broad popular resistance among the islanders who had vivid memories of a long colonial occupation that had ended only shortly before, in August 1945. In fact, the troubles began a year before April 1948.

On March 1, 1947, crowds gathered in different locations on Jeju to mark the anniversary of the March First uprising of 1919. The March First movement is a formative event in modern Korean history, when tens of thousands of ordinary Koreans took to the streets to protest against Japan's colonial occupation. The largely peaceful protest was held simultaneously in a multitude of locations across the country, urban and rural, and it was part of the forceful rise of an appeal for self-determination on a global scale following the end of the First World War and Woodrow Wilson's intervention at the Paris Peace Conference, also employing the rhetoric of self-determination. Historians view this time as the origin of decolonization in the history of the global South, and also as the onset of the American Century – the century defined by the preponderance of American power in place of Europe's crumbling imperial powers. In the political history of Korea, 1919 is regarded as the initiatory moment in the making of Korea's modern polity and political society. After the peaceful uprising was violently crushed by the colonial police and military forces, the leaders of the movement, then exiled to China, established a provisional government in Shanghai.[6] The 1919 uprising was largely based on the voluntary participation of ordinary people, young and old and women and men, who acted freely and politically in the public world to reclaim it as their own, in a way that closely resonates with how Hannah Arendt describes the concept of political action.[7] The Jeju islanders who joined the 1947 anniversary gatherings to commemorate this momentous event, which happened during the dark colonial era, did so in protest against the postcolonial conditions they confronted, which appeared to them as a return to the dark times. The US Military Government reacted to the 1947 protest with excessive coercive force, and this provoked heightened resistance from the islanders, who responded with a general strike. The Military Government regarded what was unfolding in Jeju as a challenge to its authority and the island as a whole as a subversive place.[8]

It quickly deployed extra police troops from the mainland to this "red island," as well as armed groups of anti-communist paramilitaries. In this way, as prominent Jeju historian Park Chan-sik wrote, "The March First of 1947 became the most formative background to the April Third eruption a year later."[9]

Soon after their concerted assault against several police outposts on April 3, 1948, the communist partisans were entrenched in the relatively inaccessible mountainous areas at the center of the island, thereby beginning to exert their influence on the hillside villages, while the government's counterinsurgency forces took control of communities in the lowlands and along the coast. The standoff between the highlands-based partisan groups and the counterinsurgency troops controlling the coastal areas continued until the end of the Korean War in 1953, resulting in great hardship, especially for the villagers in the highlands of Jeju, who were caught between the forces in the mountains and those in the coastal region. For these islanders, the 4/3 incident refers principally to the extreme chaos and terror that they experienced during those years, which resulted in over 25,000 dead and missing – about 10 percent of the Jeju population at the time. It also addresses the wounds induced in the lives of the survivors and a deep sense of betrayal, not merely in regard to the power of the state but also that which still exists between and within communities.

The lead testimony in *Now We Speak Out* is given by a local *simbang*, a common reference to a specialist in shamanism among the islanders, a strong tradition in Jeju. The *simbang* says:

Nearly every family [in Jeju] keeps some grievous spirits of the tragic dead from the time of the Incident. If you listened to their stories, you would discover that nearly all these dead were innocent people. They were neither on that side nor on this side; ensconced in between the two sides, they were simply trying to escape a brutal fate. Some escaped to the mountains to preserve their lives and never came back; others met death while staying quietly at home. Each time I opened a *kut* [shamanic rite], I heard these stories. In *kut* for families who had people working for the police or the government, you would hear more about people killed by the mountain [partisan] side; in other homes, stories were mostly about the victims of the government side. Many dead had no this or that side origin. I heard from [the spirit of] a man how his death had been caused by his relative by law. His relative had had a grudge against him because of an old marriage dispute between the two families.[10]

The making of these testimonies, first in the space of a local newspaper and later as a book, is regarded among the island's intellectuals as one of the most important public events in recent decades and as an event that put an end to the island's long-held silence about its past experience. Such public historical testimonial actions advanced in Jeju earlier and more forcefully than in other parts of South Korea. They were a pioneering and exemplary local initiative, which subsequently encouraged many other similar public efforts of historical accountability elsewhere in Korea. In this sense, it is not an exaggeration to say that the act of speaking out, as represented by the emergence of *Now We Speak Out*, marked a decisive change in the sociopolitical landscape of South Korea. We may consider this act in a broader historical perspective, as an important intervention in the making of a post-Cold War world in the Asian context. The 1948 chaos in Jeju was, in many ways, a prelude to the crisis of Korea's civil war in 1950. It was also a manifestation of the politics of the Korean War on a smaller scale, just as the Korean War itself was, as mentioned earlier, emblematic of the politics of the Cold War as a global civil war. Seen from this angle, the fate of Jeju in 1947–1953 is part of a much broader crisis of the time relating to the concurrence of decolonization and the Cold War in Asia and beyond, including, among other things, the troubles in Taiwan, the Malaysian emergency, and the violence of the First Indochina War in Vietnam. The island witnessed one of the first violent manifestations of the postcolonial Cold War; in recent years, it has emerged as one of the first and most powerful witnesses to the living legacies of this tragic global history.

However, what is interesting about *Now We Speak Out* is not merely its exemplary status as an act of historical witnessing in the chronological sense. The initiative also demonstrates a distinct way to testify to the violence of the Cold War. This act introduces a number of testimonies to the reality of the April Third violence, as it was experienced in different localities and by a variety of historical actors – for instance, a secondary-school student in town, a village farmer, a former prisoner, and a former mountain partisan. Each of these testimonies provides a rare glimpse of the hitherto unknown historical reality, and as a whole they are meant to provide a view of the era from multiple perspectives. The story from the local village shaman is brought into this act as the opening testimony, ahead of all other original accounts, as if it were meant to be a general introduction to the rest of the stories that follow.

The efficacy of shamanism as an initiatory act in historical testimony, as manifested in the organization of *Now We Speak Out*, draws upon the islanders' everyday lives during the long Cold War. The anthropologist Kim Seong-nae notes the unique place of the local religious culture of shamanism in the history and legacy of political violence. Kim conducted fieldwork in a northeastern Jeju coastal village at the end of the 1980s. Her research initially focused on gender questions in the islanders' cultural life, especially the significance of shamanism in the daily lives of the island's women. This is a religious form existing alongside rituals of ancestor worship, which also takes up an important place in the routines of the islanders' family and communal lives. The anthropologist changed her research focus, however, after discovering fragments of historical violence in the shamanic rituals she was attending. Kim had no knowledge of the 1948–1953 violence at that time, nor had she encountered any traces of this past outside the ritual context. Through this experience, Kim later came to conclude that shamanism in Jeju is a powerful, distinct institution of historical memory.[11]

This clearly shows that the particular structure of *Now We Speak Out*, in which a testimony by a local shaman plays a pivotal role in opening up the space of testimonial and revelatory acts, is grounded in the lived cultural milieus of the island's communities. Before the 1990s, knowledge of the postcolonial violence in Jeju was strictly a taboo subject both in Jeju and in South Korean society at large. Evidence suggests that this was the case even within a neighborhood and among the kin – a condition that is sometimes expressed as the impossibility of grieving. On occasions of domestic ancestral death remembrance rites called *jesa*, for instance, families took care in containing the eruption of lamentations among the participants in fear that they might include exclamations of indignation against the authorities, and that their neighbors might overhear these dangerous words. The Jeju-born writer Hyun Ki-young depicts, in his celebrated story *Suni Samchon* (Aunt Suni), the cultural institution of *jesa* as a principal site of historical memory. The story's background is Bukchon, a village in the northeast of Jeju, which suffered the tragedy of a large-scale massacre at the hands of the government's counterinsurgency forces on January 17, 1949. Since the killing affected nearly every household in the village, each year, on the anniversary of the incident, a multitude of domestic death-day rites take place in Bukchon – all separately yet all simultaneously. Hyun writes:

Lamentations were heard from many houses. Then the village dogs started barking. That was how people opened their death-day ceremonies. Rituals were held in many village homes, in the same hour and on the same day. The rite for our grandfather was one of them, and I knew it started when I heard the lamentation by my father's sister. Following hers came the wailing of my grandfather's first daughter-in-law and then that of my father's sister's niece. Each year, in the evening of the eighteenth day of the second lunar month, our entire village was engulfed by sad and loud lamentations emanating from many houses, while the spirits of the dead, some five hundred of them, quietly descended to the village to receive the foods prepared by their families.[12]

What is striking about the stories introduced here is the fact that each of them draws upon, respectively, one of the two important institutions of death commemoration in Korea's religious cultural tradition: domestic ancestral death-day rites (*jesa*) and shamanic death consolation rites (*kut*). The *Aunt Suni* story unfolds from within the context of an ancestral rite. *Now We Speak Out* begins with accounts of complications in family genealogy as these are revealed in shamanic consolation rites. In both cases, historical testimonial actions appear to require a ritualized space of remembrance for their enunciation, a milieu in which the living are expected to commune or communicate with the dead.

Two Faces of Ancestors

Aunt Suni begins with the return of a middle-aged man, who has settled in Seoul, to his birth village in Jeju for the purpose of joining the death-day rite for his grandfather after many years of absence.[13] A number of relatives gather for the evening's ceremony, where the visitor hears the sad news that Suni, a relative on his father's side, was recently found dead on her plot of land. He is shocked to learn that the small stone-walled plot is where Suni buried her two children who were killed in tragic circumstances at the height of the April Third violence. He starts wondering if the tragedy of 1949 that befell her family had anything to do with the mysterious circumstances of Suni's death. He imagines that Suni had actually endured the existence of the living dead ever since she had buried the bodies of her children at the corner of her garden plot. These thoughts about Suni and her past emerge in the atmosphere of a death-day rite and amid the soft-spoken, intimate conversation among his relatives about the family's past. The participants feel relatively at ease recalling even the turbulent years of the late 1940s – something the islanders would rarely do in other circumstances. When his elderly relatives reminisce about the family's past, the stories of the April Third incident unavoidably seep into their recollections. Listening to these stories, the returnee from Seoul is awakened to the fact that the violent events of the past are deeply entrenched in the lives of his family today.

Among those gathered for the day's ceremony is his late father's younger sister's husband. This man objects to the way in which other guests speak about the brutality of the government's counterinsurgency measures against the villagers, insisting that these measures would not have been necessary unless there were atrocities committed by the mountain-based insurgents. While making this protest, his language changes from the Jeju dialect he adopted during the past years to a dialect used in a region in North Korea with which he had been familiar before he settled in Jeju. This incident brings back another memory of 1948–1949 to the returnee: how his father and other senior relatives on his paternal side reacted to the request from the man from the northern part of Korea when the latter expressed his wish to marry his future spouse. The suitor arrived on the island as a member of an anti-communist youth group consisting mostly of youths displaced from their homes in North Korea – the paramilitary group that was introduced to the island as part of the counter-insurgency actions of 1948 and which the survivors of the April Third incident today associate with exceptional brutality. The returnee recalls that there was no possibility for the family to respond negatively to the suitor's approach at that time and also that his family survived, unlike many other families in the village, partly thanks to the marriage and his family's consequent ties of kinship to a member of an anti-communist paramilitary group.

Although rendered in a fictional form, *Aunt Suni* draws upon real historical events. First published in 1978, the appearance of this story was part of the politically gloomy yet artistically vibrant South Korea of the 1970s, during which, as Youngju Ryu shows in her magisterial depiction of the time, the country's literary world waged a critical fight against the state's authoritarian and increasingly dictatorial politics grounded in a militant ideology of anti-communism.[14] The story presents the event of *jesa* (ancestral death commemorative rites), or more specifically *gijesa* (domestic death-day rites usually held at the home of the primogeniture descendant for ancestors four generations removed from below), as its primary narrative context. In this respect, some literary critics call *Aunt Suni* a good example of "*jesa* literature," a distinct genre of modern Korean literature that employs the traditional culture of ancestral death commemoration as a key element of an unfolding narrative. This genre employs the organization of death-day rites as a context within which an opening is provided to a history that is otherwise forbidden from narration. The idea is that ancestral rites provide a quasi-liminal space that is set apart from the everyday order, and that this ritualized space is congenial to the release of repressed historical memories – memories that are, within the routine public order of daily life, not to be exposed. The prominence of the ancestral death ritual as a context for historical reckoning and remembrance is also associated with the fact that kinship in Korea is traditionally a ritual community and a unity based on the common practice of ancestral remembrance rites, from the domestic group consisting of a stem family to expanding circles of kindred that are centered on varying parameters of patrilineal ancestors.

Note also, however, that the story about Suni presents the family's ancestral rite as being part of many like events of death commemoration taking place in the locality simultaneously. The story takes note of this unusual ritual atmosphere. The visitor from Seoul recalls: "That was the hour to do the death-day ceremony; ceremonies took place in many family homes, at the same hour and on the same day." These simultaneous, multiple household-based death-commemorative ceremonies within a confined community are alien to Korea's traditional culture of commemoration and indicative of the fact that an extraordinary event of mass deaths exists in the community's past history. As such, they are a distinct feature in the communities that suffered mass violence during the war. The multiplicity of the ritual events generates an eerie atmosphere in the community and, in a kin-based local community, makes the annual lunar-day event a recurrently poignant reminder of the collective tragedy suffered by the community as a whole.[15] These occasions are sad events for the families and the community; however, there are also other hidden, even more critical elements in these commemorative events, which concern the structure of traditional domestic death commemoration. If the victims of violence died young and unmarried, they were usually not entitled, under the traditional customary law of Korea, to join the space of *jesa*. The details of these victims (i.e., the times and circumstances of their death) also risk being unrecorded in the family genealogical records; sometimes, even their names were erased from these records.

As a way to counter these problems in the family's ritual commemorative order caused by untimely death, the ritual known as a "spirit marriage" was practiced fairly widely in parts of postwar Korea. The marriage brings together the spirits of two young individuals who died unmarried in a posthumous matrimonial union. It typically involves an agreement between the families of the dead youths, followed by a complex ritual usually overseen by a specialist in shamanism, who in this context plays the role of a facilitator of the matrimonial union. The ritual procedure closely resembles a traditional marriage procedure, including an exchange of intent and gifts between the two families as well as a fortune-telling of the compatibility between the prospective bride and groom based on their dates and times of birth. The posthumous marriage enables the groom's family to find a child (often from their circle of relatives) who can be adopted by the married couple and who thereafter can perform periodic death-day commemorative rites on their behalf. If the victims of violence were married at the time of death but died without leaving behind a descendant, the entitlement of the deceased to death commemorative rituals is also in crisis, although less severely so than in the case of the unmarried death. Hence, the practice of posthumous child adoption without an accompanying posthumous spirit marriage was also not uncommon in parts of Korea during the postwar years.[16]

The postwar practice of posthumous adoption was often fraught with conflicts among people involved in it, however. Adoptions typically took place among close collateral relatives (most often, involving a child of the deceased man's male sibling), and the adoptee was expected not only to assume ritual obligations but also, if available, to inherit the properties that belonged to his new family line. Against the background of civil war, however, what was inherited involved not only properties and ritual statuses but also political legacies. In the logic of associative guilt described earlier, the newcomers to a family line had to shoulder the burden of their new family's politically negative, socially stigmatizing ancestral heritage. For this reason, the episodes of posthumous adoption after the Korean War abound with stories of bitter disagreements within and between families, between the donor and the receiving family. One family I knew had felt obliged to hand over one of their children to their collateral family line that was cut short by the war, and they had been encouraged to do so by their lineage elders. Privately, however, they were pained by the idea not merely because it meant the sorrow of parting with their beloved child, but also because it meant a possibly ominous prospect for the child who might have a tough life ahead from being associated, through the adoption, with a politically dangerous ancestor, as it were. In the atmosphere of radicalized anti-communism after the war, this ominous prospect was not just a remote possibility.

Another difficulty faced by postwar families in the domain of death commemoration is related to the organization of Korea's traditional ancestral rites. In order to perform the rite, it is necessary to know the time of death, for the death-day rite has to be held according to the precise place of death in the lunar calendar. In light of this, testimonies of war experience that have recently been made available in South Korea amply show how uncertainties about the circumstances of death or disappearance induced great anxieties for the surviving families. Many families who confronted this situation took the missing person's date of disappearance from home as the date of the person's death. The traditional rule of death commemoration makes this option a haphazard and incomplete practice, however, failing to dispel the sense of impropriety and lack of closure entirely, and the desire to know the right time of death remains strong in many bereaved families even today. Without knowing the exact day of death, moreover, the missing person's status in the family and public genealogical records also remained incomplete and, for that matter, the entire order of the family genealogical record was left in suspension. The absence of bodies also complicated postwar domestic death commemoration. The customary practice of ancestor worship principally consists of both the domestic death-day commemorative rites held at home and the periodic ceremony held at the ancestral graves, which usually brings together a wider network of kindred. The tomb visits may involve a relatively small group of collateral kin or may be done as part of a larger gathering of relatives who together visit a multitude of family graves located in the ancestral village. On these occasions, for families with missing relatives, the absence of graves for their loved ones becomes materially evident, which can be an agonizing experience for them. The failure to have an appropriate burial for a relative is understood to be a moral failure of the concerned kin group as a whole, and, moreover, is sometimes associated with threats of what some observers call ancestral affliction – negative ramifications of an ancestor's ill state of being on the descendants' health and material well-being. Roger Janelli and Dawnhee Yim Janelli, in their ethnography based in a single-lineage village of a central South Korean region, make astute observations as to how the people of this village conceptualize the possibility and reality of ancestral affliction related to events of tragic death suffered during the Korean War.[17] As a response, it is common in Jeju and elsewhere to find graves that the locals describe as *hŏtmyo* ("empty grave" or "fictive grave"), a grave made without the deceased's body. These empty graves typically contain old clothing and other personal objects that belonged to the missing dead. The burial of these objects involves a funerary procedure that is very much akin to a real funeral. The procedure is overseen by either a village elder, who is familiar with Confucian ritual texts and oration, or a specialist in shamanism, who is believed to be able to call the soul of the missing dead to the latter's personal objects before these objects are put in the coffin and entombed. When completed, these fictive graves are treated with the same respect and care as is given to real graves, although this does not mean that by making these graves, the families are able to entirely put to rest their concerns and anxieties about their missing relatives. Another notable practice in this regard is found in the island of Jeju. Referred to as a "*jesa* even the raven are unaware of" (i.e., a secretly held rite unknown even to relatives and neighbors), the locals extended this traditional custom – which was originally meant for, among others, dead fishermen whose bodies were lost at sea – to the commemoration of their loved ones whose bodies had been lost amid the chaos of mass political violence.[18]

Postwar communities dealt with the war-induced moral, material, and spiritual crises in the sphere of death commemoration in diverse and, at times, inventive ways. Although spirit marriages, posthumous adoptions, and fictive tombs were all significant means by which families sought to counter the war-generated crises in their domestic culture of death commemoration, it was, nevertheless, the *kut*, the shamanic rite, which stood as the most prominent, popular means of dealing with war-caused crises in family and kinship relations. Notable here is Kim Seong-nae's work on Jeju shamanism, mentioned earlier, which focuses on the ritual act called locally "the lamentations of the dead."[19] In a family-based performance, the lamentations of the dead typically begin with a tearful narration of the moments of death, the horrors of violence, and the expression of indignation against the unjust killing. Later, the ritual performance moves on to the stage where the spirits, exhausted with lamentation and somewhat calmed, engage with the surroundings and the participants. They express gratitude to their family for caring about their grievous feelings, and this is often accompanied by magical speculations about the family's health matters or economic prospects. When the spirits of the dead start to express concerns about their living family, this is understood to mean that they have become somewhat free from the grid of sorrows, which the Koreans express as a successful "disentanglement of grievous feelings."

The act of disentanglement is never complete, however. On the next occasion that the family hosts a spirit consolation rite, therefore, it is likely for a similar scene of the spirits of the dead expressing sorrows to be repeated, although over time the expression may become less intense. The ritual for lamenting souls is a type of ancestral rite in that it invites primarily the spirits of the dead related in ties of kinship to the ritual-hosting family. Spirits who appear in the ancestral ritual within *kut*, however, are not the same as those invited to *jesa*, the domestic ancestral death-day commemorative rite. The category of ancestors in the former context is broader in scope than that in the latter. The difference has several distinct, although ultimately interrelated, aspects. First, the institution of *jesa* is typically restricted to the family's genealogical past traced according to the dominant lineage ideology, which in this case is patrilineal descent, although exceptions do exist. The idea of ancestors in shamanism, in contrast, is open to the ritual host's broad historical relational milieu, including matrilateral and sometimes affinal ties. Observers of Korea's traditional popular religions explain the difference between these two institutions of death commemoration in several ways. Laurel Kendall highlights the aspect of gender – the fact that shamanic rituals tend to attract particularly active participation by women, although not exclusively so, in contrast to the ancestral rites of *jesa* in which male descendants usually take up an organizing role.[20] Also relevant is the deep political history of Korea's kinship system – the fact that this system was bilateral in character before Korea's neo-Confucian revolution of the thirteenth century onward. As Martina Deuchler shows, this revolution was both political and social in character, with the aim of realizing a new political order through a radical reform of the existing loose, flexible bilateral kinship order to one that takes patrilineal descent as the singularly meaningful organizing ideology.[21] Key to this revolution was the transformation of the ancestral rite to an institution that was exclusively for the patrilineal genealogical past. Seen together, these two points about the difference between *jesa* and *kut* show that the category of ancestors in *kut* is relatively free from the ideology of the dominant moral order, compared to that within the institution of *jesa*, whether we consider this relative freedom in a sociological (as an aspect of gender) or historical (an incomplete neo-Confucian revolution) perspective.

This idea of freedom and the related structural difference between the two traditionally preeminent institutions of death commemoration explain how Kim Seong-nae came to discover shamanism in Jeju as a distinct theater of historical memory. If *kut* was relatively free from the dominant ideology of the neo-Confucian moral order in traditional times, the same can be said about modern times and with regard to the dominant ideology of anti-communism in the second half of the twentieth century. A similar idea may apply to the organization of *Now We Speak Out*, which advances the structural specificity of shamanism in the domain of death commemoration to an initiatory act of historical truth telling.

The aesthetics of shamanism continued to play a pivotal part in the subsequent developments in Jeju in relation to its 1948–1953 history and memory. Nowadays, in April of each year, the island as a whole transforms into a public world of commemoration (see later discussion), involving a number of local events that subsequently culminate in a province-wide memorial gathering. Throughout the past two decades, these civic actions have always involved public performances adopting elements of local shamanic traditions of spirit consolation. The lamentations of the dead are traditionally a familial ritual, as noted earlier. Today, they are a crucial part of the public sphere of Jeju, having broken out of the domestic space. In a family-based ritual, the spirits of the dead share their grievous feelings and unfulfilled wishes with their kin and, later, thank the latter for helping to disentangle their remorse, which then triggers the spirits' gesture of overcoming their grievances in the form of engaging with their living relatives' health and economic well-being. In rituals on a wider scale that involve participants beyond the family circle, as now happens in April, the lamentations typically include the spirits' confused remarks about how they should relate to the strangers gathered for the occasion, which later typically develop into remarks of appreciation and gratitude. The spirits thank the participants for their demonstration of sympathy to the suffering of the dead, who have no blood ties to them and to whom therefore, the participants have no ritual obligations. If the occasion is sponsored by an organization that has a particular moral or political objective, moreover, some of the invited spirits may proceed to make gestures of support for the organization. Thus, the spirit narration from the victims of a massacre may explicitly invoke concepts such as human rights if the ceremony is sponsored by a local civil rights activist group, or other contemporary issues, such as gender equality if the occasion is supported by a network of feminist activists. These examples show that the lamentations of the dead can engage with the diverse aspirations of the living and those expressed by different social groupings. They also indicate that this cultural form can extend from the milieu of intimate communal relations to the broader public domain. In recent Jeju history, this process of extension has been crucial to the empowerment of civic activism in relation to the history of the April Third violence.

Several astute observers of Korea's modern political history have indeed noted that South Korea's recent democratic transition is not to be considered separate from the aesthetic power of ritualized lamentations.[22] During the 1990s, South Korea's civil rights activist groups disseminated the voices of the victims of state violence as a way of mobilizing public awareness and support for their cause, and they employed forms of popular shamanic spirit consolation rites to enable the dead victims' messages to materialize. The lamentations of the dead have been, according to the eminent South Korean anthropologist Kim Kwang-ok, a principal aesthetic instrument in Korea's "rituals of resistance."[23] The voices of the dead are considered both as evidence of political violence and as an appeal for collective actions for justice. Political activism in South Korea has been so intimately tied to the ritual aesthetics of lamenting spirits of the dead that even an academic forum might not do without the aesthetic form. The annual assembly of Korean anthropologists chose the cultural legacy of the Korean War as the conference's main theme in 1999, and that event included a grand shamanic spirit consolation rite dedicated to all the spirits of the tragic dead from the war era. In these situations, the history of mass war deaths is not merely a subject of academic debate or collective social actions; rather, it takes on a vital agency of its own that influences the course of communicative actions about the past.

The emergence of such rites from the sphere of kinship into the public world has been a principal element in the process of democratic transition. Between the past and the present, a radical change has taken place in that the living no longer have to fear what the dead have to say about history and historical justice. What is continuous in time, however, is that the understanding of political reality, at the grassroots level, is expressed through the communicability of historical experience between the living and the dead. The rituals displaying the lamenting spirits of the dead have continued to play a formative role in various sectors of civic activism to date. In Jeju, this activism has focused on the moral rehabilitation of the casualties from the April Third Incident as innocent civilian victims, in place of their previous classification as communist insurgents or sympathizers. These rehabilitative initiatives have since spread to other parts of the country and have resulted in the legislation in 2000 of a special parliamentary inquiry into the April Third Incident. This was followed by legislation passed in May 2005 on the investigation of incidents of Korean War civilian massacres in general. These initiatives led to forensic excavation activity on a national scale involving numerous suspected sites of mass burials in the subsequent years. The 2005 legislation includes an investigation of the roundup and summary execution of alleged communist sympathizers in the early days of the Korean War – an estimated 200,000 civilians, led by the government-supported Truth and Reconciliation Commission.[24]

These dark chapters in modern Korean history were relegated to non-history under the previous military-ruled authoritarian regimes, which defined anti-communism as one of the state's prime guidelines; since the early 1990s, in contrast, these hidden histories of mass deaths have become one of the most heated and contested issues of public debate, and their emergence into public discourse is, in fact, regarded by observers as a key feature of Korea's political development.[25] A notable aspect of this development is that the claims for historical truth were first raised locally before they became a national public issue.[26] This was evidently the case with the activities of the bereaved families of the Korean War civilian massacres in the early postwar years that we saw in Chapter 1. As a close observer of the contemporary public history of the Korean War in South Korea, Park Myung-lim, argues, the moral and political solidarity among the families of the victims of state violence played a pivotal role in the advent of public actions for historical truth and justice.[27] The province of Jeju is exemplary in terms of this development. It initiated an institutional basis for a sustained documentation program for the victims of the April Third atrocities and province-wide memorial events; and it continues to excavate suspected mass burial sites and plans to preserve these sites as historical monuments. The provincial authority also hopes to develop these activities to promote the province's public image as "an island of peace and human rights."

These laudable achievements of Jeju islanders were made possible by their sustained community-based grassroots mobilization, which was networked through active nongovernmental organizations and civil rights associations, including an association for the victims' families. For those active in the family association, the beginning of the 1990s was a time of sea change. Before 1990, the association was officially called the Anticommunist Association of Families of the Jeju April Third Incident Victims and, as such, was dominated by families related to a particular category of victims – local civil servants and paramilitary personnel killed by the communist militia. This category of victims, by current estimations, amounts to about 20 percent of the total civilian casualties. The rest were the victims of the actions of government troops, police forces, or paramilitary groups, and were previously classified as communist subversives or "red elements." Since 1990, the association has gradually been taken over by the families on the majority side, relegating the family representatives from the anti-communist association era to a minority status within the association. This was "a quiet revolution," according to a long-time observer of the association; a result of long, sometimes heated negotiations between different groups of family representatives.[28] During the transition from a nominally anti-communist organization to one that intends to "go beyond the blood-drenched division of left and right," the association faced several crises: some family representatives with anti-communist family backgrounds left the association, and some new representatives with opposite backgrounds refused to sit with the former. Similar conflicts also existed at the village level.

Nevertheless, the association's resolute stand that its objective is to account for all atrocities from all sides, communist or anti-communist, has been conducive to preventing the conflicts from reaching an implosive level. Equally important was the fact that many family representatives (particularly from the villages in the highland region, which suffered both from the pacification activity of the government troops and from the retributive actions of the communist partisan groups) had casualties on both sides of the conflict within their immediate circle of relatives. The observer mentioned earlier, for instance, lost his father to violence committed by the police and his elder brother to that perpetrated by the partisans. At the village level, people who had close relatives as victims on both sides of the conflict often played a formative role. Also important was the role of the war-veteran villagers, who, after undergoing the violence of the state's counterinsurgency warfare, as mentioned in the previous chapter, took part in the theater of the Korean War and helped to rescue this state from the threat of annihilation. The democratization of the family association was a liberating experience for the families on the majority side, including those who were members of it before the change. Under the old scheme, some of the victims of the state's anti-communist terrorism were registered as victims of the terror perpetrated by communist insurgents. This was partly caused by the prevailing notion that the violent "red hunt" campaign would not have happened had there been no "red menace." The "quiet revolution" since the 1990s meant that these families are now free to grieve for their dead relatives of 1948–1953 publicly and in a way that does not falsify the history of their mass deaths.

New Ancestral Stones

This development has resulted in a cosmic change in the islanders' domestic and communal death-commemorative activities. Actually, it would be more accurate to say that changes in their domestic activities and those in the wider society were closely interacting, encouraging and reinforcing each other. The end of the Cold War resulted in notable changes in the fabric of ancestral remembrance. Many communities in Jeju have recently begun to introduce the previously outlawed "red" ancestral identities into their communal ancestral rituals, thereby placing their memorabilia in demonstrative coexistence with those of other "ordinary" ancestors. This process has resulted in the rise of diverse, inventive new ancestral memorials across communities in Jeju and elsewhere in Korea in recent years.

In February 2008, *The New York Times* reported a story from a village in the southwestern region of Korea, under the heading "A Korean village torn apart from within mends itself."[29] The mending was partly achieved through a community-wide project to erect a village ancestral stone. This village, named Gurim ("the forest of pigeons") after an ancient legend, is famous in the area for the production of traditional earthenware. Maintaining a traditional village structure typical of the area and comprising a few lineage-based kindred groups, Gurim's elderly residents have bitter memories of the Korean War (see Chapter 2). Situated at the mouth of a rugged mountain area, the village was vulnerable, even before the Korean War broke out, to reciprocal violence from the communist partisans who had taken shelter in the mountains and from the counter-insurgency actions in the area by South Korea's national police. This precarious situation resulted in tragic incidents of vengeful violence within the village between individuals and households who suffered from the communist partisans and those who lost relatives to counter-insurgency actions. When the village was swept into the changing hands of military occupation during the initial phase of the Korean War, the violence was magnified in intensity and its brutality radicalized, as it began to involve the armed power of the occupying forces.

The people of Gurim speak proudly of their long-held tradition, *daedong'gye* – a type of village assembly, which in the past worked as an informal local governing body. Consisting of representatives of the

community's six major family groups, the village assembly recently produced a book about the settlement's past and present based on the local
people's vernacular knowledge of its history. The book includes a history
of the village assembly for the last four centuries, the village's folkloric
tradition, and the turmoil it underwent during the colonial era and then
during the war. The last depicts a community helplessly exposed to the
war's chaotic violence, and it includes several incidents of mass killings,
which, perpetrated by both Northern and Southern forces, also instigated
vengeful violence among the locals. The publication of this book was part
of broader efforts among the residents of this village, spearheaded by the
multi-lineage village assembly, to come to terms with the destruction of
war. The book's prologue says:

> Bringing this book into light, the people of Gurim are preparing other works in the
> hope of going beyond the wounds of history which our nation as a whole had to
> painfully undergo. Our objective is to console the souls of those who fell victim to
> the conflicts of war and to bring some comfort to the descendants of these tragic
> victims who had to conceal their sorrows during the past decades. We plan to erect
> a memorial stone that we hope will provide a means with which we forgive and
> reconcile with each other. It will be to our great satisfaction if this book can
> contribute to bringing about the spirit conducive to communal reconciliation
> and peace.[30]

Similar initiatives were undertaken by other communities in the same
region. In the district of Naju, which was hard hit during the war both by
the Northern and the Southern armed groups, families related to the
victims of anti-communist state violence and those to the victims of
violence committed in the name of revolutionary justice against sympathizers with the Southern regime recently met to create a joint local
association of bereaved families of the Korean War. This move was
facilitated by the idea that both groups of victims of war are equally
yangmin (innocent civilians), despite the differences in the identities of
the perpetrators, and the related notion that the identities of the victims
should be liberated from the separation imposed on them by the perpetrators' identities. The association prided itself in representing the tragedy
of war in an encompassing way and, according to one investigator, "having transcended the ideology of anticommunism by refusing to separate
the victims of the Left from those of the Right."[31] According to another
researcher, who investigated the activity of these families leading to the
construction of a memorial stone in the early 2000s:

> The memorial stone in Bongwang displays the names killed by the [South
> Korean] army and police as well as the victims of the violence perpetrated by
> the Left. The way in which these families succeeded to shake off the ideology of

anticommunism was due to their commitment to bring the memory of the tragic dead to the public sphere irrespective of how and by whom their lives had been violated.[32]

This and other reports also mention an interesting shift in the structure of local Korean War commemorations. Until the end of the 1990s, the idea that the two groups of civilian war victims, people who fell to the violence perpetrated by the political right and by the left, could be brought together in communal memorial actions was alien to most communities; whereas, in the 2000s, the same idea began to take root in public opinion as a legitimate way forward. As in Gurim, this idea had huge relevance not only for shaking off the political history of anti-communism, but also for recovering a sense of local integrity and communality among the local inhabitants. In other words, the act of bringing the memories of the dead together was a way of bringing the living back together, away from the long divisive history that the community had undergone for the past two generations.

Elsewhere in Korea, rehabilitative initiatives also advanced within individual kin groups. In the Andong district, several local lineage groups sought to restore their hitherto stigmatized family ancestral heritages of the political left from the colonial time. These included Kim Jae-bong, Lee Jun-tae, and Kwon Oh-seol, all prominent members of Korea's early communist movement. The lineage group's rehabilitative initiative involved discussions with the elders and in broader family assemblies. These groups prepared (sometimes in competition with each other) documents that detailed the contribution of the particular family's ancestors to resistance against colonial domination. Their efforts included the publication of a "Collection of Essays," a traditional means for a kin group to preserve and demonstrate its ancestral relics. These collections typically feature essays and letters written by ancestral figures of recent times together with the literary works by the lineage group's more distant ancestry. Such family-initiated activities included preparing appeals to the government. In these appeals, families expressed their hope that the state would recognize their ancestor's patriotic merit, arguing that this person's anti-colonial activism outweighed his or her specific ideological orientation toward a socialist revolution, which, during the colonial time, was far from an illegitimate property, unlike the postcolonial and post-Korean War era.

In some cases, the kin-based publication and commemoration initiatives were developed in collaboration with the activities of local historians. In an essay that he wrote to endorse a lineage group's collection of ancestral writings, which included the prison letters of Kwon Oh-seol, who was prominent in Korea's communist youth movement in the 1930s, the historian and director of the Andong Museum of Independence Movement, Kim Hui-gon, highlights the imperative "to consider the socialist movements during the colonial era separately from the political order established in North Korea after the liberation from colonialism."[33] Elsewhere, the historian argues against the prevailing narrative order of the previous postwar era, in which the history of anti-colonial resistance is constricted by the ideology of anti-communism, relegating the resistance activities of socialist or communist orientations to oblivion and to the exteriority of legitimate national histories. Such "cracks between anticolonialism and anticommunism," according to another commentator, resulted in disparities in local historical accounts between names remembered in association with the locality's resistance against the colonial order, on the one hand, and, on the other, those recorded as local heroes of resistance against colonialism.[34] According to these historians, local historical records of colonial experience have long been distorted by the experience of the Korean War. Kim Hui-gon notes further that the vitality of anti-colonial resistance in the area can be traced to the area's strong tradition of neo-Confucianism. He mentions that most of the area's radical nationalist (socialist, communist, and anarchist) intellectuals shared the same family roots with its conservative nationalist intellectuals, and that this common root was the area's long tradition of Confucian moral training and ethical self-enlightenment: the emphasis in the Confucian tradition on the virtue of self-cultivation brought the local intelligentsia to learn about radical modern ideas, thus resulting in the growth of "radical Confucian scholars."[35] On the basis of this assessment, it is even argued that the "descendants of the neo-Confucian tradition also played a major role in socialist and communist political movements. This was against the common knowledge that these movements are usually led by repressed classes."[36]

The last is an interesting remark. Other studies of radical political movements in places in Asia under colonial domination show how students of Confucianism played a pivotal role in initiating these movements. The work of Hue-Tam Ho Tai, the eminent historian of modern Vietnam, for instance, presents a gripping account of how the Vietnamese revolution first took root in the colonial context through the initiative of "prodigal sons" – the descendants of landowning, Confucian families who, after renouncing their inherited feudal heritage, began to explore a path of political modernity other than the form imposed on the nation by the colonial authority.[37] In any case, the point raised in the previously mentioned study of a common heritage between the political left and right is relevant for grasping the present-day kin-based popular initiative to reconstitute the lineage's genealogical legacy in a more inclusive form, recovering the normativity of the ancestral relic on the political left. Several communities in Andong recently erected new ancestral memorial stones. One of them is for Kwon Oh-seol, which stands at the entrance to his home village. The inscription on the stone says: "You are standing in the place of birth of a distinguished man who was not in fear of extreme hardship in pursuing his struggle for national liberation. Here is where the patriotic individual spent his childhood, before he dedicated his life to the cause of anti-imperialism and recovery of national independence." The new "Collection of Essays" prepared by this man's descendants features the patriotic revolutionary's past relics at the end of the volume, after introducing the literary work of the lineage's founding ancestor and those of other prominent scholars in the following generations. The composition of this book situates the life and work of the recent revolutionary ancestor as part of and in line with the lineage's long tradition of scholar ancestors and their exemplary lives according to Confucian ethics. It also introduces a number of funerary and commemorative speeches dedicated to the revolutionary ancestor by his relatives. These texts of funerary oratory offer a firm impression that the revolutionary has recovered, within the moral community of his kinship, his full normative historical status.

Another notable aspect of these family-based activities to restore the normativity of their family history is a tendency to explain the family's hardship in modern times via a deeper genealogical trajectory. In the collection of essays that includes the writings of Kwon Oh-seol, for instance, the life history of this recent ancestor is included along with historical episodes of the lineage group's distant ancestors from the sixteenth to eighteenth centuries. Many of these distant ancestors and their families suffered calamities (*hwa*, in the Sino-Korean vocabulary), while being mired in the vicious court politics of the old Chosun dynasty.[38] In regard to these distant and recent lineage ancestors, the essays commonly emphasize the disposition of *jŏlŭi* (roughly, "fidelity to virtue") and the inevitability in history that, in due time (sometimes, even two centuries later), their virtuous acts would be recognized and their names restored. This narrative form is intended to deliver the sense, on the one hand, that the politically troubled record of the family's modern-day ancestors should not be considered in terms of the language of modern politics, but rather in moral terms, as a revelation of the ethical commitment kept in the family's long tradition of virtuous ancestors. On the other hand, such a mode of narrating the past also constitutes a public statement that it is this moral aspect of their recent ancestral relics, not their political meanings and ramifications, that the family is intent on preserving as its genealogical heritage.

In other places around the Andong area, the effort to rehabilitate hitherto outlawed family and lineage ancestors developed in a more cautious way – as was the case with the Anh lineage group (whose story was featured in Chapter 4) in relation to their two important anti-colonial and communist intellectual ancestors. Unlike Kwon Oh-seol, these two men of the Anh family survived the colonial time and were settled in North Korea after 1948, acting in the country's public political arena. Although neither of them came back to their home village during the war nor participated in the local politics of war, it was difficult for people of this lineage group to undertake a commemorative project in ways that other lineage groups in the area set out to do. When they assembled for their periodic ancestral rituals, there was a series of heated debates among members of the Anh lineage about what the family could do about the memory of their two communist ancestors. Although this debate continues to this day, the group has meanwhile reached a tentative consensus to erect a new stone in the family's ancestral graveyard. Erected in 2004, the surface of the dark granite stone displays a genealogical chart of the lineage group. It lists the names of all of the group's patrilineal ancestors and their lines of descent from the apical ancestor of eight generations back. The apical ancestor is on one side of the stone at the far-right corner; on the other side are names closer to contemporary times. In the middle of the latter side are inserted the names of the group's two prominent ancestors of modern times – the names that for long were a source of stigmatization for the lineage as a whole and whose existence once led several of the group's living descendants into extreme life crises. According to a member of the lineage's oldest line of descent:

We built this in 2004 after great difficulty. Some of us were unhappy about it, and some of my senior relatives still blame me for having proposed the idea in the first place. One of them told me, "Are you out of your mind? All of us, and especially you, have made it our life's quest to sever our ties with the two elders. And now you want to tell the world that these communist elders are your proud ancestors?" I don't blame him. When I come here, I also feel uneasy. I know the world is different now, and I also know that it is my duty to honor all our ancestors. But each time I come here, I do feel unsettled when I see the two names on the stone and the lines connecting their names to the whole family.

Erecting these ancestral stones was far from a smooth process. Both Anh's and Kwon Oh-seol's family groups experienced torrents of disputes while preparing their stones. Some were in fear of the consequences of erecting a memorial stone for troubled ancestors, and the possible negative repercussions the action might bring to their lives and the family as a whole. Others were more concerned about the enduring wounds existing within the family that they believed were caused by the legacy of these ancestors. These wounds had many forms, as detailed earlier, including the separation of families during the war and public discriminations in their postwar lives.

Many new ancestral shrines and memorials have also been erected recently in Jeju. Most prominent is a large memorial site completed in 2010 and located at the center of the island, in Jeju Peace Park, which is intended to commemorate the victims of the political violence that the islanders experienced from 1948 to 1953. The site consists of a state-of-the-art museum complex, beautifully conceived memorial sculptures, and a large chamber that shelters many thousands of tablets inscribed with the names of the victims. It attracts many visitors from mainland Korea and from overseas. In April each year, Jeju Peace Park holds a province-wide commemorative event in the presence of notable guests, the media, and families of victims. Whereas the place is regarded as a public memorial dedicated to the victims of the April Third Incident, this is not necessarily the case for the locals. Many islanders relate to the events hosted at the park as an extension of their ancestral remembrance rites held in their homes or in their villages. This is illustrated by the way in which some islanders bring to the Peace Park memorial their household utensils that are kept in their home exclusively for ancestral death-day rites. What is a public monument to outside visitors, for bereaved families is principally another place where their ancestral memories are kept, although this is not to deny the fact that some families continue to feel reluctant to take part in the Peace Park events or even refuse to do so. This is partly because they associate the Peace Park with the authority of the state (the upkeep of the park premises is financed by the central and provincial governments), the very authority that is culpable for the violence and hardship they endured.

Equally remarkable were some local initiatives. The village of Hagui in the northwestern district of Jeju Island completed a village ancestral shrine in the beginning of 2003. The residents of this village are proud of their thousand-year-long settlement history as well as several heritage sites existing in the environs of the village. The sites include those relating to resistance by their distant ancestors in the fifteenth century against the Mongol invasion, which speaks of Hagui's distinguished role as "a frontier defender of the island of Jeju against foreign invaders arriving from the northern sea."[39] The initiative to erect a new ancestral stone had another material cultural background relating to a much more recent crisis of war. Across the communities in Jeju are found local war cemeteries and accompanying memorials dedicated to the "patriotic spirits" – combat police and other personnel who fell during the time of the April Third crisis. The fallen include fighters from "civil organizations," which in this context refers to members of paramilitary anti-communist youth groups that took part in the 1948 counterinsurgency war. These memorials have long been a source of moral alienation and silent indignation for the locals, who are living close to a resting place for the strangers who were associated with the violence perpetrated against their own families.

New ancestral shrines in Jeju arose, in part, in reaction to this distorted landscape of war commemoration and as a way of changing it into a more accountable form. The shrine in Hagui consists of a white vertical stone located at the center, and on each side of it, two horizontal stones made of black granite are inlaid. The inscription on the white stone reads, in Chinese characters, "Shrine of Spirit Consolation." The two black stones on the left side commemorate the patriotic ancestors from the colonial era ("stone for virtuous ancestors") and the patriotic fighters from the village during the Korean War ("stone for patriotic spirits"). The two black stones on the right side ("stones for spirit consolation") commemorate the hundreds of villagers who fell victim to the protracted counterinsurgency campaigns waged in Jeju before and during the Korean War.

The "virtuous ancestors" include names associated with anti-colonial activities of socialist or communist persuasions – names that rarely appear in the existing historical accounts, local or national. The rehabilitation of the village's ancestral heritage of the political left from colonial times provided an important basis on which Hagui's further initiatives of communal reconciliation could evolve. The rehabilitative process was intended to recover the community's historical genealogical identity more truthfully, free from the grid of ideological polarity that conditioned public life during the previous era. As such, it was hoped that its dynamics and moral legitimacy would extend to the history of destruction in the postcolonial era, thereby legitimizing the public appearance of hitherto stigmatized historical traces from the latter. In addition to this temporal dimension based on genealogical thinking, the initiative also had a spatial dimension, intended to free the local history from the dominant paradigm of national history as inscribed in the local landscape of war commemoration.

The completion of this stone has a complex historical background, including the division of the village into two separate administrative units in the 1920s, which the locals now understand as a divide-and-rule strategy by the Japanese colonial administration at the time, and the distortion of this division during the chaos following the April Third uprising. Hagui's elders recall that the village's imposed administrative division developed into a perilous situation at the height of the counterinsurgency military campaigns. The zero-sum logic of these campaigns set people in one part of the village, labeled then as a "red" hamlet, against those in the other, who then tried to dissociate themselves from the former. After these campaigns were over, Hagui was considered a politically impure and subversive place in Jeju, just as the whole island of Jeju was known as a "red" island to mainland South Koreans. A document published in 1986 for anti-communist public education argues that "The characteristics of local communities [in Jeju] are that once someone in the community's leadership position was affected by communism, due to the tight webs of kinship and residential ties in the island communities, it was inevitable that members of the entire lineage and the entire village were to become members of the communist party."[40] In the impoverished, distorted conditions of this political society, Hagui villagers seeking employment outside the village experienced discrimination because of their place of origin, and this aggravated the existing grievances between the two administratively separate residential clusters. The people on one side felt it was unjustified to blame them for what they believed the other side of the village was responsible for, while the other side found it hard to accept that they should endure accusations and discrimination even within a close community.[41] It was against this background that some Hagui villagers petitioned the local court, proposing the assignment of new, separate names for the two village units. Their intention was partly to bury the stigmatizing name of Hagui, and also to eradicate signs of affinity between the two units. This was just after the end of the Korean War in 1953. Since then, the village of Hagui has been separated in official documents into Dong-gui and Gui-il, two invented names that no one liked, but which were, nevertheless, necessary.

This historical trajectory resulted in a host of conundrums in the villagers' everyday lives. A number of them suffered from the extrajudicial system of associative culpability, which prevented individuals with an allegedly politically impure genealogical background from obtaining employment in public sectors or enjoying social mobility in general; some of them also had to endure sharing the village's communal space with someone who was, they believed, culpable for their predicament. This last point relates to the enduring wounds of the April Third history within the community, caused by the villagers' complex experience with the counterinsurgency's actions, including being coerced into accusing close neighbors of supporting the insurgents.[42] Madame Kim Jung-a lost her parents to violence committed by the insurgents, which involved acts of complicity by some villagers. She now lives in Tokyo and recalls her early years in a village next to Hagui: "How could anyone even pretend to understand the fury and sorrow of people like my grandmother who had to confront the faces of those culpable along her daily routines in the village, day after day?"[43] These hidden histories are occasionally pried open to become an explosive issue in the community when, for instance, two young lovers protest over why their families oppose their relationship so ferociously, without telling them any intelligible reason for doing so.

The details of these intimate histories of the April Third violence and their contemporary traces still remain a taboo subject in Hagui and its environs even today. The most frequently recalled, excitedly recited episodes are instead related to festive occasions. One time, before the villagers began to discuss the idea of a communal shrine, the two units of Hagui joined in an inter-village sporting event and feast, which was periodically organized by the district authority. They had done so on many previous occasions, but this time, the two football teams of Dong-gui and Gui-il both managed to reach the semifinals, and each was hoping to win the final. During the competition, the residents of Dong-gui cheered against the team representing Gui-il, supporting the team's opponent from another village instead, and the same happened with the residents of Gui-il in a match involving the team from Dong-gui. This experience was scandalous, according to the Hagui elders I spoke to, and they contrasted the explosively divisive situation in the village with an opposite initiative taking place in the wider world. At the time of the inter-village feast, the idea of joint national representation in international sporting events was under discussion between South Korea and North Korea. The village was going against the stream of history, according to the elders, and they said that the village's shameful collective representation on the district football grounds provided the momentum for thinking about a communal project that might help to bring the divided villages closer together.

In 1990, the village assembly in Dong-gui and its counterpart in Gui-il agreed to revive their original common name and to shake off their nominal separation of the past four decades. They established an informal committee responsible for the rapprochement and reintegration of the two villages. One of the first initiatives of this committee was an intervention in the village's lunar New Year celebration. The two settlements of Hagui each have a communal house where the village elders spend their daytime together; these elders agreed to visit each other's communal house alternately on the lunar New Year opening days to offer well-wishes to one another. This seemingly small step taken by the village had powerful consequences. It facilitated exchanges between the youths of the coastal settlement and those of the hillside community; it also helped to improve relations among the Hagui-born residents in Japan, especially in Osaka. Encouraged by this development, in 2000, the committee proposed to the village assemblies the idea of erecting an ancestral shrine based on donations from the villagers and from those living elsewhere. When the shrine was completed in 2003, the Hagui villagers held a grand opening ceremony in the presence of many visitors from elsewhere in the country and from overseas. The stone, which is dedicated to the 303 village victims of the April Third violence, delivers the following poetic message:

> When we were still enjoying the happiness of being freed from the colonial misery,
> When we were yet unaware of the pains to be brought by the Korean War,
> Did come to us the dark clouds of history, whose origin we still don't know after all those years.
> Then, many lives, so many lives, were broken and their bodies were discarded to the mountains, the fields and the sea.
> Who can identify in this mass of broken lives a death that was not tragic?
> Who can say in this mass of displaced souls some souls have more grievance than the others?
> What about those who couldn't even cry for the dead?
> Who will console their hearts that suffered all those years only for one reason that they belonged to the bodies who survived the destruction? . . .
> For the past fifty years,
> The dead and the living alike led the unnatural life as wandering souls, without a place to anchor to.
> Only today,
> Being older than our fathers and aged more than our mothers,
> We are gathered together in this very place.
> Let the heavens deal with the question of fate.
> Let history deal with its own portion of culpability.
> Our intention is not to dig again into the troubled grave of pains.
> It is only to fulfill the obligation of the living to offer a shovel of fine soil to the grave.
> It is because we hope someday the bleeding wounds may start to heal and we may see some sign of new life on them . . .
> Looking back,
> We see that we are all victims.
> Looking back,
> We see that we all are to forgive us all.
> In this spirit,
> We are all together erecting this stone.

For the dead, may this stone help them finally close their eyes.
For us the living, may this stone help us finally hold hands together.[44]

Society at Peace

Ten years after the inauguration of the new ancestral stone in Hagui, July 2013 marked the sixtieth anniversary of the Korean War Armistice. In the run-up to the anniversary, several notable public events were taking place on both sides of the partitioned Korea, which are formally still at war, with a peace treaty yet unrealized, two generations after the guns went silent on July 27, 1953. South Korea invited friends from across the world, surviving veterans of the Korean War from the Americas, Europe, and Africa. These honored visitors were escorted on a tour of the National War Cemetery and the National War Museum, both in Seoul, as well as the United Nations Cemetery in the Southern port town of Pusan, and the heavily fortified frontier with North Korea along the Armistice line. While this celebration of international friendship was underway south of the 38th parallel, on the Northern side, two large-scale construction projects were being completed in North Korea's capital of Pyongyang. Built by the country's army and youth volunteers, the two new cultural sites, the Museum of Fatherland Liberation War and the Graves of Heroes of Fatherland Liberation War, opened to the public on Victory Day, as Armistice Day is called in North Korea. The opening ceremony brought in delegates from the country's traditional international allies, most notably from China. The Chinese delegates were given pride of place throughout the Victory Day festivities and were escorted to the Korea-Chinese Friendship Tower located at the center of Pyongyang. On the surface of this neo-Gothic tower is written

The martyrs of the Chinese People's Volunteers who defeated our common enemy together with us under the banner of "Resist America, Aid Korea, Protect Family and Defend the Country" – your eternal honor and the international friendship between the people of Korea and the people of China forged in blood shall shine over this country and this land forever.

The delegates then traveled further north of the capital city to visit the Graves of the Chinese Volunteers to the Korean War. They brought wreaths to place on the grave of Mao Anying, Mao Zedong's eldest son, killed in October 1950 in a napalm attack by a South African fighter jet.[45]

While these affirmations of old friendships were underway, inventions of new friendships were also in progress. In June 2013, South Korea and China agreed to repatriate to China the remains of the fallen Chinese Korean War volunteers, which had been held in South Korea. In the following years, several hundred such remains were brought back to China through this agreement, with ceremonies of military honor on both the Korean and Chinese sides. Their long overdue homecoming was made to coincide with the spring Tomb-sweeping Day, an important traditional seasonal marker for both China and Korea, when people visit and clean their ancestral graves. A similar initiative to mend old enmities existed between North Korea and the United States. From 1996 to 2002, the two countries joined together in an effort to search for the remains of US servicemen missing in action since the Korean War. Approximately 200 remains were recovered from different parts of North Korea under this historic initiative, before it was abruptly discontinued in January 2002. This was immediately after that year's State of the Union address by President George W. Bush, who branded North Korea as part of "the axis of evil" countries together with Iran and Iraq.

These two separate diplomatic events involving the fallen from the Korean War, between China and South Korea on the one hand and between the United States and North Korea on the other were interconnected in their unfolding. In preparation for the fiftieth anniversary of the outbreak of the Korean War in 2000, the South Korean government launched a national campaign to find the hitherto unrecovered remains of the fallen Korean War soldiers, estimated to number more than 100,000, and created a special forensic taskforce within the country's armed forces for this purpose. Continuing to this day, the forensic mission was modeled on the activity of the Joint POW/MIA Accounting Agency of the United States, the organization in charge of accounting for the country's missing servicemen from various overseas wars, including the Korean War. South Korea's own MIA work attracted considerable attention from the country's public, and its activities have recently expanded to other categories of Korean War combatants, such as student volunteers and conscripts. The recent initiative concerning the remains of the fallen soldiers of the Chinese People's Volunteer Army in Korea arose as part of the growing public interest in the recovery of the remains of the Korean War fallen in general. It also represents the changing landscape of international ties in today's northeast Asia. According to the South Korean army spokesperson, the repatriation of Chinese remains to China was intended to "heal the wounds of war and improve the relations between the two countries a step further."[46] This claimed "healing" initiative is perhaps best illustrated in the place where the remains of Chinese volunteer soldiers are sheltered before being repatriated to their homeland and, subsequently, reinterred in the Graves of the Martyrs of the Resist America, Aid Korea War in Shenyang, Liaoning Province. Located near the Korean War Armistice line, this cemetery for the

North Korean and Chinese fallen soldiers has recently parted with its long-held name, the Cemetery of the Enemies.

The situation changed again the run-up to the Korean War anniversaries in 2018. At the beginning of the year, threats of war loomed large on the Korean peninsula, with news about it making international headlines for weeks without interruption. Belligerent rhetoric was exchanged between Pyongyang and Washington, and Korea witnessed the largest concentration of US naval and aerial strategic forces since the war ended in July 1953. These followed North Korea's completion of its intercontinental nuclear strike capability against the United States. The risk of war was real, and the escalating tensions between the world's most powerful nation and one of its poorest were becoming increasingly worrisome. Since then, the atmosphere has once again changed dramatically. After the inter-Korean summit on April 27 and the ensuing Trump–Kim meeting in Singapore on June 12, there emerged some possibilities for entering into a lasting peace on the peninsula. This peace on the Korean peninsula must involve the opening of diplomatic ties between the United States and North Korea, as well as a long-delayed agreement to end the Korean War. The two Koreas are still in a state of war two generations after the guns went silent after the 1953 Korean Armistice Agreement. This Korean War end game will probably have to involve China. The Korean War was principally a fratricidal war fought among the Koreans; yet, men of the two most powerful countries in today's world, China and the United States, killed each other there too.

The turn of events was so abrupt that many observers expressed disbelief at what was unfolding. The current South Korean president Moon Jae-In's diplomatic maneuvers between Washington and Pyongyang contributed to bringing about this change. Donald Trump's highly personalized politics also played a part – both in the drum-beating for war and in the subsequent overture of peace to Pyongyang. China's taking part in the international sanction regime against North Korea exerted considerable pressure on the reclusive country's precarious economy. The results are remarkable. As I write the end of this chapter, North Korea is celebrating this year's anniversary of their Victorious Fatherland Liberation War, their term for the Korean War. In stark contrast to previous years, 2018's anniversary events in Pyongyang are conspicuously void of the usual anti-US imperialist slogans. In South Korea, a number of high-profile global political and opinion leaders gathered in Jeju to discuss the prospects of peace and co-prosperity in the Korean peninsula. The two Koreas' Red Cross organizations resumed negotiations over the question of reuniting families separated since the time of the Korean War. Pyongyang and Washington are in dialogue about other humanitarian issues, including resuming the recovery from North Korea of the remains of American servicemen missing in action from the Korean War, an initiative that has been dormant for many years. The last is significant. We know how central MIA repatriations had been in the process leading to the normalization of relations between the United States and another of its major former antagonists in Asia, Vietnam, in 1993.[47] The young leader of North Korea flew to Singapore via China on a Chinese plane, but the meeting was purely between North Korea and the United States with no space in it for North Korea's powerful and singular Asian ally, China. We may witness more of such dramas in the coming months – dramas in which the weak plays a hard game with the strong and in between strong powers.

North Korea has long-running experience in such theatrics of power. Throughout the Cold War, especially since the Sino-Soviet split in the late 1950s, it had maneuvered shrewdly between its two powerful northern neighbors, Soviet Russia and China.[48] Now its place is squarely within the milieu of geopolitical competition between China and the United States. North Korea is probably aiming to strike some sort of balance in relation to these two powerful states, using its traditionally intimate alliance with China to interest the United States on the one hand and, on the other, using the thawing of its relationship with the United States, as well as those with South Korea and Japan, to keep China anxiously interested. The North Korea of today may still retain elements of a totalitarian society[49]; economically, however, it is now a heavily marketized and market-driven place.[50] Kim Jong-un knows this well, and he has given his word to his people that he is going to deliver to them an economically comfortable future.

Shortly before the inter-Korean summit on April 27, 2018, and the subsequent change in atmosphere on the Korean peninsula from a prelude to another war to an overture to peace, the province of Jeju held another annual, island-wide commemoration of the victims of the 1948–1953 massacres. Thousands of people from nearly all villages, highland and coastal, gathered in the Peace Park located in the central highlands of this volcanic island. This was a rare occasion when the islanders came together on a nearly universal scale, and the reason for their coming to the beautifully landscaped Peace Park that day was both individual and collective. Each participant had close ties with some of the names inscribed on the Peace Park's gigantic chamber for the victims of the 1948–1953 massacre. Many were related to those commemorated at the Cemetery of Missing Persons, consisting of rows and rows of empty graves with gravestones that record the missing person's name and his or her village of origin. The participants joined the official memorial event, which involved messages of condolence from politicians and government officials. When this was over, the people of Jeju dispersed to visit, separately, the chamber of names and the cemetery of the missing. At this point, the atmosphere changed noticeably. The event continued to be a public commemoration for the officials and the outside visitors who proceeded to pick flowers from the bundle of chrysanthemums prepared by the provincial government, and lay them on the stone tablet prepared in front of the chamber of names. For the families of the victims, however, the moment was the beginning of their rite of ancestral remembrance – that is, the very reason they had come to the place that day.

People opened the bundles of fruits and drink they had brought with them and lay the offerings at specific locations – underneath the tablets with their relatives' names inside the chamber or in front of specific graves in the cemetery of missing persons. Some families had brought a full set of ceremonial utensils – heavy copperware they use exclusively for ritual meals offered to ancestors (see the Conclusion to this volume). After making food offerings and kowtowing to the grave or the tablet, the families came together according to their village origins and shared the food they had brought with them in a wider group with neighbors and other visitors. Then, the ambience changed once again, departing from the solemn atmosphere of the earlier formal commemorative event, followed by the chaotic dispersal of family groups to all corners of the park premises. I cherished the conviviality of these moments: there was an explosion of conversation – about the price of spring onions and tangerines, about novice members of the village from the mainland and from further afield, about Chinese tourists, and about a long-awaited visit to relatives in Japan. In one corner, several elders and youths were engaged in conversation about the imminent inter-Korean summit that had been announced shortly before. Their conversations included conflicts between China and Japan over an obscure island southwest of Jeju – one of the vicious territorial disputes taking place in today's East Asia that are undermining the region's security. In another corner, an elderly woman, whose youngest son recently married a woman from southern Vietnam, was boasting to her friends about her daughter-in-law. She said that she was surprised to hear from her daughter-in-law in the morning that the young foreign woman knew why her mother-in-law was coming to the Peace Park and that her family in Vietnam also had people missing from war and missing from home burial. Her friends responded appreciatively to this remark, with one of them complaining that her own daughter-in-law, despite being born and bred in Korea, allegedly had no interest in what her affinal family had gone through in the past. Then, all the women of the group said, in one voice, how nice it was that the president of the Republic of Korea took the trouble to join the anniversary gathering that day to say warm consoling words to the people of Jeju.

Following the day's seventy-year commemorative gathering for the 1948 tragedy, a week-long shamanic rite was held on the premises of the Peace Park. Presided over by several renowned ritual specialists of the island, these "great rites for spirit consolation and regeneration" were intended to provide a public meeting place for the living and the dead. Each day, spirits of a particular village area were called upon in the presence of participants from the same place. Each day, a huge number of bowls, each containing modest amounts of buckwheat gruel, were prepared on the offering tables on behalf of the invited spirits of the dead. At the closing of the day's rite, the names of the victims at a specific locale were read aloud, to which the local participants reacted with intense interest. Turning clockwise, by the end of the week, the consolation rite covered nearly all the different local districts of the island, ending on the last day with a final rite on behalf of the souls still lost and missing. The idea was to bring all the spirits of the tragically dead from the 1948–1953 violence into one single public space, together with their surviving relatives, while respecting all their different and specific local roots and environments, only within which a proper commemorative and consolation rite can traditionally take place.

The whole occasion was marked by an artful combination of the traditional and the modern. It was also an equally elaborate meeting of the two political forms of human sociality that we have discussed in this book, in part with reference to Lewis Henry Morgan's distinction between *societas* and *civitas*. Peace Park is emblematic of Jeju's civil society and its power. It was made possible after a difficult struggle by a multitude of the region's civic association groups, including intellectuals, writers and artists, student groups, and the local media. Their long struggle focused on mobilizing these groups into a concerted force and, based on this, on obtaining from the state recognition of its culpability for the tragedy of 1948. The park as a whole is a gesture and statement of reconciliation between state and society, an achievement that is rare in the contemporary world. In recent years, the idea of civil solidarity in Jeju has expanded into an international landscape, taking on the character of what some observers call global civil society. In 2013, for instance, the island's annual April commemoration included a forum on Cold War violence together with civil activists and scholars from Taiwan, Indonesia, and Guatemala. In subsequent years, the transnational solidarity initiative expanded to Okinawa, Vietnam, and elsewhere. Alongside these developments, the April commemoration demonstrates a powerful idea of social peace, in which families and villages play a part as importantly as civil groups, both regional and international. In this environment, we may say that the work of *societas* and that of *civitas* join hands to create an extraordinary political space, parting with the ideology of the modern world that separates the two. This space is a realm of freedom for families, in which they can perform what they do at home or in their village space for the dead in full view of the public world. What they do is far from an invasion of private interests, or what Hegel called family feelings, into civic and public space. On the contrary, it is a manifestation of the family's desire for freedom from itself – from the monster that has seeped deep into the life of human kinship during the Cold War, and which turned the amity of kinship into a weapon of containment politics.

Looking back, I wonder whether it is precisely thanks to its capacity to enable such expressions of freedom that Peace Park truly merits its name. If peace is considered merely an antonym of war, it does not take much imagination to render the entire history of the Cold War, as some observers do, as a long peaceful time – a time during which the then entrenched system of the balance of power successfully prevented the eruption of a large-scale armed crisis between powerful nations and the groupings of international alliance these nations led. The historical reality of the postcolonial Cold War defies such a simplistic, vacuous concept of peace. This is not only because the era of political bipolarity involved the shattering crises of civil war and other radical forms of political violence. It is also because, for communities that experienced the early Cold War in a violent way, a peaceable life, a life without the fear of violence and persecution, meant above all a resolution of conflicts in the sphere of everyday life – an ideal that remained a distant goal throughout the "long peace" of the Cold War. A grounded understanding of the global Cold War cries out for a different concept of peace, one that can bring into the concept's premises the aspirations of those for whom the era of the long peace was, in actuality, a long and enduring crisis in the moral and political life of community. Some in Jeju express this concept of peace as the virtue of the ordinary – "the aspiration to return to ordinary life, free from history of despairs."[51] A veteran observer of Jeju defines it as the related virtue of communal life – as the miracle of a new history taking off when "we offer first our hands of consolation to [our neighbors] who are alone in their sadness."[52] We can add to this concept of peace the determination of people of a war generation to shield and protect their next generations from bearing the burden of history – the determination to free the sphere of everyday life from the politics of associative guilt.[53] The making of this peace requires vigorous engagement between the world of kinship and the public world, and the continuous assertion of the right to be related in kinship as a vital political question.

A recent province-wide commemoration of the victims of the April Third violence opened with the following invocation to the souls of the dead:

> Please come in, samchun,
> Jokae, I have come.
> Samchun!
> Jokae!
> Today, all the samchon in the world of the dead and all the jokae
> in this world are gathered together.

In the local Jeju language, *samchun*, which roughly translates to uncles and aunts, and *jokae* (nieces and nephews) refer to broad contiguous relations that incorporate ties of residence as well as those of kinship. In the context of the commemoration rite, the invited spirits of the dead – namely, all the victims of violence between 1948 and 1953 – stand as aunts and uncles for the living participants in the ceremony – that is, all the people of Jeju.

Conclusion

The idea of friendship is embedded in the constitution of modern society, and celebrations of friendship abound in the historical landscape of modern warfare. The old battlefields of the First World War in Western Flanders and Northern France are dotted with monuments representing political friendship. Here, the fallen soldiers of catastrophic trench warfare rest in peace in neatly landscaped cemeteries that are arranged in discrete national groupings. While honoring their sacrifice, these sites of memory also celebrate the guiding norms of modern society and politics: the principles of individuality, equality, and fraternity. The First World War dead are buried in separate individual graves, unlike in the previous era where such privilege in war burial was available only to people of high birth or those of exceptional merit. Their graves are identical to one another, irrespective of differences in class and other traditional social backgrounds – thus, the principle of equality or what some call the "democracy of death."[1] Seen as a whole, these graves constitute an object of reverence in the civil religion of modern nationalism, considered to embody the integrity of the fraternal political community in the name of which they sacrificed their lives. Recently, amid the centennial commemoration of 1914–1918, efforts have been made to enlarge this idea of fraternity.

One of the opening ceremonies of the First World War centenary was held in a relatively obscure military cemetery in the village of Saint-Symphorien near Mons, in Belgium. In contrast to other better-known WWI cemeteries further west, the St. Symphorien Military Cemetery is a mixed graveyard where fallen German soldiers lie together with the fallen of the Commonwealth.[2] As such, it is regarded as an appropriate place for contemplating the evolution of Europe over the past hundred years and the novel sense of political friendship, the European identity, which has emerged during this process. A rather different development is also observed in present-day Europe. The number of monuments to international friendship mushroomed in the former Eastern Bloc countries following the end of the Second World War. Typically made to celebrate the heroic sacrifices of the Soviet army in the liberation of Europe from German occupation, these monuments had been an important symbolic object in the making of socialist international solidarity in the postwar years. Since the implosion of the Soviet order at the beginning of the 1990s, however, the public meaning of these built forms has undergone a radical transformation. In many places in Eastern and Central Europe, these monuments are now an unwanted or highly contested reminder of an era of domination by a foreign power and of repression by the regimes supported by this expansionist power.[3]

It is broadly against this background of rapidly changing vistas of political friendship that the very concept of friendship is now attracting renewed interest in contemporary social science scholarship. The question of how to bring out friendship-like solidarity and like-mindedness among otherwise unrelated individuals – a subject that goes back as far as the time of Aristotle – is once again prominent in today's public and academic discourses. Political theorists advance friendship as a key normative property of democratic public order, which, defined as the virtues of the common public good and the art of reciprocity, can function as the knot that ties together individual citizens who are otherwise strangers to one another.[4] Some advance a theory of friendship as part of a general critique of the idea of social order advocated by the utilitarian philosophical tradition, which postulates that human subjects are inherently self-serving and self-seeking beings. Others are more interested in freeing the concept of friendship from the burden of modern history, especially from that of the age of nationalism. In *The Politics of Friendship*, for instance, Jacques Derrida strives to envision a democratic political order based on an open and broad sense of public or political friendship. The first step in doing so, according to him, is to separate the concept of political friendship from the idea of fraternity, which Derrida sees as the invention of modern nationalism and an unfortunate legacy.[5] Political friendship is also an intensely debated concept in some circles of international relations theory today.[6] Focused primarily on interstate relations in the Western world, this research trend tends to define itself against the traditionally dominant school of thought during the time of the Cold War, which places power and the balance of power among the key concepts in international studies. These debates center on the same question as that found in all deliberations on friendship, social or international – whether the thing called the state, like the being called the individual, is prefigured to pursue its self-interests and these interests only, or whether this thing, like all social individuals, is bound to cohabit the world sociably with others. The interest in friendship in international relations theory tries to move beyond the idea that the international system is a fundamentally anarchic entity (Hobbes's "all against all" idea), characterized by the contest of power among selfish actors pursuing their narrow interests relentlessly.[7] Some of the scholars who pursue this interest also tend to be critical of theories influenced by the German constitutional theorist Carl Schmitt and his notion of modern political sovereignty based on a radical friend/enemy dichotomy.[8] They question whether the idea of friendship in international relations is necessarily dependent on this dyadic scheme of friends versus enemies, arguing that in Schmitt's theory of the political, the notion of friend remains unjustifiably obscure and ill-defined compared to the arguably relative clarity of the concept of the enemy.[9]

These contemporary deliberations on the politics of friendship broadly represent the atmosphere of the post-Cold War world, in which the old certainties about friends and enemies are no longer. Among its other notable features, the Cold War is distinct from other major transnational political forms known in modern history, such as colonialism, in that it had a globally encompassing friends-versus-enemy formation. It promoted an unprecedented expansive transnational solidarity on each side of the global political divide among territorially-based state entities and peoples. The result was a bifurcation of the human world based on the universalization of the politics of enmity on the one hand and, on the other, the globalization of the politics of friendship – a condition that the eminent German historian Reinhart Koselleck defines as a global civil war.[10] The current fascination with the politics and morality of friendship interacts with the passing of the age of the Cold War and the related imperative today of having to chart a new horizon of political friendship, whose constitution is not dependent on the existence of a common enemy, real or imaginary.

The concept of friendship, in modern political history and theory, interacts closely with the prevailing friends-versus-enemy contrast of a specific era. It is worth noting, however, that in a broader tradition of modern social thought, the concept of friendship relates to the idea of kinship more intimately than to the relationship of enmity: kinship is a milieu of relations we believe we are born into, thus making up ascribed and given relationships, in contrast to friendship, which is something we build up in the course of our lives, that is, an achieved and acquired relationship. Kinship was central to the moral and political order of a premodern collective; in small-scale tribal societies or in traditional agrarian societies before the rise of the "modern family" that is sheltered behind the "high walls of privacy" against community.[11] Friendship is a formative aspect of personal life and interpersonal relations, the primary manifestation of intimate human relationships in modern individual society; that is, an alternative in modern society to what kinship is in traditional society. It is widely assumed in the history of modern social thought that kinship retreats in relevance during the transition from traditional community to modern society, and that friendship fills the vacuum left by the retreat of kinship functions. These prevailing assumptions about kinship may not accord with the ways in which kinship relations are actually understood and practiced in modern history; however, they are nevertheless constitutive of the ideology of modern politics and society. Seen in this light, the rationality of modern politics is not merely a politics of friendship. It is also a politics against kinship, which leads to the understanding that a critical theory of friendship calls for an effort to rethink the expungement of human kinship from the constitutive space of the modern public world.[12]

This is not intended to belittle the significance of the fact that different forms of "familism" – new ideologies of familial or patriarchal order – were part and parcel of the making of the modern civic bond in Europe and in its colonies. Camille Robcis explores the negotiation between individual liberty and social solidarity in the making of the French republican social contract. Enshrined in the Civil Code of 1904, she argues that the social contract, despite the fact that it celebrates the voluntary agreement among autonomous individuals, nevertheless advances conservative images of family and conjugality as the center of the public social bond.[13] Jürgen Habermas has provided an enlightening revelation regarding the way in which family and kinship relations lost their public and political features during the bourgeois socioeconomic revolution in Northern Europe. He shows how the privatization of family relations was integral to the legal sanctification of private property and the political empowerment of those who own private properties.[14] From a different angle, Benedict Anderson in his classic study of nationalism asks how claims for unity by an artificial body such as a nation can have moral force as powerful as the claim of the family, which, according to him, "has traditionally been conceived as the domain of disinterested love and solidarity."[15] Derrida also sees a close affinity between fraternity and kinship, and his main concern in the work mentioned earlier is how to enable "a friendship which goes beyond this proximity of the congeneric double, beyond kinship, the most as well as the least natural of kinships."[16] Future democratic politics must move beyond the principle of fraternity, according to Derrida, and at the core of this progression is a genuine, complete liberation of friendship from the specter of kinship.

Turning to a different spectrum, we find that kinship versus friendship is also a theme of considerable importance in the growing literature on colonial modernity and political subjectivity. Earlier, we saw Dipesh

Chakrabarty's critique of the tradition of European liberal political theory: by showcasing Bengali ideas of citizenship, which, according to him, are grounded in traditional indigenous patrilineal descent ideology, rather than the ideology of possessive individualism and political brotherhood imported from the imperial metropolis. Closer to the subject of this book, Naoko Shimazu looks at the personal experiences of Japanese soldiers during the Russo-Japanese War of 1904–1905, arguing that for many ordinary Japanese conscript soldiers, family and local belongings, rather than their national *kokumin* identity or that as subjects of the celestial emperor, remained "the most significant source of identity."[17]

Beyond these diverging observations on kinship and friendship in contemporary social and international studies, we can witness one of the most powerful renderings of the ethics of kinship in relation to the politics of friendship – back in the historical landscape of the First World War. Not all monuments of modern wars celebrate only the ideal of fraternal community, and notable exceptions do exist. In the vista of WWI burial, the German war cemetery in Vladslo, Western Flanders, has a unique composition. Its uniqueness is not confined to the fact that those buried there are German in origin. The place is well known among students of WWI cultural history, as the magnificent German expressionist artist Käthe Kollwitz's moving sculpture *Die Eltern* (The Parents) is found within the cemetery premises. The sculpture is a self-image of Kollwitz and her husband, Karl, grieving over the loss of their child, Peter, who was buried in the cemetery together with some 25,000 of his former comrades-in-arms. Visitors experience a landscape of remembrance that is starkly different from other nearby sites of the WWI dead. The Vladslo cemetery is structurally no different from the rest: the fallen soldiers here are buried in identical graves that are arranged in a neat and orderly fashion, as is typical of modern war cemeteries. The aesthetics of equality and fraternity emanate from this place as elsewhere. Seen together with *Die Eltern*, however, these aesthetic certainties are no longer clear: it is not certain whether this place is a site of memory or one of mourning, following the historian Jay Winter's powerful observation on the ambiguity of war commemoration. According to Winter:

What does separate the Kollwitz memorial from so many others, either of religious or secular inspiration, is its sheer simplicity, and the power to escape from the notation of a particular school of art or ideology. Her memorial to her son Peter has a timelessness derived from her gift for taking an older religious frame of references and remolding it to suit a modern catastrophe.

Winter's interpretation of *Die Eltern* concentrates on the traditional-religious and secular-modern contrast, which has been a subject of heated debate in the scholarship of First World War cultural history. The debate has been, to a significant degree, in reaction to the eminent literary critic Paul Fussell, who viewed the Great War as a cultural earthquake, not merely a political disaster. Fussell focuses on what he calls the rise of modern memory – a radical shift from a strongly Romanticism-inspired aesthetic preference, after the catastrophic experience of the industrial war of 1914–1918, to a harsh critical modernist orientation. The modern memory is more spatial than temporal, relating to the "simultaneity of multiple distant events that were shared by hundreds of thousands of men in battle and witnessed by the civilian population who attempted to draw those events together into a single coherent pattern."[18] A number of scholars have subsequently responded to Fussell's modern memory thesis.[19] Winter focuses on the cultural condition in postwar European societies in which the advent of modernist criticism coexisted with a strong revival of traditional religious symbols and ideas. He shows how ordinary grieving families sought solace in the traditional icons of regeneration and resurrection, irrespective of the flowering of critical secular aesthetics in highbrow literature and art. Winter's reading of *Die Eltern* extends his findings on the spatiotemporal coexistence of the traditional and the modern, and the religious and the secular, in the constitution of the postwar European landscape of bereavement and commemoration: The Vladslo cemetery is a sublime example of the presence of the past in the present. Kollwitz's *Die Eltern* draws upon the long German tradition of Christian art – most notably, the iconography of *Vesperbild* (Pietà) since the fourteenth century and especially Holbein's 1571 painting *Christ in the Tomb*. This deeply tradition-inspired artwork is integrated in a place, which is supposed to embody the constitutive principles of modern society and politics – individuality, equality, and fraternity.

We may approach the structure of Vladslo cemetery from yet another angle, however. *Die Eltern* may be considered as having elements of religious art if seen from the perspective of the history of art. However, the immediate way in which this sculpture exerts an impact on the visitors to the cemetery is rather an aura of intimacy and loss in the milieu of close relations with which they all can sympathize. Indeed, Winter observes: "Through the monument to her son Peter, [Kollwitz] brought commemorative art to a level beyond that of most of her contemporaries ... At [Vladslo], on their knees, Käthe and Karl Kollwitz suggest a family which includes us all, and that may be precisely what she had in mind. *The most intimate here is also the most universal*" (emphasis added).[20] Seen in this light, *Die Eltern* is an intrusion of family grief into a space to which it is uninvited – the space that is emblematic of the virtues of modern political friendship and which is, therefore, exclusive of traditional family feelings and kinship morality. As such, it undermines the aesthetic certainty of political friendship, perhaps more effectively than any critical philosophical deliberations on the politics of fraternity.[21]

Other efforts to make the aesthetics of kinship into a meaningful element in reflections on war exist within the tradition of modernist art. In 1952, Pablo Picasso completed his last composition dedicated to the theme of war and peace. Installed in the curved vaulting of the village chapel in Vallauris, Southern France, Picasso's two-piece mural, *War and Peace*, follows his 1951 oil-on-plywood, *Massacre in Korea*, as well as the larger and better-known, *Guernica*, completed in 1937. *Massacre in Korea* takes on a bifurcated composition: a group of naked women and children on the left side of the composition in confrontation with a horde of heavily armed robotic soldiers on the right. In the space between these two contrasting parts is featured, in the distance, what appears to be a mass grave. *War and Peace* also consists of two parts that are named *War* and *Peace*, and are made to face each other in the vaulting. The *Peace* panel depicts, according to the inscription available at the National Picasso Museum at Vallauris, "a tightrope walker as a symbol of the fragile nature of peace ... and, under an orange tree, a family calmly and happily enjoying themselves in the sunshine."[22] It also shows "mothers and playing children, around the central figure of Pegasus, pulling a plough at the bidding of one child and so personifying the fertile world of peace."[23] A considerable body of art history literature delves into the symbolic language of *Massacre in Korea* or that of *War and Peace* separately. If seen together, however, the communal effervescence in *Peace* may appear to be in dialogue with the lethal terror in *Massacre* – as if the lives lost in *Massacre* were summoned back in *Peace*.[24]

Turning to *Peace* and to the image of "a family calmly and happily enjoying themselves" underneath the orange tree, we may ask how this scene of convivial intimacy and domesticity relates to the political question of peace as a counterforce to the power of war. The group of individuals depicted here consists of a woman who is breastfeeding an infant and a man tending the hearth and preparing a meal. Another man is immersed in writing, and the woman is reading a book while breastfeeding. According to one art historian, the *Peace* panel depicts "an apolitical golden age in which figures symbolizing maternity and culture are warmed by an olive-branched sun."[25] With this note, the historian contrasts *Massacre in Korea*, which, according to her, is a deeply political artwork (Picasso expressing his anti-American sentiment and communist identity; see following discussion) compared to *War and Peace*, in which the painter allegedly toned down his politics in preference for art.

I find this conclusion problematic. The issue is not about the freedom of art from politics, but rather about viewing the image of domestic conviviality as apolitical. This image may appear idyllically innocent and obliviously apolitical if seen on its own, but it cannot be interpreted as such if considered in relation to the larger composition. Seen as part of the didactic statement on the power of war, the image of intimate sociality comes alive with powerful meanings about the experience of war and the struggle for peace. I believe that the conviviality of domestic life portrayed in *Peace* is meant to be perspectival. Imagine that this imagery is seen not by just any spectators but those who, having experienced the destruction of war, are trying to bring together fragmented pieces of their lives. Then, the seemingly apolitical scenery of ordinary life near the hearth appears to be either a life they can recall from a time that the history of war has made a prehistory, or one in a distant, unforeseeable future, the prospect of reaching which seems so far beyond their strength. The image depicts such an ordinary life situation, but one that has become an ideal to attain and which will require extraordinary human will to live on with the hope of attaining it. Seen in this way, the image of domestic life comes alive as a powerful statement against the politics of war from the specific perspective to which the sorrows of war are integral. Indeed, South Korean art historian Young-taik Park remarks on a notable tradition in the postwar South Korean art world in which artists concentrate on peaceable images of familial lives. These include the work featured on the cover of this book, *The Kim Family after the Korean War* (1990), by one of the country's renowned contemporary artists, Ok-sang Lim. The art historian notes that the keyword for these artworks is aspiration (for the future) rather than representation (of historical reality), arguing that "these Korean War-generation artists are preoccupied with the theme of family because of their desire to recover [through art] their families that have been broken apart by war." These works constitute, according to him, "an aesthetical reaction to the violence and madness of the [political] system."[26]

Massacre in Korea created a small storm in wartime South Korea. General MacArthur's office in Japan was alert and its public relations officers reacted swiftly against it. Indignant reactions also came from South Korean artists. Before the war, Picasso was extremely popular among many of these artists, who were attracted to his artwork as part of their strong interest in the broader spectrum of the modernist art movement. After *Massacre in Korea* appeared to the public in Europe and the news reached wartime Korea, however, Picasso quickly became a dangerous name to be associated with in South Korea's art community, being nearly synonymous with pro-communism. Some artists publicly declared a break with Picasso, accusing him of appeasing the communist world and regretting their previous interest in his work. They accused Picasso of corrupting the artistic spirit with his ideological preferences, pointing out that, if he had a right mind and an objective understanding of the Korean War's realities, the perpetrators of violence against innocent civilians depicted in the painting should have pointed to the communists and them only. Subsequently, books about Picasso's artwork, especially those about his anti-war art, became a dangerous object in postwar South Korea up until the mid-1970s. The history of the massacre in Korea has been a taboo subject for longer than Picasso's *Massacre in Korea*. Even today, many years after the end of the Cold War that conditioned Korea's civil war, the structure of emotion that led to the condemnation of *Massacre in Korea* has not entirely become a thing of the past and continues to curb a true understanding of the scale and magnitude of the history of the massacre in Korea. The rehabilitation of the victims of the massacre as innocent victims of state violence continues to face formidable objections from some circles in South Korea's political society, despite the laudable progress the country has made during the past two decades on the front of political democracy. The country's civil society is still divided on the meaning of the Korean War and on ways to come to terms with its tragic legacy. This situation may relate to the specific fact that the global civil war that we habitually call the Cold War has not yet seen a genuine ending in the Korean peninsula. It may also be due to the more general propensity in the public history of modern warfare and in the constitution of modern political society that privileges, while dealing with the legacy of war, the idea of heroic political friendship over the reality of the tragic political life of human intimacy. One thing that is clear, however, is that the understanding of the massacre in Korea is transforming today, true to the spirit of the artist who sought to capture its tragic nature and the tragedy's afterlife in an extraordinary message of peace.

It is one of the enduring myths of modern politics that the milieu of human kinship makes up a private sphere of life, having no remarkable place in the advancement of the structure of political society. This myth even has it that the horizon of modern society and politics would emerge when kinship retreated from the public world to the private sphere. The historical experience of Cold War modernity in the outposts of the global conflict does not sit easily with such an idle assumption about modern political life. Nor do processes of political development beyond the age of extremes that arise in such places – in which the recovery of the public world requires the voice of kinship to be heard loud and clear. This voice of kinship reverberates from the shiny copperware utensils that the villagers bring to the Jeju Peace Park memorial events for their ancestors and when the mourners assert their rights to engage in the public space as an extension of their domestic space. It is heard in the care these mourners give to unwrapping these objects, and in the fleeting moments in which these caring and dignified acts appear to the public view – moments in which the morality of kinship declares its sovereign status free from the politics of being guilty by association. This freedom, for the living, means the recovery of the right to grieve and commemorate the dead without fearing the harmful political consequences of doing so. For the dead and the missing, it means recovering the right to exist in the world of kinship without endangering this world by being part of it. The political life of kinship after the massacres in Korea has been a long struggle to reclaim the inalienable rights of the memory of the dead to an intimate existence among the living – what Emile Durkheim once called *the rights of the soul*.[27] The rights of the soul in this context meant, for the dead, the recovery of their rights to exist in the world of kinship, and have been, for the living, equal in meaning to the recovery of their civil rights in political society. This long march to peace continues on the island today, two generations after the terrifying knock of civil war was first heard loudly on the door, driven by the magnitude of a multitude of aspirations to recover the amity of kinship, which in this context is equal in meaning to the ideal of society at peace.

Notes

INTRODUCTION

1. This story is from Wan-suh Park's *Kyŏul nadŭli* (A winter journey), featured in her collection of stories *Baebanŭi yŏrŭm* (The treacherous summer), (Paju: Munhakdong'ne, 1999), pp. 11–29.
2. This story by Wan-suh Park is entitled "In the Realm of Buddha," included in *The red room: stories of trauma in contemporary Korea*, trans. by Bruce Fulton and Ju-chan Fulton (Honolulu: University of Hawaii Press, 2009). The original Korean title of the short story is *Buch'ŏnim gŭnch'ŏ*, meaning "in the environs of Buddha." The title entails an upsurge of hitherto repressed intimate memories in a religious space and, at the same time, an inability to really enter into the religious domain due to unresolved complications in past memories.
3. Sung-chil Kim, *Yŏksa ap'esŏ: han sahakjaŭi 6.25ilgi* (In face of history: a historian's diary of 6.25 [Korean War]), (Seoul: Chang'bi, 2009).
4. Wan-suh Park, *Who ate up all the shinga?: an autobiographical novel*, trans. by Young-nan Yu and Stephen Epstein (New York: Columbia University Press, 2009).
5. Han Kang, "While the U.S. talks of war, South Korea shudders: there is no war scenario that ends in victory," *The New York Times*, October 7, 2017.
6. Allan Young, "W. H. R. Rivers and the anthropology of psychiatry," *Social Science and Medicine*, Vol. 36 (1993), pp. ii–vii.
7. Allan Young, *The harmony of illusions: inventing post-traumatic stress disorder* (Princeton, NJ: Princeton University Press, 1995).
8. Most notable here is the eminent South Korean writer Choi In-hun, whose 1960 work *Gwangjang* (The square) approaches the Korean War as a series of crises in the webs of intimate human relations in close relation to the turbulent geopolitical condition of the time. See In-hun Choi, *The square: a novel*, trans. by Seong-Kon Kim (McLean, IL: Dalkey Archive Press, 2014). See also Gil-on Hyun, *Gwangye* (Relations), (Seoul: Koryŏwŏn, 2001).
9. It is interesting to note that some scholars adopt this three-dimensional concept of relationship, which is at once social and political, or the related notion of "intimacy" as a political and profoundly politicized concept, in telling microhistories of colonial violence. See, for instance, Nayoung Aime Kwon, *Intimate empire: collaboration and colonial modernity in Korea*

and Japan (Durham, NC: Duke University Press, 2015); and Timothy Brook, *Collaboration: Japanese agents and local elites in wartime China* (Cambridge, MA: Harvard University Press, 2005). See also Heonik Kwon, "Excavating the history of collaboration," *The Asia-Pacific Journal*, Vol. 6, Issue 7 (July 2, 2008), available online at https://apjjf.org/-Heonik-Kwon/2801/article.html.

10. See Chapter 2 for Reinhart Koselleck's idea of *Weltbürgerkrieg* – a "world civil war" with reference to the Cold War. See also David Armitage, *Civil wars: a history in ideas* (New Haven, CT: Yale University Press, 2017).

11. Jian Chen, *Mao's China and the Cold War* (Durham: University of North Carolina Press, 2000).

12. Steven H. Lee, *The Korean War* (New York: Longman, 2001).

13. Dong-choon Kim, *The unending Korean War: a social history*, trans. by Sung-ok Kim (Larkspur, CA: Tamal Vista Publications, 2009), p. 38.

14. Chan-sung Park, *Maŭllo gan hankukjŏnjaeng* (The Korean War that went into villages), (Paju: Dolbegae, 2010).

15. Lewis H. Morgan, *Ancient society* (New York: Henry Holt, 1907); Meyer Fortes, *Kinship and the social order: the legacy of Lewis Henry Morgan* (Chicago: Aldine, 1969).

16. "The laws of the heaven" and "the human laws" are my translations of the Sino-Korean concepts, *chŏnlyun* and *inlyun*.

17. Among the combatant casualties were 520,000 North Korean soldiers, 100,000 South Korean soldiers, 900,000 Chinese soldiers, and 36,940 Americans. Bruce Cumings, *The Korean War: a history* (New York: Modern Library, 2010), p. 35.

18. This is how Marshall Sahlins tries to redefine kinship in his recent attempt to depart from a radically relativist, constructivist view to kinship such as David Schneider's. See Marshall Sahlins, *What kinship is – and is not* (Chicago: University of Chicago Press, 2013). Also Andrew Shryock, "It's this, not that: how Marshall Sahlins solves kinship," *HAU: Journal of Ethnographic Theory*, Vol. 3, No. 2 (2013), pp. 271–279.

19. See Heonik Kwon, "Ghosts of war and the spirit of cosmopolitanism," *History of Religions*, Vol. 48, No. 1 (2008), pp. 22–42.

20. Cited from Linda Colley, "What gets called 'civil war'?" *The New York Review of Books*, Vol. 64, No. 10 (2017), pp. 42–43.

21. On the notion of microhistory, see Carlo Ginzburg, "Microhistory: two or three things that I know about it," *Critical Inquiry*, Vol. 20, No. 1 (1993), pp. 10–35. Microhistory aims to ask big questions in small places and, in this regard, closely resonates with the purpose of ethnography, which, according to Clifford Geertz, intends to "draw large conclusions from small, but very densely textured facts." Cited from Clifford Geertz, *The interpretation of cultures* (New York: Basic Books, 1973), p. 28.

22. Morgan, *Ancient society*, pp. 65–67. Central to Morgan's broad thesis is the observation: "In civilized society the state assumes the protection of persons and of property. Accustomed to look to this source for the maintenance of personal rights, there has been a corresponding abatement of the strength of the bond of kin. But under gentile society the individual depended for

security upon his gens. It took the place afterwards held by the state, and possessed the requisite numbers to render its guardianship effective. Within its membership the bond of kin was a powerful element for mutual support. To wrong a person was to wrong his gens; and to support a person was to stand behind him with the entire array of his gentile kindred." Quoted from Morgan, *Ancient society*, p. 76.

23. Although these scholars were based primarily in Britain and their works were principally grounded in parts of Africa that were under the indirect rule of the British imperial power, the ideas they advanced had a much broader origin, developed in close interaction with ideas raised by Morgan in the mid-nineteenth century as well as those by Emile Durkheim, who, while leading the early French sociological school in the early twentieth century, pursued an interest in the constitutive mechanisms of social integration as part of his general interest in the nature of human solidarity. These ideas were formative of the interwar-era political theory of kinship, which focused squarely on the close relationship between systems of kinship and forms of political order, which was Morgan's question, as an empirical sociological question, following Durkheim, rather than a question of human social evolution as was the case with Morgan.

24. According to a typical view expressed with respect to this, the "political organization of the Nuer is totally unformulated. They have no explicit institutions of government or administration. Such fluid and intangible political structure as they exhibit is a spontaneous, shifting expression of their conflicting loyalties. The only principle of any firmness which gives form to their tribal life is the principle of genealogy." Cited from Mary Douglas, *Purity and danger: an analysis of concepts of pollution and taboo* (London: Routledge, 1966), p. 143.

25. E. E. Evans-Pritchard, "The Nuer of the southern Sudan," in Meyer Fortes and E. E. Evans-Pritchard (eds.), *African political systems* (London: Oxford University Press, 1940), pp. 272–296. The expressions of thick versus thin relations are drawn from Avishai Margalit's *The ethics of memory* (Cambridge, MA: Harvard University Press, 2002).

26. In the depths of human evolution, according to Peter Wilson, kinship and friendship are mutually constitutive categories: "kinship ... signals friendship, while friendship realizes and confirms kinship." Cited from Peter J. Wilson, *The domestication of the human species* (New Haven, CT: Yale University Press, 1988), p. 35. See also Peter Goodrich's stimulating discussion of friendship "as a category of kinship" and why this ancient idea is missing from contemporary deliberations on friendship in his "Veritie hidde: amity, law, miscellany," *Law and Humanities*, Vol. 11, No. 1 (2017), pp. 137–155.

27. It is observed that the family of nations idea also has a dark history. During the colonial age, the idea applied only to a handful of powerful, expansionist states of the time, while expunging other weaker political groups from the "family" and relegating their status to a protectorate. See Harald Kleinschmidt, "The family of nations as an element of the ideology of colonialism," *Journal of the History of International Law*, Vol. 18 (2016), pp. 278–316. Others explore how

a similar idea is reinvented after the Second World War. See David Mole, "Discourses of world kinship and the United Nations: the quest for a human family" (PhD thesis, London School of Economics, 2009).

28. Max Gluckman, *Custom and conflict in Africa* (Oxford: Blackwell, 1955).

29. Thomas Borstelmann, *Apartheid's reluctant uncle: the United States and southern Africa in the early Cold War* (New York: Oxford University Press, 1993).

30. Fred Halliday, *The making of the second Cold War* (London: Verso, 1987).

31. Signe Howell and Roy Willis (eds.), *Societies at peace: anthropological perspectives* (London: Routledge, 1989).

32. Roger D. Masters, "World politics as a primitive political system," *World Politics*, Vol. 16, No. 4 (1964), pp. 595–619.

33. Hedley Bull, *The anarchical society: a study of order in world politics* (New York: Columbia University Press, 1977).

34. See Tim B. Mueller, "The Rockefeller Foundation, the social sciences, and the humanities in the Cold War," *Cold War Studies*, Vol. 15, No. 3 (2013), pp. 108–135. Also Francis Stonor Saunders, *The cultural Cold War: the CIA and the world of arts and letters* (New York: Free Press, 2000).

35. Notable was the polarization between the efforts to further universalize the phenomenon of kinship (as in the structuralist theory of the French anthropologist Claude Lévi-Strauss, based on the idea of universal incest avoidance), and those to radically pluralize it (with the idea that there are as many kinship rules as there are cultures, as advocated by the American anthropologist David Schneider): David Schneider, *American kinship: a cultural account* (Chicago: University of Chicago Press, 1980); and Claude Lévi-Strauss, *The elementary structures of kinship* (Boston, MA: Beacon Press, 1969).

36. Pierre Bourdieu, *Outline of a theory of practice* (Cambridge: Cambridge University Press, 1977), pp. 34–35.

37. Peter P. Schweitzer, "Introduction," in Peter P. Schweitzer (ed.), *Dividends of kinship: meaning and uses of social relatedness* (London: Routledge, 2000), p. 9.

38. For instance, questions regarding whether the concept of kinship belongs to biology (e.g., natural process of procreation) or to culture (i.e., specific and non-generalizable ideas about how we come into the world) continue to attract heated debate not only in anthropology but also in areas such as social studies of biomedical technologies. For an excellent review of the history of kinship studies in anthropology, see Janet Carsten, *After kinship* (Cambridge: Cambridge University Press, 2004), and also Schweitzer's introduction to *Dividends of kinship*, pp. 1–32.

39. Fortes, *Kinship and the social order*, p. 219.

40. See Sharon Herbarch, "Afghan families divided, villages uprooted," *Los Angeles Times*, July 26, 1992; and Hussein Tahiri, "Divided Afghans will never accept one master," *The Sydney Morning Herald*, October 22, 2010.

41. Fortes, *Kinship and the social order*, p. 237.

42. Maurice Bloch, "The long term and the short term: the economic and political significance of the morality of kinship," in Jack Goody (ed.), *The character of kinship* (Cambridge: Cambridge University Press, 1973), pp. 75–87.

43. Fortes, *Kinship and the social order*, p. 77.
44. See, for instance, Christine Sylvester, "Experiencing war: an introduction," in Christine Sylvester (ed.), *Experiencing war* (London: Routledge, 2010), pp. 1–7.

MASSACRES IN KOREA

1. *Daegu Maeil Sinmun* (Daegu Daily Gazette), July 10, 1950.
2. *Daegu Maeil Sinmun* (Daegu Daily Gazette), July 29, 1960. The funerary address was based on the 1925 poem *Ch'ohon* (Calling the souls), composed by the well-known South Korean literary figure Kim So-wŏl. The poem's title derives from the traditional Korean mortuary custom of calling the soul of the dead to the deceased person's funerary clothing before it is interred together with the body.
3. Adam Roberts, "The civilian in modern war," *Yearbook of International Humanitarian Law*, Vol. 12 (2009), pp. 13–51.
4. Ibid., p. 38.
5. Cited from Peter Gatrell, *The making of the modern refugee* (Oxford: Oxford University Press, 2013), p. 2.
6. Kyung-li Park, *Sijang'gwa jŏnjaeng'* (The market and the war), (Seoul: Nanam, 1993), p. 321.
7. Wan-suh Park, *Baebanŭi yŏrum* (The treacherous summer), (Paju: Munhakdongne, 2006), p. 282.
8. Chan-sung Park, *Maŭllo gan hankukjŏnjaeng* (The Korean War that went into villages), (Paju: Dolbegae, 2010), p. 8.
9. Stathis N. Kalyvas, *The logic of violence in civil war* (Cambridge: Cambridge University Press, 2006).
10. Ibid., pp. 333–336.
11. Steven H. Lee, *The Korean War* (New York: Longman, 2001), p. 60.
12. See Sahr Conway-Lanz, *Collateral damage: Americans, non-combatant immunity, and atrocity after World War II* (New York: Routledge, 2006).
13. Charles J. Hanley, Sang-Hun Choe and Martha Mendoza, *The bridge at No Gun Ri* (New York: Henry Holt, 2001).
14. Dong-choon Kim, "Hankukjŏnjaeng' 60nyŏn, hanbandowa segye (Sixty years after the Korean War, the Korean peninsula and the world)," *Yŏksabipyŏng* (Historical criticism), No. 91 (2010), pp. 161–163.
15. Marilyn B. Young, "Remembering to forget," in Mark P. Bradley and Patrice Petro (eds.) *Truth claims: representation and human rights* (New Brunswick, NJ: Rutgers University Press, 2002), p. 20.
16. Ki-jin Kim, *Ggŭtnaji anŭn jŏnjaeng: gukminbodoyŏngmaeng, busan kyŏngnam jiyŏk* (The unfinished war: national guidance alliance, Pusan-Kyungnam region), (Seoul: Yoksabipyŏngsa, 2002), pp. 19–22.
17. The expression "suspected traitors" is cited from Gavan McCormack, "Korea at 60," *The Asia-Pacific Journal*, Vol. 6, Issue 9 (September 1, 2008), available online at https://apjjf.org/-Gavan-McCormack/2869/article .html. See also his *Cold war, hot war: an Australian perspective on the Korean War* (Sydney: Hale and Iremonger, 1983).

18. Su-kyoung Hwang, "South Korea, the United States and emergency powers during the Korean War," *The Asia-Pacific Journal*, Vol. 12, Issue 5 (February 3, 2014), available online at https://apjjf.org/2014/12/5/Su-kyoung-Hwang/4069/article.html.
19. Ibid., p. 4.
20. Daegŏmchalchŏng josaguk (National Prosecutor's Office Investigation Bureau), *Jwaiksagŏnsillok*, 11gwŏn (Chronicle of leftist incidents, Vol. 11), (Seoul: National Prosecutor's Office, 1975). Cited from Jinsilgwa hwahoi uiwŏnhoi (National Truth and Reconciliation Commission), *Jinhwaui 2007nyŏn sangbangi josabogosŏ* (Truth and Reconciliation Commission investigation report for the first half of 2007), (Seoul: Truth and Reconciliation Commission, 2007), p. 192.
21. Ibid.
22. The British journalist Alan Winnington also reported on the latter incident. See Alan Winnington, *I saw the truth in Korea* (London: People's Press, 1950).
23. Gurimji pyŏnchan wiwŏnhoi (Editorial Committee of Gurim Chronicles), *Honam myŏngchon Gurim: Gurimsaramduli sonsu ssŭn maŭlgongdongche iyagi* (A distinguished village in Honam region: stories of a village community written by the villagers themselves), (Seoul: Libuk, 2006), p. 373.
24. Ibid.
25. Keun-sik Chung et al. (eds.), *Gurim yŏngu: maŭlgongdongcheŭi gujowa byŏndong* (Gurim studies: structure and change in village community), (Seoul: Kyunginmunhwasa, 2003).
26. Dong-choon Kim, *The unending Korean War: a social history*, trans. by Sung-ok Kim (Larkspur, CA: Tamal Vista Publications, 2009), pp. 97–108.
27. Ibid., pp. 199–200.
28. Ibid., pp. 257–258.
29. Ibid., p. 258.
30. Among the most relevant are: Taik-lim Yun, *Inryuhakjaŭi gwagŏyŏhaeng: han ppalgaeng'i maŭlŭi yŏksarŭl chatasŏ* (An anthropologist's journey to history: in search of a red village), (Seoul: Yŏksabipyŏngsa, 2003); In-ju Pyo et al. (eds.), *Jŏnjaeng'gwa saramdŭl: araerobutŏŭi hankukjŏnjaengyŏngu* (War and peoples: studies of the Korean War from below), (Seoul: Hanul, 2003); Gwi-Sook Gwon, *Giŏkŭi jŏngch'i: daeryanghaksalŭi sahoijŏk giŏkgwa yŏksajŏk jinsil* (Politics of memory: social memories and historical truths of mass violence), (Seoul: Munhwakgwa jisŏngsa, 2006).
31. Park, *Maŭllo gan hankukjŏnjaeing* (The Korean War that went into villages), p. 57.
32. Ibid., p. 63.
33. Jinsilgwa hwahoi uiwŏnhoi (National Truth and Reconciliation Commission), *Hankukjŏnjaeing jŏnhu minganin jipdanhŭisaeng gwanlyŏn 2007nyŏn yuhaebalgul bogosŏ* (2007 recovery report on mass civilian victims around the Korean War period), Vol. 1 (Seoul: Hakyŏnmunhwasa, 2008), p. 236.
34. Ibid., p. 237.
35. Yun, *Inryuhakjaŭi gwagŏyŏhaeng* (An anthropologist's journey to history), p. 176.

36. Ibid., p. 178.
37. Ibid., p. 177.
38. Ibid., pp. 182–190.
39. Ibid., p. 190.
40. Jeong-ran Yoon, "Hankukjŏnjaenggi gidokkyoin haksalui wŏningwa sŏng-gyŏk (The causes and characteristics of the massacres of Christians during the Korean War)," in Kyung-hak Kim, et al. (eds.), *Jŏngjaenggwa giŏk* (War and memories), (Seoul: Hanulakademi, 2005), pp. 76–112.
41. See Dong-man Suh, *Bukjosŏn sahoijuŭi chejesŏngripsa 1945–1961* (History of the building of socialist system in North Korea), (Seoul: Sŏnin, 2005), pp. 466–471; and Jon Halliday and Bruce Cumings, *Korea: the unknown war* (London: Viking, 1988) pp. 99–110. Scattered testimonial evidence exists concerning the violence that was perpetrated by communist forces in parts of North Korea after the retreat of United Nations forces. See, for instance, the experience of Yŏnguhoi, a secret political group in wartime northern Korea that grew out of the traditional indigenous religious group-ing Chŏndogyo, in Donghak Yŏnguhoi (Association of Donghak Friends), *Yŏnguhoi bisa* (Unknown histories of Yŏnguhoi), 1989.
42. Kim, "Hankukjŏnjaeng' 60nyŏn, hanbandowa segye (Sixty years after the Korean War, the Korean peninsula and the world)," p. 273.
43. Sun-gwon Hong, *Jŏnjaeng'gwa gukga pp'okryok* (War and state violence), (Seoul: Sonin, 2012), p. 177.
44. "Lee Won-sike sahyŏng'hwakjŏng (Death sentence to Lee Won-sik)," *Hankuk Ilbo* (Korea Daily), December 8, 1961.
45. Nan Kim, *Memory, reconciliation, and reunions in South Korea: crossing the divide* (Lanham, MD: Lexington, 2016).
46. See Marilyn B. Young, "Bombing civilians from the twentieth to the twentieth-first centuries," in Yuki Tanaka and Marilyn B. Young (eds.), *Bombing civi-lians: a twentieth-century history* (New York: New Press, 2009), pp. 154–174.
47. Sung-chil Kim, *Yŏksa ap'esŏ: han sahakjaŭi 6.25ilgi* (In face of history: a historian's diary of 6.25 [Korean War]), (Seoul: Changbi, 2009).
48. Ibid., p. 258.
49. "Yangmin, biyangminŭro gyŏkron (Disputes over innocent civilians or non-innocent civilians)," *Daegu Maeil Sinmun* (Daegu Daily Gazette), June 16, 1960.
50. These quotes are from *Daegu Maeil Sinmun* (Daegu Daily Gazette), May 27, 1960.
51. *Daegu Maeil Sinmun* (Daegu Daily Gazette), June 16, 1960.

BAD GEMEINSCHAFT

1. See, for instance, Maurice Bloch, *Placing the dead: tombs, ancestral villages, and kinship organizations in Madagascar* (London: Seminar Press, 1971).
2. Do-young Lee, *Jukŭmŭi yebigŏmsok: yangminhaksal jinsangjosa bogosŏ* (The deadly preventive custody: investigative report of [the Korean War] civilian massacres [in Jeju]), (Seoul: Mal, 2000), p. 76.
3. Ibid., pp. 46–47.

4. Ibid., p. 77. Concerning incidents in Gŏchang, see Min-young Rho and Hee-chung Kang, *Gŏchang yangminhaksal: gŭ ithyŏjin p'iulŭm* (Civilian massacres in Gŏchang: its forgotten cries), (Chungju: Onnuri, 1988).

5. Lee, *Jukŭmŭi yebigŏmsok* (The deadly preventive custody), p. 46.

6. See Charles R. Kim, *Youth for nation: culture and protest in Cold War South Korea* (Honolulu: University of Hawai'i Press, 2017).

7. Gwang-taek Kim, *Bumonim yŏngjone* (On our parents' memorial table), pamphlet of the Daegu Association of Bereaved Families, p. 4.

8. The quote is from Sung Chul Yang, *Korea and two regimes: Kim Il Sung and Park Chung Hee* (Cambridge, MA: Schenkman Publishing Company, 1981), p. 241.

9. Some observers explain the coup leaders' strong interest in cracking down on the rising expression of social grievances in this particular sphere in terms of their perceived need to show the United States they would be committed to anti-communist politics once in power. See Hyung-Tae Kim, "A sŭlpŭn son, namedo bukedo 'baekjoilson'irose (The tragic descendant, we have 'one hundred ancestors and a single descendant' in the north as well as in the south)," *Hangyŏre sinmun* (Hangyŏre News), November 30, 2012.

10. On *La Violencia*, see Michael Taussig, *Law in a lawless land* (New York: The New Press, 2003).

11. This happened in Geochang, the site of a large-scale civilian massacre by South Korean counterinsurgency forces in February 1951, where families of victims excavated the mass graves three years after the incident and reburied the remains in two separate collective tombs for male and female victims. "Bigŭkŭi yŏksarŭl kaenda 3 (Excavating the tragic history 3)," *Pusan Ilbo* (Pusan Daily), May 11, 1960.

12. One Hundred Ancestors and One Single Descendent Association of Families, *Baejoilsonyŏngryŏng je52jugi hapdonguiryŏngje* (The fifty-second collective commemoration of the ancestors of the One Hundred Ancestors and One Descendent Families), document prepared by the family association for the occasion in 2009, pp. 13–14.

13. Bruce Cumings, *The origins of the Korean War: liberation and the emergence of separate regimes, 1945–1947* (Princeton, NJ: Princeton University Press, 1981).

14. Bruce Cumings, *Parallax visions: making sense of American-East Asian relations at the end of the century* (Durham, NC: Duke University Press, 1999).

15. The South Korean historian Kang Man-gil argues that the civil triumph of the late 1980s is a culmination of the powerful legacy that the earlier-era events had left in the collective memory. See Man-gil Kang, *A history of contemporary Korea* (Folkestone: Global Oriental, 2006).

16. George Mosse, *Fallen soldiers: reshaping the memory of the World Wars* (Oxford: Oxford University Press, 1990).

17. Ibid., p. 7.

18. Christine Sylvester, "Experiencing war: an introduction," in C. Sylvester (ed.), *Experiencing war* (London: Routledge, 2010), pp. 1–7.

19. Laura Sjoberg, *Gendering global conflict: toward a feminist theory of war* (New York: Columbia University Press, 2013), p. 271.

20. Aleida Assmann, *Cultural memory and Western civilization* (Cambridge: Cambridge University Press, 2011).

21. Stéphane Audoin-Rouzeau and Annette Becker, *14–18, retrouver la Guerre* (Paris: Gallimard, 2000).
22. Christopher E. Goscha and Vatthana Pholsena, "The experience of war: four Sino-Indochinese perspectives," *European Journal of East Asian Studies*, Vol. 9, Issue 2 (2010), pp. 189–199.
23. Edward Miller and Tuong Vu, "The Vietnam War as a Vietnamese war: agency and society in the study of the Second Indochina War, *Journal of Vietnamese Studies*, Vol. 4, No. 3 (2009), pp. 1–16.
24. Bao Ninh, *The sorrow of war* (New York: Vintage, 1987).
25. Notable examples are Robert K. Brigham, *ARVN: Life and death in the South Vietnamese army* (Lawrence: University Press of Kansas, 2006), and Nha Ca, *Mourning headband for Hue: an account of the battle for Hue, Vietnam 1968*, trans. by Olga Dror (Bloomington: Indiana University Press, 2014).
26. Brigham, *ARVN: Life and death in the South Vietnamese army.*
27. Lewis H. Morgan, *Ancient society* (New York: Henry Holt, 1907).
28. Michael Carrithers, Steven Collins and Steven Lukes (eds.), *The category of the person: anthropology, philosophy, history* (Cambridge: Cambridge University Press, 1985).
29. Clifford Geertz, *The interpretation of cultures* (New York: Basic Books, 1973), pp. 389–390.
30. Quoted from an interview featured in *The Kyunghyang Sinmun* (Kyunghyang Daily), February 25, 2001. See also Hyun Gil-on, *Gwangye* (Relations), (Seoul: Koryŏwŏn, 2001).
31. The expression "selfless person" is cited from Steven Collins, *Selfless persons: imagery and thought in Theravada Buddhism* (Cambridge: Cambridge University Press, 1990).
32. Carrithers, Collins and Lukes (eds.), *The category of the person.*
33. C. W. Mills, *The sociological imagination* (New York: Oxford University Press, 1959).
34. Moreover, the concept addresses a form of historical realism. Although the residues of war wounds lodged in the web of human relations may not be as tangible as those found in human bodies, these were "no less real than is the tangible in-between of a commonly experienced world of things," as Peter Fuss writes of Hannah Arendt's conception of community. See Peter Fuss, "Hannah Arendt's conception of political community," in Melvyn A. Hill (ed.), *Hannah Arendt: the recovery of the public world* (New York: St. Martin's Press, 1979), p. 162.
35. Keith Hart, *The memory bank: money in an unequal world* (London: Profile Books, 2000).
36. Song-chil Kim, *Yŏksa apesŏ* (Facing history), (Seoul: Changbi, 1993).
37. Ibid., pp. 184–186.
38. See Nancy Abelmann, *Echoes of the past, epics of dissent: a South Korean social movement* (Berkeley: University of California Press, 1996); Bruce Cumings, *Korea's place in the sun: a modern history* (New York: W. W. Norton, 1997), pp. 337–393; Hagen Koo, *Korean workers: the culture and politics of class formation* (Ithaca, NY: Cornell University Press, 2001); Namhee Lee, *The making of minjung: democracy and the politics of representation in South Korea*

(Ithaca, NY: Cornell University Press, 2009). See also Charles K. Armstrong (ed.), *Korean society: civil society, democracy, and the state* (New York: Routledge, 2007); and Gi-Wook Shin and Paul Chang (eds.), *South Korean social movements: from democracy to civil society* (New York: Routledge, 2011).

39. Bruce Cumings, "Civil Society in West and East," in Armstrong (ed.), *Korean society*, pp. 9–32.
40. Ibid.
41. Ibid., p. 9.
42. Anthony Giddens, *The third way: renewal of social democracy* (Cambridge: Polity Press, 1998).
43. Mary Kaldor, *Global civil society: an answer to war* (Cambridge: Polity, 2003), pp. 50–77.
44. Ibid.
45. Ibid., p. 70.
46. Ibid., p. 61.
47. Ibid., p.72. See also Mary Kaldor, *The imaginary war: interpretation of East-West conflict in Europe* (Oxford: Blackwell, 1990).
48. Quoted from Tony Judt, *Reappraisals: reflections on the forgotten twentieth century* (New York: Penguin, 2008), p. 371. The object of Judt's review is: John Lewis Gaddis, *The long peace: inquiries into the history of the Cold War* (New York: Oxford University Press, 1987).
49. Mary Kaldor, *New and old wars: organized violence in a global age* (Stanford, CA: Stanford University Press, 2001).
50. Ibid., p. 29.
51. Ibid., p. 30.
52. Heonik Kwon, *The other Cold War* (New York: Columbia University, 2010).
53. Niklas Olsen, "Carl Schmitt, Reinhart Koselleck and the foundations of history and politics," *History of European Ideas*, Vol. 37, No. 2 (2011), p. 199.
54. Among prominent examples are: Odd Arne Westad, *The global Cold War: Third World interventions and the making of our times* (Cambridge: Cambridge University Press, 2005); Robert J. McMahon, *The Cold War in the Third World* (New York: Oxford University Press, 2013); and Hajimu Masuda, *Cold War crucible: The Korean conflict and the postwar world* (Cambridge, MA: Harvard University Press, 2015).
55. Neni Panourgiá, *Dangerous citizens: the Greek left and the terror of the state* (New York: Fordham University Press, 2009), pp. 23–30.
56. The term "international civil war" is from André Gerolymatos, *Red Acropolis, black terror: the Greek Civil War and the origins of Soviet–American rivalry, 1943–1949* (New York: Basic Books, 2004), pp. 187–228.
57. Paul G. Pierpaoli, Jr., *Truman and Korea: the political culture of the early Cold War* (Columbia: University of Missouri Press, 1999), p. 8.
58. Gerolymatos, *Red Acropolis*, p. 231.
59. Ibid., pp. 6, 8.
60. The quote is from Mark Mazower, "Introduction," in M. Mazower (ed.), *After the war was over: the family, nation, and state in Greece, 1943–1960* (Princeton, NJ: Princeton University Press, 2000), p. 14. The works mentioned here include: Gwi-ok Kim, *Isan gajok, 'bangong jŏnsa'do 'ppalgaeng'i'*

do anin (Divided families: neither "anticommunist warriors" nor "red communists"), (Seoul: Yŏksabipyŏngsa, 2004), pp. 203–206; Taik-lim Yun, *Inryuhakjaŭi gwagŏyŏhaeng: han ppalgaeng'i maŭlŭi yŏksarŭl chatasŏ* (An anthropologist's journey to history: in search of a red village), (Seoul: Yŏksabipyŏngsa, 2003), pp. 214–219.

61. Yun, *Inryuhakjaŭi gwagŏyŏhaeng* (An anthropologist's journey to history), pp. 214–222.

62. This is the message that Marcel Mauss, one of the greatest anthropologists of the last century, intended to get across in his classic, *Seasonal variations of the Eskimo: a study in social morphology* (Abingdon: Routledge, 1979).

63. Ferdinand Tönnies, *Community and society*, trans. by Charles P. Loomis (East Lansing: Michigan State University Press, 1957), p. 34.

64. Similar patterns of family-based public unity are known from the existing literature of modern warfare. For instance, Jay Winter writes movingly about the broad mutual assistance network formed among bereaved families in post-First World War France. Jay Winter, "Forms of kinship and remembrance in the aftermath of the Great War," in J. Winter and E. Sivan (eds.), *War and remembrance in the twentieth century* (Cambridge: Cambridge University Press, 1999), pp. 40–60.

65. The phrase "bond of bereavement" is quoted from Judith Butler, *Antigone's claims: kinship between life and death* (New York: Columbia University Press, 2000). According to a song composed by a member of the Daegu association of Korean War bereaved families:

> Ferocious wind pierces through our heart,
> With sad memories of lullabies,
> Let's stand together,
> The children of victims of massacres.

PEACE IN THE FEUD

1. See Taik-lim Yun, *Inryuhakjaŭi gwagŏyŏhaeng: han ppalgaeng'i maŭlŭi yŏksarŭl chatasŏ* (An anthropologist's journey to history: in search of a red village), (Seoul: Yŏksabipyŏngsa, 2003).

2. "Red ideology" is my translation of the expression in local dialect, *bŏlgŏn sasang*.

3. Peter Gatrell, *The making of the modern refugee* (Oxford: Oxford University Press, 2013), p. 2.

4. Ibid.

5. Valérie Gelézeau, Koen De Ceuster and Alain Delissen, "Introduction," in V. Gelézeau, K. De Ceuster and A. Delissen (eds.), *De-bordering Korea: tangible and intangible legacies of the Sunshine Policy* (London: Routledge, 2013), p. 1.

6. Quoted from the radio program *Isangajok* (Separated families), Korea Broadcasting System, September 11, 2005.

7. Margaret MacMillan, *Nixon and Mao: the week that changed the world* (New York: Random House, 2008). The expression "the long 1970s" is

quoted from Chen Jian, "China's changing policies toward the Third World and the end of the global Cold War," in Artemy M. Kalinovsky and Sergey Radchenko (eds.), *The end of the Cold War and the Third World: new perspectives on regional conflict* (London: Routledge, 2011), pp. 101, 119.

8. See Yongho Kim, *North Korean foreign policy: security dilemma and succession* (Lanham, MD: Lexington Books, 2011), pp. 35–52; and Chin O. Chung, *P'yongyang between Peking and Moscow: North Korea's involvement in the Sino-Soviet dispute, 1958–1975* (Tuscaloosa: University of Alabama Press, 1978).

9. Don Oberdorfer, *The two Koreas: a contemporary history* (London: Warner Books, 1999).

10. *Kŭmsugangsan*, 10 (1990), p. 14.

11. James A. Foley, "'Ten million families': statistics or metaphor?" *Korean Studies*, Vol. 25, No. 1 (2001), pp. 96–110.

12. See, for instance, Roger L. Janelli and Dawnhee Yim, "South Korea's great transformation (1960–1995)," *Haksulwŏnnonmunjip* (Proceedings of the Korean National Academy of Sciences), Vol. 55, No. 1 (2016), pp. 53–120.

13. The acclaimed figure of "ten million divided families" may also represent how the Koreans customarily express the condition of multitude; that is, in this context, their perceived severity of war-caused human displacement and consequent crisis in familial life.

14. Kwang-ok Kim, "Jŏntongjŏk gwangye'ŭi hyundaejŏk silch'ŏn (Modern practice of traditional relations)," *Hankukmunhwainlyuhak* (Korean cultural anthropology), Vol. 33, No. 2 (2000), pp. 7–48.

15. Daehanjŏksipjasa (Korea Red Cross), *Isangajokchatgi 60nyŏn* (60 years in search for separated families), (Seoul: Daehanjŏksipjasa, 2005).

16. Tessa Morris-Suzuki, *Exodus to North Korea: shadows from Japan's Cold War* (Lanham, MD: Rowman and Littlefield, 2007).

17. John Borneman, *Being in the two Berlins: kin, state, nation* (Cambridge: Cambridge University Press, 1992).

18. Charles Stafford, *Separation and reunion in modern China* (Cambridge: Cambridge University Press, 2000), pp. 156–173.

19. Sheila Miyoshi Jager and Jiyul Kim, "The Korean War after the Cold War: commemorating the Armistice Agreement in South Korea," in S. M. Jager and R. Mitter (eds.), *Ruptured histories: war, memory, and the post-Cold War in Asia* (Cambridge, MA: Harvard University Press, 2007), p. 234.

20. For an excellent overview of this history, see Nan Kim, *Memory, reconciliation, and reunions in South Korea: crossing the divide* (Lanham, MD: Lexington, 2016).

21. Choon Soon Kim, *Faithful endurance: an ethnography of Korean family dispersal* (Tucson: University of Arizona Press, 1988).

22. See also Kyung-ja Kang, "Gohyangŭi gajok, bukŭi gajok (Families in the homeland, families in North Korea)," in Noriko Ijichi et al. (eds.), *Gohyangŭi gajok, bukŭi gajok* (Families in the homeland, families in North Korea), trans. by Kyung-ja Kim (Seoul: Sŏnin, 2015), pp. 121–168.

23. See the "Tales of families and home villages" available at the South Korean government's online portal for separated families: https://reunion .unikorea.go.kr/reunion/jsp/user/uh/uho0101L.

24. Gwi-ok Kim, *Isan gajok, 'bangong jŏnsa'do 'ppalgaeng'i' do anin* (Divided families: neither "anticommunist warriors" nor "red communists"), (Seoul: Yŏksabipyŏngsa, 2004).

25. Eun Cho, "Jŏnjaenggwa bundanŭi ilsanghwawa giŏkŭi jŏngchi: 'wŏlnam'gajokgwa 'wŏlbuk'gajok janyŏdŭlŭl jungsimŭro (The routinization of war and partition and the politics of memory: testimonies by children of south-crossing and north-crossing families)," in Gwi-ok Kim, et al. (eds.), *Jŏnjaengŭi giŏkgwa naengjŏnŭi gusul* (Memories of war and testimonies to the Cold War), (Seoul: Sŏnin, 2008), p. 63.

26. Kim, *Isan gajok*, pp. 198–200.

27. Asaea jayumunje yŏnguso (Asian research institute of the question of freedom), *Ban'gong gyemong dokbon* (Readings in anticommunist enlightenment), (Seoul: Asaea jayumunje yŏnguso, 1967), p. 200.

28. Su-jong Lee, "Making and unmaking the Korean national division: separated families in the Cold War and post-Cold War eras," Unpublished doctoral thesis (University of Illinois at Urbana-Champaign, December 2006).

29. Hui-gon Kim, "Hangukdokripundonggwa jŏntongmyŏngga (Korean independence movement and traditional families)," *Gukgabohunchŏ haksulnonmunjip I* (The Korean Ministry of Patriots and Veterans Affairs collection of academic papers, Vol. 1), (Daejeon: Daejeon University, 2005), p. 460. The role of kinship ties in local political mobilization is observed in the context of anti-colonial activities as well. The historian Park Chan-sung, for instance, asks why during the popular uprisings against Japan's colonial rule in March 1919, some single-lineage villages were particularly effective in mobilizing protesters. See Chan-sung Park, *1919, daehanmingukŭi chŏt bŏnjjae bom* (1919, Korea's first spring), (Paju: Dasan Books, 2019), pp. 265–275.

30. Min-young Rho and Hui-jong Kang, *Gŏ changyangminhaksal, gŭ ithyŏ jin p'iul ŭm* (Civilian massacre in Gŏchang, its forgotten cries), (Chongju: Onnuri, 1988), pp. 76–83.

31. Ibid., p. 85.

32. Max Gluckman, *Custom and conflict in Africa* (Oxford: Blackwell, 1955).

33. Quoted from a private account of the village's history, "Gailesŏ itŭn il (What happened in Gail)," compiled and kept by a local writer.

34. Concerning the idea that people of these two villages consider they are genealogically related through generations of intermarriage, a local historian testified that "We have different surnames, yet we share each other's blood. You may consider us as descendants from the same roots." See the publication that came out of a village history project conducted by a local university: Andong Daehakgyo Andong Munwah Yŏnguso (Research Institute of Andong Culture, Andong University), *Andong Gail maul* (Gail village of Andong), (Seoul: Yemunsŏwŏn, 2006), p. 260.

GUILT BY ASSOCIATION

1. Geoffrey Robinson, *The dark side of paradise: political violence in Bali* (Ithaca, NY: Cornell University Press, 1995).
2. Ibid., pp. 294, 300.
3. Heonik Kwon, *Ghosts of war in Vietnam* (Cambridge: Cambridge University Press, 2008).
4. Stephan Feuchtwang, *After the event: the transmission of grievous loss in Germany, China and Taiwan* (Oxford: Berghahn, 2011). See also Sylvia Li-Chun Lin, *Representing atrocity in Taiwan: the 2/28 incident and white terror in fiction and film* (New York: Columbia University Press, 2007), pp. 47–72.
5. Greg Grandin, *The last colonial massacre: Latin America in the Cold War* (Chicago: University of Chicago Press, 2004), p. 14.
6. Polymeris Voglis, *Becoming a subject: political prisoners during the Greek Civil War* (Oxford: Berghahn, 2002), pp. 7–8.
7. Ibid., pp. 6–10.
8. Michel Foucault, *Discipline and punish: the birth of the prison*, trans. by Alan Sheridan (New York: Penguin, 1991), p. 224.
9. Ibid., pp. 216–217.
10. Young-min Cho, "Jŏnhyangjedowa gamokŭi yaman (The system of ideological conversion and the barbarity of the prison system)," in Byung-chon Lee and Gwang-il Lee (eds.), *20segi hangukŭi yaman* (The twentieth-century barbarities in Korea), (Seoul: Ilbit, 2001), p. 125.
11. See Jae-il Suh, Jŏnhyang'gongjakgwa ŭimunsa (Questionable deaths in ideological conversion attempts), *Report by the Truth Commission on questionable deaths* (Korean Truth Commission on Questionable Deaths, 2014), pp. 586–622.
12. Cho, "Jŏnhyangjedowa gamokŭi yaman (The system of ideological conversion and the barbarity of the prison system)," p. 114.
13. Foucault, *Discipline and punish*, p. 224.
14. Balázs Szalontai, *Kim Il Sung in the Khrushchev era: Soviet–DPRK relations and the roots of North Korean despotism, 1953–1964* (Washington, DC: Woodrow Wilson Center Press, 2005), pp. 221–223.
15. Ibid., p. 222.
16. Seong-hoon Han, *Jŏnjaeng'gwa inmin* (War and people), (Seoul: Dolbege, 2012), pp. 125–128.
17. Elazar Barkan, "Individual versus group rights in Western philosophy and the law," in Nyla R. Branscombe and Bertjan Doosje (eds.), *Collective guilt: international perspectives* (Cambridge: Cambridge University Press, 2004), p. 309. See also Emile Durkheim, "Two laws of penal evolution," T. A. Jones and Andrew T. Scull (trans.) *Economy and Society*, Vol. 2, No. 3 (1973 [1900]), p. 298.
18. Frederic William Maitland, "Criminal liability of the hundred," *The Law Magazine and Review*, Vol. 7 (1882), pp. 367–380.
19. Quoted from Larry May, *The morality of groups: collective responsibility, group-based harm, and corporate rights* (Notre Dame, IN: University of Notre Dame Press, 1987), p. 8. See also Elazar Barkan, "Individual versus group rights," p. 311.

20. Joseph W. Koterski, "Introduction," in Karl Jaspers, *The question of German guilt*, trans. by E. B. Ashton (New York: Fordham University Press, 2000), p. xi.
21. Durkheim, "Two laws of penal evolution," p. 296.
22. *Yŏnjwaje* formally ended in South Korea in 1988. The outlawing of this institutional practice was one of the first legal reforms undertaken by the democratically elected legislative body after the fall of military rule in 1987. Commentators in Korea hailed the reform as dramatic progress in the country's legal history. However, it is observed that the penalization of family relations continued even in the 1990s, although less intensively and systematically than in the previous postwar decades. The sociologist Cho Eun argues that *yŏnjwaje* in South Korea truly ended only in the mid-2000s. See Eun Cho, "Bundanŭi gin gŭrimja (The long shadows of the national partition)," in Han-hui Ham, et al. (eds.), *Gusulsaro ilnŭn hankukjŏnjaeng* (Reading the Korean War through oral histories), (Seoul: Humanist, 2011), p. 213.
23. John Lord O'Brian, "Loyalty tests and guilt by association," *Harvard Law Review*, Vol. 61, No. 4 (1948), p. 599.
24. Mun-gu Lee, *Gwanchonsupil* (Essays on Gwanchon), (Seoul: Munhakgwa jisongsa, 1996).
25. Sung-mi Cho and Gwi-ok Kim, "Wŏlbukin yugajokŭi bangongjŏk ŏkapgwa 'wŏlbuk'ŭi ŭimich'egye (Anticommunist repressions against the families of individuals who moved to North Korea and the meanings of 'moving to North')," in Gui-ok Kim (ed.), *Isan gajok, 'bangong jŏnsa'do 'ppalgaeng'i' do anin* (Divided families: neither "anticommunist warriors" nor "red communists"), (Seoul: Yŏksabipyŏngsa, 2004), p. 178.
26. Notable are In-ju Pyo et al. (eds.), *Jŏnjaeng'gwa saramdŭl: araerobutŏŭi hankukjŏnjaengyŏngu* (War and peoples: studies of the Korean War from below), (Seoul: Hanul, 2003); *Jŏnjaeng'gwa saramdŭl* (War and people), (Seoul: Hanul Academy, 2003); and Kyung-hak Kim et al. (eds.), *Jŏnjaeng'gwa giŏk* (War and memories), (Seoul: Hanul Academy, 2005).
27. Hankukjŏnjaegjŏnhu   Minganinhaksal   Jinsangkyumyŏng Bŏmkukminuiwŏnhoe (All-national Committee on the Investigation of Civilian Massacres Before and After the Korean War), *100man minganinhaksal, gŭ bŭlaekbaksŭrŭl yŏlda* (Massacre of a million civilians, opening its black box), (Seoul: Uinmedia, 2006), p. 34.
28. Do-young Lee, *Jukŭmŭi yebigŏmsok: yangminhaksal jinsangjosa bogosŏ* (The deadly preventive custody: investigative report of [the Korean War] civilian massacres [in Jeju]), (Seoul: Mal, 2000), p. 79.
29. Ibid., pp. 32–35.
30. "*Kudetaro jungdandoin yŏksaŭi hyŏnjang* (The history disconnected by military coup)," *Mal* (Parole), March 2000, p. 34.
31. The second half of the 1970s was a particularly critical time in this respect. Threatened by the fall of South Vietnam to North Vietnam in March 1975, the South Korean state administration revamped its anti-communist social campaigns through a series of measures. These included the implementation of the so-called Social Safety Law in July 1975, which made it easier for the police and security agents to

detain, interrogate, and inspect anyone they regarded as political and ideological suspects.

32. *Jindotaimjŭ* (Jindo Times), June 26, 2009; *Kyunghyang Sinmun* (Kyunghyang Daily), November 15, 2009.

33. Cited from Won-gyu Lee, "Jŏsŭngkkot (Flowers in the world of the dead)," *Silchŏnmunhak* (Praxis literature), (Autumn 1989), pp. 177–178.

34. Foucault, *Discipline and punish*, p. 138.

35. Ibid., p. 141.

36. Ibid., p. 221.

37. See Alasdair MacIntyre, "The virtues, the unity of a human life, and the concept of a tradition," in Lewis P. Hinchman and Sandra K. Hinchman (eds.), *Memory, identity, community: the idea of narrative in the human sciences* (Albany: State University of New York Press, 1997), pp. 241–243.

38. This choice to highlight the autonomous, displaced "modern" self in historical inquiry is also a methodological choice, related to the fact that "what Foucault calls his '[historical] nominalism' is par force of a kind of methodological individualism. It treats collectives such as the State or abstractions like 'man' or 'power' as reducible, for purposes of explanation, to the individuals that comprise them." Cited from Thomas R. Flynn, "Foucault and historical nominalism," in Harold A. Durfee and David F. T. Rodier (eds.), *Phenomenology and beyond: the self and its language* (Dordrecht: Kluwer Academic Publishers, 1989), p. 134.

39. Michel Foucault, "Qu'est-ce qu'un auteur?!" in his *Dits et écrits 1, 1954–1975* (Paris: Gallimard, 2001), pp. 810–811.

40. Maryon McDonald, "Medical anthropology and anthropological studies of science," in U. Kockel, M. Nic Craith and J. Frykman (eds.), *A companion to the anthropology of Europe* (Oxford: Wiley-Blackwell, 2012), pp. 459–479.

41. Flynn, "Foucault and historical nominalism,", p. 138.

42. Foucault, *Discipline and punish*, p. 30.

43. *Discipline and punish* was based on the lectures Foucault delivered at the Collège de France in 1972–1973. His lecture notes, later published as *The punitive society*, however, show some remarkable differences from *Discipline and punish*. For instance, *Discipline and punish*'s obsession with the body as the object of power is largely absent from the notes. See Michel Foucault, *The punitive society: lectures at the Collège de France, 1972–1973* (London: Palgrave, 2015).

44. Foucault, *Discipline and punish*, p. 31.

45. Ibid., p. 207.

46. Ibid., p. 200.

47. Ibid., p. 198.

48. Ibid., p. 7.

49. Arthur M. Schlesinger, Jr., *The vital center: the politics of freedom* (Boston, MA: Houghton Mifflin, 1962), p. xiii.

50. Quoted from Cynthia Hendershot, *Anti-communism and popular culture in mid-century America* (Jefferson, NC: McFarland, 2003), p. 13.

51. Douglas Field, "Introduction," in D. Field (ed.), *American Cold War culture* (Edinburgh: Edinburgh University Press), pp. 3–4.

52. Walter LaFeber (ed.), *The origins of the Cold War 1941–1947: a historical problem with interpretations and documents* (New York: John Wiley, 1971), pp. 165–167.

53. Ron Robin, *The making of the Cold War enemy: culture and politics in the military-intellectual complex* (Princeton, NJ: Princeton University Press, 2001), p. 168.

54. O'Brian, "Loyalty tests and guilty by association," pp. 597, 599.

55. Quoted from Young-ik Yu, "Unam Rhee Syngmanŭi kaehyŏk, gŏnguk sasang (Syngman Rhee's thoughts about reform and state-building)," *Aseahakbo* (Asian studies journal), No. 20 (1997), p. 40.

56. Asaea Jayumunje Yŏnguso (Asian research institute of the question of freedom), *Ban'gong gyemong dokbon* (Readings in anticommunist enlightenment), (Seoul: Asaea jayumunje yŏnguso, 1967), p. 385. The expression "reddened" is my translation of *gongsanjuŭie muldŭlmyŏn*, meaning literally "dyed in communism."

MORALITY AND IDEOLOGY

1. Chang-dong Lee, *Soji* (Letters to the dead), (Seoul: Munhakgwa Jisŏngsa, 2003, originally published in 1987), p. 258.

2. Amy Murrell Taylor, *The divided family in Civil War America* (Chapel Hill: The University of North Carolina Press, 2005), p. 124.

3. These include the ill-fated love story written by Delphine Baker, the women's rights campaigner and a humanitarian activist during the civil war. The story features two fictional characters, the daughter of Abraham Lincoln and the son of Jefferson Davis, whose amorous relationship was broken by the national crisis in which their fathers stood as contending leaders.

4. Taylor, *The divided family in Civil War America*, p. 63.

5. According to Pham Duy's powerful popular lyric, "Brothers":

> There were two soldiers, both of one family,
> Both of one race – Vietnam,
> There were two soldiers, both of one family,
> Both of one blood – Vietnam.
> There were two soldiers who lay upon a field,
> Both clasping rifles and waiting.
> There were two soldiers who one rosy dawn
> Killed each other for Vietnam.

6. Cited from Joshua Parthow, "War pulls apart Afghan families," *The Washington Post*, April 11, 2011.

7. See Mujib Mashal, "I will kill him: Afghan commander targets son, a Taliban fighter," *The New York Times*, May 15, 2016.

8. Sheila Miyoshi Jager, *Narratives of nation building in Korea: a genealogy of patriotism* (New York: M. E. Sharpe, 2003), p. 136.

9. Sheila Miyoshi Jager and Jiyul Kim, "The Korean War after the Cold War: commemorating the Armistice Agreement in South Korea," in S. M. Jager

and R. Mitter (eds.), *Ruptured histories: war, memory, and the post-Cold War in Asia* (Cambridge, MA: Harvard University Press, 2007), p. 234.

10. Ibid., p. 242. See also Roland Bleiker and Young-Ju Hoang, "Remembering and forgetting the Korean War: from trauma to reconciliation," in Duncan Bell (ed.), *Memory, trauma and world politics: reflections on the relationship between past and present* (London: Palgrave, 2006), pp. 195–212.

11. Choon Soon Kim, *Faithful endurance: an ethnography of Korean family dispersal* (Tucson: University of Arizona Press, 1988). On the other hand, it can also be said that the phenomenon of family separation has somewhat contributed to keeping the ideology of familial solidarity alive even in a highly urbanized, industrialized society such as contemporary South Korea.

12. Hyangjin Lee, *Contemporary Korean cinema: identity, culture and politics* (Manchester: Manchester University Press, 2000), p. 139.

13. Heonik Kwon and Byung-Ho Chung, *North Korea: beyond charismatic politics* (Lanham, MD: Rowman & Littlefield, 2012), pp. 18–26.

14. See, for instance, Carol Delaney, "Father state, motherland, and the birth of modern Turkey," in Sylvia Yanagisako and Carol Delaney (eds.), *Naturalizing power: essays in feminist cultural analysis* (New York: Routledge, 1995), pp. 177–199.

15. Ernest Gellner, *Nations and nationalism* (Oxford: Blackwell, 1986), pp. 181–188.

16. Benedict Anderson, *Imagined communities: reflections on the origin and spread of nationalism* (London: Verso, 2006).

17. The expressions of "thick" versus "thin" relations are cited from Avishai Margalit, *The ethics of memory* (Cambridge, MA: Harvard University Press, 2002).

18. Anderson, *Imagined communities*, p. 217.

19. Ibid., pp. 217–218.

20. For a discussion of related phenomena in pre-1989 Germany, see John Borneman, *Belonging in the two Berlins: kin, state, nation* (Cambridge: Cambridge University Press, 1992), pp. 284–312.

21. See Charles K. Armstrong, *The Koreas* (New York: Routledge, 2007), p. 167.

22. Je-do Oh, "Gŏsujaŭi jŭngŏn (Testimonies by puppet individuals)," *Ban'gong jisik ch'ongsŏ* (Collection of anticommunist knowledge) Vol. 1, (Seoul: Hŭimang Publisher, 1969), p. 5.

23. The expression, "patriotism based on anticommunist democratic spirit," is cited from the national manifesto of patriotic anti-communist civic education (*kukmin gyoyuk hŏnjang*) issued by the South Korean government on December 5, 1968. The manifesto asserted, among other things, the routinization of anti-communism in everyday life. See Kyunggido kyoyuk yŏnguwŏn (Institute of pedagogical research, Kyuinggi province), *Kukmin gyoyuk hŏnjang inyŏm guhyŏnmit ban'gong kyoyuk silchŏn saryejip* (The realization of the national manifesto and examples of anti-communist educational practice), (Suwŏn: Kyunggido kyoyuk yŏnguwŏn, 1971), pp. 261–284.

24. Ibid., p. 309.

25. Christina Klein, *Cold War Orientalism: Asia in the middlebrow imagination, 1945–1961* (Berkeley: University of California Press, 2003).

26. Ibid., p. 37.

27. Ibid., pp. 47–48.
28. Ibid., p. 50.
29. Ibid., p. 37.
30. Ibid., p. 11.
31. Ibid., pp. 191–222.
32. Eleana J. Kim, *Adopted territory: transnational Korean adoptees and the politics of belonging* (Durham, NC: Duke University Press, 2010), p. 76.
33. Eleana Kim, *The origins of Korean adoption: Cold War geopolitics and intimate diplomacy*, US-Korea Institute Working Paper, October 2009.
34. Im-ha Yoo, *Hanguk sosŏlŭi bundan iyagi* (Stories of partition in Korean novels), (Seoul: Ch'aeksesang, 2006), pp. 49–56.
35. Ibid., p. 54.
36. As to postwar cultural production in North Korea, it is also observed that "traditional family values are commonly treated as the most powerful cultural force." Cited from Lee, *Contemporary Korean cinema*, p. 139.
37. Asaea Jayumunje Yŏnguso (Asian research institute of the question of freedom), *Ban'gong gyemong dokbon* (Readings in anti-communist enlightenment), (Seoul: Asaea jayumunje yŏnguso, 1967), p. 17.
38. Ibid., pp. 188–189.
39. Ibid., p. 188.
40. Ibid., pp. 187–188.
41. For an analysis of the film version of this epic story, see Lee, *Contemporary Korean cinema*, pp. 129–135.
42. Bruce Cumings, *The Korean War: a history* (New York: Modern Library, 2010), p. 290.
43. Gregory Henderson, "Korea," in G. Henderson, R. N. Lebow and J. G. Stoessinger (eds.), *Divided nations in a divided world* (New York: David Mckay, 1974), p. 43.
44. Lee, *Soji* (Letters to the dead).
45. David Kehr, "Revisiting the Korean War in a tale of two brothers," *The New York Times*, September 3, 2004.
46. Je-kyu Kang, Ji-hun Han and Sang-don Kim, *Taegukgi hŭinalimyo* (Waving the taegukgi), (Seoul: Communication Books, 2004), pp. 32–33.
47. Ibid., p. 33.
48. Robert R. Williams, *Hegel's ethics of recognition* (Berkeley: University of California Press, 1997), p. 274.
49. Ibid.
50. Ibid.
51. Shlomo Avineri, *Hegel's theory of the modern state* (Cambridge: Cambridge University Press, 1972), p. 134.
52. Bruce Cumings, *North Korea: another country* (New York: The New Press, 2004), p. 107.
53. Mun-Woong Lee, *Bukhan jŏngch'imunhwaŭi hyŏngsŏnggwa gŭ t'ŭkjing* (The formation and characteristics of North Korean political culture), (Seoul: Institute of National Unification, 1976), p. 39.
54. Won-il Kim, *Bulŭi jejŏn* (Feast of fire), (Seoul: Munhakgwa Jisŏngsa, 1997).

55. Carl Schmitt, *Theory of the partisan: intermediate commentary on the concept of the political*, trans. by G. L. Ulmen (New York: Telos Press, 2007), p. xvi.

56. Gwi-sook Gwon, *Giŏkŭi jŏngchi: daeryanghaksalŭi sahoiǐŏk giŏkgwa yŏksajŏk jinsil* (Politics of memory: social memories and historical truths of mass murders), (Seoul: Munhakgwa Jisŏngsa, 2006), p. 59. Mr. Lim Moon-kuk of the Hanrim district, Jeju, survived both the counterinsurgency terror campaign during the April 3 crisis in 1948–1949 and again, in 1953, the preemptive state terror against the survivors of earlier state violence – such as what befell the victims now buried in the One Hundred Ancestors and One Single Descendent cemetery (see Chapter 1). In August 1953, having survived these two rounds of state violence, unlike many of his relatives and neighbors in his highland village, he volunteered to join South Korea's national army, believing that otherwise, he would surely face another life and death crisis and that he and his family would not have the extraordinary luck to live through this one. Cited from his testimony featured in Jeju 4·3 Je50junyŏn Haksul Munhwa Saŏpchujinwiwŏnhŏi (Committee on scholarly and cultural events for the fiftieth anniversary of Jeju April Third), *Jeju 4·3 yujŏkji gihaeng: ilŏbŏrin maŭlŭl chatasŏ* (Visiting Jeju April Third heritages: in search of disappeared villages), (Seoul: Hakminsa, 1998).

57. Sung-chil Kim, *Yŏksa ap'esŏ: han sahakjaŭi 6.25ilgi* (In face of history: a historian's diary of 6.25 [Korean War]), (Seoul: Chang'bi, 2009), p. 231.

58. Personal communication, April 2016. See testimonies available in Jeju 4·3 Yŏnguso (Jeju 4·3 Research Institute), *Ijesa malhaemsuda* (Now we speak out), (Seoul: Hanul, 1989), p. 51; and Kyung-ja Kang, "Gohyangŭi gajok, bukŭi gajok (Families in the homeland, families in North Korea)," in Noriko Ijichi et al. (eds.), *Gohyangŭi gajok, bukŭi gajok* (Families in the homeland, families in North Korea), trans. by Kyung-ja Kim (Seoul: Sŏnin, 2015), p. 140.

59. Samuel S. Kim, "Introduction: managing the Korean conflict," in S. S. Kim (ed.), *Inter-Korean relations: problems and prospects* (New York: Palgrave, 2004), p. 3.

THE QUIET REVOLUTION

1. George Mosse, *Fallen soldiers: reshaping the memory of the world wars* (Oxford: Oxford University Press, 1990).

2. Cited from ibid., p. 27.

3. Philip J. Kain, *Hegel and right: a study of the Philosophy of Right* (Albany: State University of New York, 2018), pp. 91–93.

4. Roberto Esposito, *Communitas: the origin and destiny of community*, trans. by Timothy Campbell (Stanford, CA: Stanford University Press, 2009).

5. For an eye-opening discussion of this concept of ordinary lives, see Veena Das, *Life and words: violence and the descent into the ordinary* (Berkeley: University of California Press, 2007).

6. 1919 is also a distant origin of the Korean War in that after the failure of the March First uprising, the anti-colonial movement of Korea became increasingly bifurcated into their so-called left and right trajectories and orientations.

7. Hannah Arendt, *The human condition* (Chicago: University of Chicago Press, 1958).

8. Young-sun Huh, *Jeju 4·3ŭl mutnŭn nŏege* (To you who ask about Jeju 4·3), (Paju: Sŏhaemunjib, 2014), p. 59.

9. Chan-sik Park, "1947nyŏn 3·1sagŏnŭi yŏksajŏk sŏnggyŏk (The historical character of the March First incident in 1947)," *4.3gwa pyŏnghwa (4.3 and peace)*, Vol. 27 (2017), p. 14.

10. Jeju 4·3 Yŏnguso (Jeju 4·3 Research Institute), *Ijesa malhaemsuda* (Now we speak out), (Seoul: Hanul, 1989), pp. 21–22.

11. Seong-nae Kim, "Lamentations of the dead: the historical imagery of violence in Cheju Island, South Korea," *Journal of Ritual Studies*, Vol. 3, No.2 (1989), pp. 251–285. Also Seong-nae Kim, "The work of memory: ritual laments of the dead and Korea's Cheju massacre," in Janice Boddy and Michael Lambek (eds.), *A companion to the anthropology of religion* (Chichester: Wiley Blackwell, 2013), pp. 223–238.

12. Ki-young Hyun, *Suni samch'on* (Aunt Suni), (Paju: Changbi, 2015, original publication in 1978), p. 55.

13. *Samch'on* or *samch'un* is a broad, flexible interpersonal referential term distinct in Jeju. In mainland Korea, the term refers primarily to a father's brother or a mother's brother. In Jeju, the term, pronounced popularly as *samch'un*, encompasses a father's siblings or a mother's siblings irrespective of gender. It can also apply broadly to any elders or seniors of a community, including relatives, neighbors, or sometimes even strangers.

14. Youngju Ryu, *Writers of the Winter Republic: literature and resistance in Park Chung Hee's Korea* (Honolulu: University of Hawaii Press, 2015).

15. For this reason, one testimony describes the day of multiple domestic ancestral rites in the village as that of a "festive holiday." Jeju 4·3 Yŏnguso (Jeju 4·3 Research Institute), *Ijesa malhaemsuda* (Now we speak out), pp. 82, 125, 140.

16. For a detailed analysis of traditional child adoption practices in the seventeenth to nineteenth centuries for the purpose of securing the ritual order, see Jae-seok Choi, *Hankukgajokjedosayŏngu* (History of Korean family system), (Seoul: Iljisa, 1983), pp. 588–669.

17. Roger L. Janelli and Dawnhee Yim Janelli, *Ancestor worship and Korean society* (Stanford, CA: Stanford University Press, 1982), pp. 156–158.

18. The Jeju writer Kim Su-yeol writes of this practice in his poem *Jochŏn halmang* (The grandmother in Jochŏn Village): "I failed to recover even my son's body. So I prepared his jesa on his birthday (not his death day), and even the raven should not know about this jesa. The rite was done merely on a bowl of fresh water." Su-yeol Kim, "Jochŏn halmang," in Jejujakgahoiŭi (Association of Writers in Jeju), *Baramchŏrŏm ggamaguichŏrŏm* (Like the wind, like the raven), (Seoul: Silchŏnmunjaksa, 1998), pp. 102–103.

19. Kim, "The work of memory," pp. 223–238.

20. Laurel Kendall, *Shamans, housewives, and other restless spirits: women in Korean ritual life* (Honolulu: University of Hawaii Press, 1985).

21. Martina Deuchler, *The Confucian transformation of Korea: a study of society and ideology* (Cambridge, MA: Harvard University Press, 1995).

22. See Kwang-ok Kim, "Jŏhangmunhwawa musokŭirye (The culture of resistance and the ritual of shamanism)," *Hanguk munhwainlyuhak* (Korean cultural anthropology), Vol. 23 (1992), pp. 131–172.
23. Ibid.
24. See the material available online at www.genocide.or.kr. See also Jae-Jung Suh (ed.), *Truth and reconciliation in South Korea: between the present and future of the Korean wars* (New York: Routledge, 2012).
25. Dong-choon Kim, *The unending Korean War: a social history*, trans. by S. Kim (Larkspur, CA: Tamal Vista Publications, 2009).
26. Myung-lim Park, *Yŏksawa jisikgwa sahoi: hangukjŏnjaeing ihaewa hanguksahoi* (History, knowledge and society: understanding the Korean War and understanding Korean society), (Seoul: Nanam, 2011), p. 296.
27. Ibid., p. 291.
28. Interview with Mr. Kim Du-yon, former chair of the association, in Jeju City, South Korea, January 2007.
29. Sang-hun Choe, "A Korean village torn apart from within mends itself," *The New York Times*, February 21, 2008.
30. Gurimji pyŏnchanwiwŏnhoi (Editorial Committee of Gurim Chronicles), *Honam myŏngchon Gurim: gurimsaramduli sonsu ssŭn maŭlgongdongche iyagi* (A distinguished village in Honam region: stories of a village community written by the villagers themselves), (Seoul: Libuk, 2006), p. 7.
31. Hyun-jong Park, "Jipdanjŏk jŏnjaenggyŏnghŏmŭi giŏkgwa ginyŏm (Memory and memorialization of collective war experience)," Master's thesis (Chonnam University, 2005), p. 62.
32. Ryung-kyung Lee, "Hankukjŏnjaeingjŏnhu jwailgwanryŏn yŏsŏngyujokŭi gyŏnghŏmyŏngu (Research on bereaved women's experience regarding [the assault] on the Left before and after the Korean War)," Master's thesis (Sungkonghoe University, 2003), p. 82.
33. Hui-gon Kim, "Kwon O-seol, gŭrŭl saeropge pyŏnggahanda (Kwon O-seol, a new view of his life), *Byŏnggoksegok* (Writings of Byŏnggok and his descendants), (Daegu: Daebosa), p. 942.
34. Byung-wook Chung, *Sikminji bulonyŏljŏn* (Chronicle of subversives against colonialism), (Seoul: Yŏksabipyŏngsa, 2013), p. 210.
35. Hui-gon Kim, *Andongŭi dokripundongsa* (History of independence movement in Andong), (Andong: Yongnamsa, 1999), p. 401.
36. Ibid., p. 402.
37. Hue-Tam Ho Tai, *Millenarianism and peasant politics in Vietnam* (Cambridge, MA: Harvard University Press, 1983).
38. Mi-young Kim, *Gail Andongkwonssi, 6baeknyŏn samŭi yŏksa* (The Kwons in Gail, Andong, a history of their lives for six hundred years), (Andong: Hankukgukhakjinhŭngwŏn, 2009), pp. 143–147.
39. Aewolup (Aewol district office), *Aewolupji* (Chronicles of Aewol District), p. 167.
40. Hankukbangonggyŏyukyŏnguwŏn (Korean Institute for Anticommunist Education), *Bangonganbojŏnsŏ* (Collections of essays on anticommunist security), p. 283.

41. See Jeju 4·3 Yŏnguso (Jeju 4·3 Research Institute), *Ijesa malhaemsuda* (Now we speak out), p. 124.

42. Ibid., p. 41.

43. Jung-a Kim, "4.3ŭi jŭngŏn (Testimony to 4.3)," *4.3gwa pyŏnghwa* (4.3 and peace), Vol. 33 (2018), p. 50.

44. A full text of this poem in Korean is available online at www.Jeju43.org/out look/outlook-1_27.asp?area=bukJeju.

45. See Heonik Kwon, "The Korean War and Sino-North Korean friendship," *The Asia-Pacific Journal*, Vol. 11, Issue 32, No. 4 (August 12, 2013), available online at https://apjjf.org/2013/11/32/Heonik-Kwon/3982/article.html.

46. *Voice of America* broadcast, March 31, 2016.

47. Michael Allen, *Until the last man comes home: POWs, MIAs, and the unending Vietnam War* (Durham: University of North Carolina Press, 2009).

48. Charles K. Armstrong, *Tyranny of the weak: North Korea and the world, 1950–1992* (New York: Columbia University Press, 2013).

49. See Patrick McEachern, *Inside the red box: North Korea's post-totalitarian politics* (New York: Columbia University Press, 2010); and Sonia Ryang, *Reading North Korea: an ethnological inquiry* (Cambridge, MA: Harvard University Press, 2010).

50. Hazel Smith, *North Korea: markets and military rule* (Cambridge: Cambridge University Press, 2015).

51. Comments on the eminent late Jeju poet Kwang-hyup Kim's lytic, "Hŭimang'ga (Song of hope)," available online at http://blog.ohmynews.com/rufdml/81329.

52. Young-hoon Kim's "Chudosa (Words of commemoration)" at the 56th province-wide commemoration of the victims of Jeju April Third incident, Jeju Peace Park, April 3, 2004.

53. Young-sun Huh, *Jeju 4·3ŭl mutnŭn nŏege* (To you who ask about Jeju 4·3), p. 239.

CONCLUSION

1. Thomas W. Laqueur, "Memory and naming in the Great War," in J. R. Gillis (ed.), *Commemorations: the politics of national identity* (Princeton, NJ: Princeton University Press, 1994), p. 151.

2. Edward Madigan, "St. Symphorien Military Cemetery, the Battle of Mons and British Centenary commemoration," *World War One centenary: continuations and beginnings* (June 13, 2013), available online at http://ww1centenary .oucs.ox.ac.uk/?p=2658. See also Heonik Kwon, "Bürgerkriegstote in Vietnam und Europa," *Mittelweg 36* (2014).

3. See Mischa Gabowitsch, Fordula Gdaniec and Ekaterina Makhotina (eds.), *Kriegsgedenken als event: der 9. Mai 2015 im postsozialistischen Europa* (Paderborn: Ferdinand Schöningh, 2017). See also Ewa Ochman, *Post-communist Poland: contested pasts and future identities* (New York: Routledge, 2013), pp. 3–5; Paul Stangl, "The Soviet war memorial in Treptow, Berlin," *Geographical Review*, Vol. 93, No. 2 (2003), pp. 230–231; and Berthold Forssman, "The controversy over Soviet monuments in eastern Europe,"

Eurotopics (April 18, 2016), available online at http://archiv.eurotopics.net/e
n/home/presseschau/archiv/magazin/kultur-verteilerseite-neu/denkmal
streit_2007_05/debatte_denkmalstreit_2007_05/.

4. See P. E. Digeser, *Friendship reconsidered: what it means and how it matters to
politics* (New York: Columbia University Press, 2016); John von Heyking and
Richard Avramenko (eds.), *Friendship and politics: essays in political thought*
(Notre Dame, IN: University of Notre Dame Press, 2008). For debates
concerning specifically American society and democracy, see
Robert Putnam, *Bowling alone: the collapse and revival of American community*
(New York: Simon and Schuster, 2000); and Danielle Allen, *Talking to
strangers: anxieties of citizenship since Brown v. Board of Education* (Chicago:
University of Chicago Press, 2004).

5. Jacques Derrida, *The politics of friendship* (London: Verso, 2006).

6. See Digeser, *Friendship reconsidered*, pp. 217–234. Also
Felix Berenskoetter, "Friends, there are no friends? An intimate reframing
of the international," *Millennium: Journal of International Studies*, Vol. 35,
No. 3 (2007), pp. 647–676.

7. Similar criticism of Hobbes's notion of the natural state has been fairly
familiar to modern anthropological research. See, for instance,
Marshall Sahlins, *Evolution and culture* (Ann Arbor: University of
Michigan Press, 1960); Signe Howell and Roy Willis (eds.), *Societies at
peace: anthropological perspectives* (London Routledge, 1989); Leslie
E. Sponsel and Thomas Gregor (eds.), *The anthropology of peace and nonviolence* (Boulder, CO: Lynne Rienner, 1994). For an interesting argument
that despite these critiques, Hobbes's presupposition on the state of nature
has had a formative impact on anthropological research, especially on
theories of exchange: Raymond Corbey, "Laying aside the spear:
Hobbesian warre and the Maussian gift," in Ton Otto, Henrik Thrane
and Helle Vandkilde (eds.), *Warfare and society: archaeological and social
anthropological perspectives* (Aarhus: Aarhus University Press, 2006), pp.
29–36.

8. Carl Schmitt, *The concept of the political* (Chicago: University of Chicago
Press, 1996).

9. Berenskoetter, "Friends, there are no friends?" pp. 670–671.

10. Reinhart Koselleck, *Futures past: on the semantics of historical time*, trans. by
Keith Tribe (New York: Columbia University Press, 2004), pp. 56–57.
Koselleck makes an emphatic observation: "Since 1945 we have lived
between latent and open civil wars whose terribleness can still be outdone
by a nuclear war, as if the civil wars that rage around the world are, reversing
the traditional interpretation, our ultimate savior from total destruction."
Cited from Koselleck, *Futures past*, p. 57.

11. Edward Shorter, *The making of the modern family* (New York: Basic Books,
1975).

12. Instead, we may understand this condition of exclusion in terms of the
specter of kinship and of kinship's haunting presence in the modern world,
following Derrida's other works on the inseparability of reason and exclusion,
and on the impossibility of perfect exclusion that he expresses with the idiom

of specters. Jacques Derrida, *Specters of Marx: the state of the debt, the work of mourning, and the new international* (London: Routledge, 1994).

13. Camille Robcis, *The law of kinship: anthropology, psychoanalysis, and the family in France* (Ithaca, NY: Cornell University Press, 2013).

14. Jürgen Habermas, *The structural transformation of the public sphere: an inquiry into a category of bourgeois society*, trans. by Thomas Berger and Frederik Lawrence (Cambridge, MA: MIT Press, 1989).

15. Benedict Anderson, *Imagined communities: reflections on the origin and spread of nationalism* (London: Verso, 2006), p. 148.

16. Derrida, *The politics of kinship*, p. viii.

17. Naoko Shimazu, *Japanese society at war: death, memory and the Russo-Japanese war* (Cambridge: Cambridge University Press, 2009), p. 281.

18. Stephen Kern, *The culture of time and space, 1880–1918* (Cambridge, MA: Harvard University Press, 1989), p. 65.

19. For a recent example, see Patrick J. Houlihan, *Catholicism and the Great War: religion and everyday life in Germany and Austria-Hungary, 1914–1922* (Cambridge: Cambridge University Press, 2015).

20. Ibid., pp. 100, 105.

21. Jay Winter, *Sites of memory, sites of mourning: the Great War in European cultural history* (Cambridge: Cambridge University Press, 1998).

22. See the document available online at www.vallauris-golfe-juan.fr/Picasso .html?lang=en.

23. See the document available online at www.all-art.org/art_20th_century/pica sso13.html.

24. Young-mok Chung, "Picassowa hankukjŏnjaeng (Picasso and the Korean War)," *Seoyangmisulsahakhoi nonmunjib* (Proceedings of the association for occidental art history), No. 8 (1996), pp. 241–258.

25. Kirsten Hoving Keen, "Picasso's communist interlude: the murals of 'War' and 'Peace'," *The Burlington Magazine*, Vol. 122, No. 928 (1980), p. 467.

26. Young-taik Park, *Gajokŭl gŭrida: gŭrimsokŭro dŭlŏon gajokŭi ŏlguldŭl* (Painting the family: faces of family that have entered into fine art), (Seoul: Bada Publisher, 2009). See also Jun-mo Chung, *Hankuk misul, jŏnjaengŭl gŭrida* (The Korean art that paints the Korean War), (Seoul: Maronie Books, 2014).

27. Cited from Emile Durkheim, *Sociology and philosophy*, trans. by D. F. Pocock (London: Cohen & West, 1953), p. xxxix.

Select Bibliography

Aewolup (Aewol district office), *Aewolupji* (Chronicles of Aewol District).

Allen, Danielle, *Talking to strangers: anxieties of citizenship since Brown v. Board of Education* (Chicago: University of Chicago Press, 2004).

Allen, Michael, *Until the last man comes home: POWs, MIAs, and the unending Vietnam War* (Durham: University of North Carolina Press, 2009).

Anderson, Benedict, *Imagined communities: reflections on the origin and spread of nationalism* (London: Verso, 2006).

Andong Daehakgyo Andong Munwah Yŏnguso (Research Institute of Andong Culture, Andong University), *Andong Gail maul* (Gail village of Andong), (Seoul: Yemunsŏwŏn, 2006).

Arendt, Hannah, *The human condition* (Chicago: University of Chicago Press, 1958).

Armitage, David, *Civil wars: a history in ideas* (New Haven, CT: Yale University Press, 2017).

Armstrong, Charles K., *The Koreas* (New York: Routledge, 2007).

Armstrong, Charles K., *Tyranny of the weak: North Korea and the world, 1950–1992* (New York: Columbia University Press, 2013).

Asaea Jayumunje Yŏnguso (Asian research institute of the question of freedom), *Ban'gong gyemong dokbon* (Readings in anti-communist enlightenment), (Seoul: Asaea jayumunje yŏnguso, 1967).

Avineri, Shlomo, *Hegel's theory of the modern state* (Cambridge: Cambridge University Press, 1972).

Barkan, Elazar, "Individual versus group rights in Western philosophy and the law," in Nyla R. Branscombe and Bertjan Doosje (eds.), *Collective guilt: international perspectives* (Cambridge: Cambridge University Press, 2004), pp.309–319.

Berenskoetter, Felix, "Friends, there are no friends? An intimate reframing of the international," *Millennium: Journal of International Studies*, Vol. 35, No. 3 (2007), pp.647–676.

Bleiker, Roland and Young-Ju Hoang, "Remembering and forgetting the Korean War: from trauma to reconciliation," in Duncan Bell (ed.), *Memory, trauma and world politics: reflections on the relationship between past and present* (London: Palgrave, 2006), pp. 195–212.

Bloch, Maurice, "The long term and the short term: the economic and political significance of the morality of kinship," in Jack Goody (ed.), *The character of kinship* (Cambridge: Cambridge University Press, 1973), pp. 75–87.

Borneman, John, *Being in the two Berlins: kin, state, nation* (Cambridge: Cambridge University Press, 1992).

Borstelmann, Thomas, *Apartheid's reluctant uncle: the United States and southern Africa in the early Cold War* (New York: Oxford University Press, 1993).

Bourdieu, Pierre, *Outline of a theory of practice* (Cambridge: Cambridge University Press, 1977).

Brook, Timothy, *Collaboration: Japanese agents and local elites in wartime China* (Cambridge, MA: Harvard University Press, 2005).

Bull, Hedley, *The anarchical society: a study of order in world politics* (New York: Columbia University Press, 1977).

Carsten, Janet, *After kinship* (Cambridge: Cambridge University Press, 2004).

Chen, Jian, *Mao's China and the Cold War* (Durham: University of North Carolina Press, 2000).

Chen, Jian, "China's changing policies toward the Third World and the end of the global Cold War," in Artemy M. Kalinovsky and Sergey Radchenko (eds.), *The end of the Cold War and the Third World: new perspectives on regional conflict* (London: Routledge, 2011), pp. 101–121.

Cho, Eun, "Jŏnjaenggwa bundanŭi ilsanghwawa giŏkŭi jŏngchi: 'wŏlnam'gajokgwa 'wŏlbuk'gajok janyŏdŭlŭl jungsimŭro (The routinization of war and partition and the politics of memory. testimonies by children of south-crossing and north-crossing families)," in Gwi-ok Kim et al. (eds.), *Jŏnjaengŭi giŏkgwa naengjŏnŭi gusul* (Memories of war and testimonies to the Cold War), (Seoul: Sŏnin, 2008).

Cho, Eun, "Bundanŭi gin gŭrimja (The long shadows of the national partition)," in Han-hui Ham et al. (eds.), *Gusulsaro ilnŭn hankukjŏnjaeing* (Reading the Korean War through oral histories), (Seoul: Humanist, 2011).

Cho, Sung-mi and Gwi-ok Kim, "Wŏlbukin yugajokŭi bangongjŏk ŏkapgwa 'wŏlbuk'ŭi ŭimich'egye (Anticommunist repressions against the families of individuals who moved to North Korea and the meanings of 'moving to North')," in Gwi-ok Kim (ed.), *Isan gajok, 'bangong jŏnsa'do 'ppalgaeng'i' do anin* (Divided families: neither "anticommunist warriors" nor "red communists"), (Seoul: Yŏksabipyŏngsa, 2004).

Cho, Young-min, "Jŏnhyangjedowa gamokŭi yaman (The system of ideological conversion and the barbarity of the prison system)," in Byung-chon Lee and Gwang-il Lee (eds.), *20segi hankukŭi yaman* (The twentieth-century barbarities in Korea), (Seoul: Ilbit, 2001).

Choe, Sang-hun, "A Korean village torn apart from within mends itself," *The New York Times*, February 21, 2008.

Choi, In-hun, *The square: a novel*, trans. by S. Kim (McLean, IL: Dalkey Archive Press, 2014).

Choi, Jae-seok, *Hankukgajokjedosayŏngu* (History of Korean family system), (Seoul: Iljisa, 1983).

Chung, Byung-wook, *Sikminji bulonyŏljŏn* (Chronicle of subversives against colonialism), (Seoul: Yŏksabipyŏngsa, 2013).

Chung, Chin O., *P'yongyang between Peking and Moscow: North Korea's involvement in the Sino-Soviet dispute, 1958–1975* (Tuscaloosa: University of Alabama Press, 1978).

Chung, Jun-mo, *Hankuk misul, jŏnjaengŭl gŭrida* (The Korean art that paints the Korean War), (Seoul: Maronie Books, 2014).

Chung, Keun-sik et al. (eds.), *Gurim yŏngu: maŭlgongdongcheŭi gujowa byŏndong* (Gurim studies: structure and change in village community), (Seoul: Kyunginmunhwasa, 2003).

Chung, Young-mok, "Picassowa hankukjŏnjaeng (Picasso and the Korean War)," *Seoyangmisulsahakhoi nonmunjib* (Proceedings of the association for occidental art history), No. 8 (1996), pp. 241–258.

Colley, Linda, "What gets called 'civil war'?" *The New York Review of Books*, Vol. 64, No. 10 (2017), pp. 42–43.

Conway-Lanz, Sahr, *Collateral damage: Americans, non-combatant immunity, and atrocity after World War II* (New York: Routledge, 2006).

Corbey, Raymond, "Laying aside the spear: Hobbesian warre and the Maussian gift," in Ton Otto, Henrik Thrane and Helle Vandkilde (eds.), *Warfare and society: archaeological and social anthropological perspectives* (Aarhus: Aarhus University Press, 2006), pp. 29–36.

Cumings, Bruce, *North Korea: another country* (New York: The New Press, 2004).

Cumings, Bruce, *The Korean War: a history* (New York: Modern Library, 2010).

Daegŏmchalchŏng josaguk (National Prosecutor's Office Investigation Bureau), *Jwaiksagŏnsillok*, 11gwŏn (Chronicle of leftist incidents, Vol. 11), (Seoul: National Prosecutor's Office, 1975).

Daehanjŏksipjasa (Korea Red Cross), *Isangajokchatgi 60nyŏn* (60 years in search for separated families), (Seoul: Daehanjŏksipjasa, 2005).

Das, Veena, *Life and words: violence and the descent into the ordinary* (Berkeley: University of California Press, 2007).

Delaney, Carol, "Father state, motherland, and the birth of modern Turkey," in S. Yanagisako and C. Delaney (eds.), *Naturalizing power: essays in feminist cultural analysis* (New York: Routledge, 1995), pp. 177–199.

Derrida, Jacques, *Specters of Marx: the state of the debt, the work of mourning, and the new international* (London: Routledge, 1994).

Derrida, Jacques, *The politics of friendship* (London: Verso, 2006).

Deuchler, Martina, *The Confucian transformation of Korea: a study of society and ideology* (Cambridge, MA: Harvard University Press, 1995).

Digeser, P. E., *Friendship reconsidered: what it means and how it matters to politics* (New York: Columbia University Press, 2016).

Donghak Yŏnguhoi (Association of Donghak Friends), *Yŏnguhoi bisa* (Unknown histories of Yŏnguhoi), 1989.

Douglas, Mary, *Purity and danger: an analysis of concepts of pollution and taboo* (London: Routledge, 1966).

Durkheim, Emile, *Sociology and philosophy*, trans. by D. F. Pocock (London: Cohen & West, 1953).

Durkheim, Emile, "Two laws of penal evolution," T. A. Jones and Andrew T. Scull (trans.) *Economy and Society*, Vol. 2, No. 3 (1973 [1900]), pp. 285–308.

Esposito, Roberto, *Communitas: the origin and destiny of community*, trans. by Timothy Campbell (Stanford, CA: Stanford University Press, 2009).

Evans-Pritchard, E. E., "The Nuer of the southern Sudan," in M. Fortes and E. E. Evans-Pritchard (eds.), *African political systems* (London: Oxford University Press, 1940), pp. 272–296.

Feuchtwang, Stephan, *After the event: the transmission of grievous loss in Germany, China and Taiwan* (Oxford: Berghahn, 2011).

Field, Douglas, "Introduction," in D. Field (ed.), *American Cold War culture* (Edinburgh: Edinburgh University Press), pp. 1–16.

Flynn, Thomas R., "Foucault and historical nominalism," in Harold A. Durfee and David F. T. Rodier (eds.), *Phenomenology and beyond: the self and its language* (Dordrecht: Kluwer Academic Publishers, 1989), pp. 134–147.

Foley, James A., "'Ten million families': statistics or metaphor?" *Korean Studies*, Vol. 25, No. 1 (2001), pp. 96–110.

Forssman, Berthold, "The controversy over Soviet monuments in eastern Europe," *Eurotopics* (April 18, 2016), available online at http://archiv.eurotopics.net/en/home/presseschau/archiv/magazin/kultur-verteilerseite-neu/denkmalstreit_2007_05/debatte_denkmalstreit_2007_05/.

Fortes, Meyer, *Kinship and the social order: the legacy of Lewis Henry Morgan* (Chicago: Aldine, 1969).

Foucault, Michel, *Discipline and punish: the birth of the prison*, trans. by Alan Sheridan (New York: Penguin, 1991).

Foucault, Michel, *Dits et écrits 1, 1954–1975* (Paris: Gallimard, 2001).

Foucault, Michel, *The Punitive society: lectures at the Collège de France, 1972–1973* (London: Palgrave, 2015).

Gabowitsch, Mischa, Fordula Gdaniec and Ekaterina Makhotina (eds.), *Kriegsgedenken als event: der 9. Mai 2015 im postsozialistischen Europa* (Paderborn: Ferdinand Schöningh, 2017).

Gatrell, Peter, *The making of the modern refugee* (Oxford: Oxford University Press, 2013).

Geertz, Clifford, *The interpretation of cultures* (New York: Basic Books, 1973).

Gelézeau, Valérie, Koen De Ceuster and Alain Delissen, "Introduction," in V. Gelézeau, K. De Ceuster and A. Delissen (eds.), *De-bordering Korea: tangible and intangible legacies of the Sunshine Policy* (London: Routledge, 2013), pp. 1–10.

Gellner, Ernest, *Nations and nationalism* (Oxford: Blackwell, 1986).

Ginzburg, Carlo, "Microhistory: two or three things that I know about it," *Critical Inquiry*, Vol. 20, No. 1 (1993), pp. 10–35.

Gluckman, Max, *Custom and conflict in Africa* (Oxford: Blackwell, 1955).

Goodrich, Peter, "Veritie hidde: amity, law, miscellany," *Law and Humanities*, Vol. 11, No. 1 (2017), pp. 137–155.

Grandin, Greg, *The last colonial massacre: Latin America in the Cold War* (Chicago: University of Chicago Press, 2004).

Gurimji Pyŏnchanwiwŏnhoi (Editorial Committee of Gurim Chronicles), *Honam myŏngchon Gurim: gurimsaramduli sonsu ssŭn maŭlgongdongche iyagi* (A distinguished village in Honam region: stories of a village community written by the villagers themselves), (Seoul: Libuk, 2006).

Gwon, Gwi-sook, *Giŏkŭi jŏngch'i: daeryanghaksalŭi sahoijŏk giŏkgwa yŏksajŏk jinsil* (Politics of memory: social memories and historical truths of mass violence), (Seoul: Munhwakgwa Jisŏngsa, 2006).

Habermas, Jürgen, *The structural transformation of the public sphere: an inquiry into a category of bourgeois society*, trans. by Thomas Berger and Frederik Lawrence (Cambridge, MA: MIT Press, 1989).

Halliday, Fred, *The making of the second Cold War* (London: Verso, 1987).

Halliday, Jon and Bruce Cumings, *Korea: the unknown war* (London: Viking, 1988).

Han, Kang, "While the U.S. talks of war, South Korea shudders: there is no war scenario that ends in victory," *The New York Times*, October 7, 2017.

Han, Seong-hoon, *Jŏnjaeng'gwa inmin* (War and people), (Seoul: Dolbege, 2012).

Hankukbangonggyŏyukkyŏnguwŏn (Korean Institute for Anticommunist Education), *Bangonganbojŏnsŏ* (Collections of essays on anticommunist security).

Hankukjŏnjaegjŏnhu Minganinhaksal Jinsangkyumyŏng Bŏmkukminuiwŏnhoe (All-national Committee on the Investigation of Civilian Massacres Before and After the Korean War), *100man minganinhaksal, gŭ bŭlaekbaksŭrŭl yŏlda* (Massacre of a million civilians, opening its black box), (Seoul: Uinmedia, 2006).

Hanley, Charles J., Sang-Hun Choe and Martha Mendoza, *The bridge at No Gun Ri* (New York: Henry Holt, 2001).

Hendershot, Cynthia, *Anti-communism and popular culture in mid-century America* (Jefferson, NC: McFarland, 2003).

Henderson, Gregory, "Korea," in G. Henderson, R. N. Lebow and J. G. Stoessinger (eds.), *Divided nations in a divided world* (New York: David Mckay, 1974), pp. 43–98.

Herbarch, Sharon, "Afghan families divided, villages uprooted," *Los Angeles Times*, July 26, 1992.

Hong, Sun-gwon, *Jŏnjaeng'gwa gukga pp'okryok* (War and state violence), (Seoul: Sonin, 2012).

Houlihan, Patrick J., *Catholicism and the Great War: religion and everyday life in Germany and Austria-Hungary, 1914–1922* (Cambridge: Cambridge University Press, 2015).

Howell, Signe and Roy Willis (eds.), *Societies at peace: anthropological perspectives* (London: Routledge, 1989).

Huh, Young-sun, *Jeju 4·3 ŭl mutnŭn nŏege* (To you who ask about Jeju 4·3), (Paju: Sŏhaemunjib, 2014).

Hwang, Su-kyoung, "South Korea, the United States and emergency powers during the Korean War," *The Asia-Pacific Journal*, Vol. 12, Issue 5 (January 30, 2014), available online at https://apjjf.org/2014/12/5/Su-kyoung-Hwang/4069/article.html.

Hyun, Gil-on, *Gwangye* (Relations), (Seoul: Koryŏwŏn, 2001).

Hyun, Ki-young, *Suni samch'on* (Aunt Suni), (Paju: Changbi, 2015, original publication in 1978).

Jager, Sheila Miyoshi, *Narratives of nation building in Korea: a genealogy of patriotism* (New York: M. E. Sharpe, 2003).

Jager, Sheila Miyoshi and Jiyul Kim, "The Korean War after the Cold War: commemorating the Armistice Agreement in South Korea," in S. M. Jager and R. Mitter (eds.), *Ruptured histories: war, memory, and the post-Cold War in Asia* (Cambridge, MA: Harvard University Press, 2007), pp. 233–265.

Janelli, Roger L. and Dawnhee Yim Janelli, *Ancestor worship and Korean society* (Stanford, CA: Stanford University Press, 1982).

Janelli, Roger L. and Dawnhee Yim, "South Korea's great transformation (1960–1995)," *Haksulwŏnnonmunjip* (Proceedings of the Korean National Academy of Sciences), Vol. 55, No. 1 (2016), pp. 53–120.

Jeju 4·3 Je50junyŏn Haksul Munhwa Saŏpchujinwiwŏnhŏi (Committee on scholarly and cultural events for the fiftieth anniversary of Jeju April Third), *Jeju 4·3 yujŏkji gihaeng: ilŏbŏrin maŭlŭl chatasŏ* (Visiting Jeju April Third heritages: in search of disappeared villages), (Seoul: Hakminsa, 1998).

Jeju 4·3 Yŏnguso (Jeju 4·3 Research Institute), *Ijesa malhaemsuda* (Now we speak out), (Seoul: Hanul, 1989).

Jinsilgwa hwahoi uiwŏnhoi (National Truth and Reconciliation Commission), *Jinhwaui 2007nyŏn sangbangi josabogosŏ* (Truth and Reconciliation Commission investigation report for the first half of 2007), (Seoul: Truth and Reconciliation Commission, 2007).

Jinsilgwa hwahoi uiwŏnhoi (National Truth and Reconciliation Commission), *Hankukjŏnjaeing jŏnhu minganin jipdanhŭisaeing gwanlyŏn 2007nyŏn yuhaebalgul bogosŏ* (2007 recovery report on mass civilian victims around the Korean War period), Vol. 1 (Seoul: Hakyŏnmunhwasa, 2008).

Kain, Philip J., *Hegel and right: a study of the Philosophy of Right* (Albany: State University of New York, 2018).

Kalyvas, Stathis N., *The logic of violence in civil war* (Cambridge: Cambridge University Press, 2006).

Kang, Je-kyu, Ji-hun Han and Sang-don Kim, *Taegukgi hŭinalimyo* (Waving the taegukgi), (Seoul: Communication Books, 2004).

Kang, Kyung-ja, "Gohyangŭi gajok, bukŭi gajok (Families in the homeland, families in North Korea)," in Noriko Ijichi et al. (eds.), *Gohyangŭi gajok, bukŭi gajok* (Families in the homeland, families in North Korea), trans. by Kyung-ja Kim (Seoul: Sŏnin, 2015), pp. 121–168.

Keen, Kirsten Hoving, "Picasso's communist interlude: the murals of 'War' and 'Peace'," *The Burlington Magazine*, Vol. 122, No. 928 (1980), pp. 464–470.

Kehr, David, "Revisiting the Korean War in a tale of two brothers," *The New York Times*, September 3, 2004.

Kendall, Laurel, *Shamans, housewives, and other restless spirits: women in Korean ritual life* (Honolulu: University of Hawaii Press, 1985).

Kern, Stephen, *The culture of time and space, 1880–1918* (Cambridge, MA: Harvard University Press, 1989).

Kim, Choon Soon, *Faithful endurance: an ethnography of Korean family dispersal* (Tucson: University of Arizona Press, 1988).

Kim, Dong-choon, *The unending Korean War: a social history*, trans. by S. Kim (Larkspur, CA: Tamal Vista Publications, 2009).

Kim, Dong-choon, "Hangukjŏnjaeng' 60nyŏn, hanbandowa segye (Sixty years after the Korean War, the Korean peninsula and the world)," *Yŏksabipyŏng* (Historical criticism), No. 91 (2010), pp. 152–181.

Kim, Eleana J., *The origins of Korean adoption: Cold War geopolitics and intimate diplomacy*, US-Korea Institute Working Paper, October 2009.

Kim, Eleana J., *Adopted territory: transnational Korean adoptees and the politics of belonging* (Durham, NC: Duke University Press, 2010).

Kim, Gwi-ok, *Isan gajok, 'bangong jŏnsa'do 'ppalgaeng'i' do anin* (Divided families: neither "anticommunist warriors" nor "red communists"), (Seoul: Yŏksabipyŏngsa, 2004).

Kim, Hui-gon, *Andongŭi dokripundongsa* (History of independence movement in Andong), (Andong: Yongnamsa, 1999).

Kim, Hui-gon, "Hangukdokripundonggwa jŏntongmyŏngga (Korean independence movement and traditional families)," *Gukgabohunchŏ haksulnonmunjip I* (The Korean Ministry of Patriots and Veterans Affairs collection of academic papers, Vol. 1), (Daejeon: Daejeon University, 2005).

Kim, Hui-gon, "Kwon O-seol, gŭrŭl saeropge pyŏnggahanda (Kwon O-seol, a new view of his life)," *Byŏnggoksegok* (Writings of Byŏnggok and his descendants), (Daegu: Daebosa).

Kim, Jung-a, "4.3ŭi jŭngŏn (Testimony to 4.3)," *4.3gwa pyŏnghwa* (4.3 and peace), Vol. 33 (2018), pp. 48–51.

Kim, Ki-jin, *Ggŭtnaji anŭn jŏnjaeng: gukminbodoyŏngmaeng, busan kyungnam jiyŏk* (The unfinished war: national guidance alliance, Pusan-Kyungnam region), (Seoul: Yoksabipyŏngsa, 2002).

Kim, Kwang-ok, "Jŏhangmunhwawa musokŭirye (The culture of resistance and the ritual of shamanism)," *Hangukmunhwainlyuhak* (Korean cultural anthropology), Vol. 23 (1992), pp. 131–172.

Kim, Kwang-ok, "Jŏntongjŏk 'gwangye'ŭi hyundaejŏk silch'ŏn (Modern practice of traditional relations)," *Hankukmunhwainlyuhak* (Korean cultural anthropology), Vol. 33, No. 2 (2000), pp. 7–48.

Kim, Kyung-hak et al. (eds.), *Jŏnjaenggwa giŏk* (War and memories), (Seoul: Hanulakademi, 2005).

Kim, Mi-young, *Gail Andongkwonssi, 6baeknyŏn samŭi yŏksa* (The Kwons in Gail, Andong, a history of their lives for six hundred years), (Andong: Hankukgukhakjinhŭngwŏn, 2009).

Kim, Nan, *Memory, reconciliation, and reunions in South Korea: crossing the divide* (Lanham, MD: Lexington, 2016).

Kim, Samuel S., "Introduction: managing the Korean conflict," in S. S. Kim (ed.), *Inter-Korean relations: problems and prospects* (New York: Palgrave, 2004), pp. 1–20.

Kim, Seong-nae, "Lamentations of the dead: the historical imagery of violence in Cheju Island, South Korea," *Journal of Ritual Studies*, Vol. 3, No.2 (1989), pp. 251–285.

Kim, Seong-nae, "The work of memory: ritual laments of the dead and Korea's Cheju massacre," in Janice Boddy and Michael Lambek (eds.), *A companion to the anthropology of religion* (Chichester: Wiley Blackwell, 2013), pp. 223–238.

Kim, Sung-chil, *Yŏksa ap'esŏ: han sahakjaŭi 6.25ilgi* (In face of history: a historian's diary of 6.25 [Korean War]), (Seoul: Chang'bi, 2009).

Kim, Su-yeol, "Jochŏn halmang," in Jejujakgahoiŭi (Association of Writers in Jeju), *Baramchŏrŏm ggamaguichŏrŏm* (Like the wind, like the raven), (Seoul: Silchŏnmunjaksa, 1998).

Kim, Won-il, *Bulŭi jejŏn* (Feast of fire), (Seoul: Munhakgwa Jisŏngsa, 1997).

Kim, Yongho, *North Korean foreign policy: security dilemma and succession* (Lanham, MD: Lexington Books, 2011).

Klein, Christina, *Cold War Orientalism: Asia in the middlebrow imagination, 1945–1961* (Berkeley: University of California Press, 2003).

Kleinschmidt, Harald, "The family of nations as an element of the ideology of colonialism," *Journal of the History of International Law*, Vol. 18 (2016), pp. 278–316.

Koselleck, Reinhart, *Futures past: on the semantics of historical time*, trans. by K. Tribe (New York: Columbia University Press, 2004).

Koterski, Joseph W., "Introduction," in Karl Jaspers, *The question of German guilt*, trans. by E. B. Ashton (New York: Fordham University Press, 2000), pp. vii–xxii.

Kwon, Heonik, *Ghosts of war in Vietnam* (Cambridge: Cambridge University Press, 2008).

Kwon, Heonik, "Ghosts of war and the spirit of cosmopolitanism," *History of Religions* Vol. 48, No. 1 (2008), pp. 22–42.

Kwon, Heonik, "Excavating the history of collaboration," *The Asia-Pacific Journal*, Vol. 6, Issue 7 (July 2, 2008), available online at https://apjjf.org/-Heonik-Kwon/2801/article.html.

Kwon, Heonik, "The Korean War and Sino-North Korean friendship," *The Asia-Pacific Journal*, Vol. 11, Issue 32, No. 4 (August 12, 2013), available online at https://apjjf.org/2013/11/32/Heonik-Kwon/3982/article.html.Kwon, Heonik, "Bürgerkriegstote in Vietnam und Europa," *Mittelweg 36* (2014).

Kwon, Heonik and Byung-Ho Chung, *North Korea: beyond charismatic politics* (Lanham, MD: Rowman & Littlefield, 2012).

Kwon, Nayoung Aime, *Intimate empire: collaboration and colonial modernity in Korea and Japan* (Durham, NC: Duke University Press, 2015).

Kyunggido kyoyuk yŏnguwŏn (Institute of pedagogical research, Kyuinggi province), *Kukmin gyoyuk hŏnjang inyŏm guhyŏnmit ban'gong kyoyuk silchŏn saryejip* (The realization of the national manifesto and examples of anticommunist educational practice), (Suwŏn: Kyunggido kyoyuk yŏnguwŏn, 1971).

LaFeber, Walter (ed.), *The origins of the Cold War 1941–1947: a historical problem with interpretations and documents* (New York: John Wiley, 1971).

Laqueur, Thomas W., "Memory and naming in the Great War," in John R. Gillis (ed.), *Commemorations: the politics of national identity* (Princeton, NJ: Princeton University Press, 1994), pp. 150–167.

Lee, Chang-dong, *Soji* (Letters to the dead), (Seoul: Munhakgwa Jisŏngsa, 2003, originally published in 1987).

Lee, Do-young, *Jukŭmŭi yebigŏmsok: yangminhaksal jinsangjosa bogosŏ* (The deadly preventive custody: investigative report of [the Korean War] civilian massacres [in Jeju]), (Seoul: Mal, 2000).

Lee, Hyangjin, *Contemporary Korean cinema: identity, culture and politics* (Manchester: Manchester University Press, 2000).

Lee, Mun-gu, *Gwanchonsupil* (Essays on Gwanchon), (Seoul: Munhakgwa jisongsa, 1996).

Lee, Mun-Woong, *Bukhan jŏngch'imunhwaŭi hyŏngsŏnggwa gŭ t'ŭkjing* (The formation and characteristics of North Korean political culture), (Seoul: Institute of National Unification, 1976).

Lee, Ryung-kyung, "Hankukjŏnjaeingjŏnhu jwailgwanryŏn yŏsŏngyujokŭi gyŏnghŏmyŏngu (Research on bereaved women's experience regarding [the assault] on the Left before and after the Korean War)," Master's thesis (Sungkonghoe University, 2003).

Lee, Steven H., *The Korean War* (New York: Longman, 2001).

Lee, Su-jong, "Making and unmaking the Korean national division: separated families in the Cold War and post-Cold War eras," Unpublished doctoral thesis (University of Illinois at Urbana-Champaign, December 2006).

Lee, Won-gyu, "Jŏsŭngkkot (Flowers in the world of the dead)," *Silchŏnmunhak* (Praxis literature), (Autumn 1989), pp. 177–178.

Lévi-Strauss, Claude, *The elementary structures of kinship* (Boston, MA: Beacon Press, 1969).

Lin, Sylvia Li-Chun, *Representing atrocity in Taiwan: the 2/28 incident and white terror in fiction and film* (New York: Columbia University Press, 2007).

MacIntyre, Alasdair, "The virtues, the unity of a human life, and the concept of a tradition," in Lewis P. Hinchman and Sandra K. Hinchman (eds.), *Memory, identity, community: the idea of narrative in the human sciences* (Albany: State University of New York Press, 1997), pp. 241–263.

MacMillan, Margaret, *Nixon and Mao: the week that changed the world* (New York: Random House, 2008).

Madigan, Edward, "St. Symphorien Military Cemetery, the Battle of Mons and British Centenary commemoration," *World War One centenary: continuations and beginnings* (June 13, 2013), available online at http://ww1centenary.oucs.ox.ac.uk/?p=2658.

Maitland, Frederic William, "Criminal liability of the hundred," *The Law Magazine and Review*, Vol. 7 (1882), pp. 367–380.

Margalit, Avishai, *The ethics of memory* (Cambridge, MA: Harvard University Press, 2002).

Mashal, Mujib, "'I will kill him': Afghan commander targets son, a Taliban fighter," *The New York Times*, May 15, 2016.

Masters, Roger D. "World politics as a primitive political system," *World Politics*, Vol. 16, No. 4 (1964), pp. 595–619.

May, Larry, *The morality of groups: collective responsibility, group-based harm, and corporate rights* (Notre Dame, IN: University of Notre Dame Press, 1987).

McCormack, Gavan, *Cold war, hot war: an Australian perspective on the Korean War* (Sydney: Hale and Iremonger, 1983).

McCormack, Gavan, "Korea at 60," *The Asia-Pacific Journal*, Vol. 6, Issue 9 (September 1, 2008), available online at https://apjjf.org/-Gavan-McCormack/2869/article.html.

McDonald, Maryon, "Medical anthropology and anthropological studies of science," in U. Kockel, M. Nic Craith and J. Frykman (eds.), *A Companion to the anthropology of Europe* (Oxford: Wiley-Blackwell, 2012), pp. 459–479.

McEachern, Patrick, *Inside the red box: North Korea's post-totalitarian politics.* (New York: Columbia University Press, 2010).

Mole, David, "Discourses of world kinship and the United Nations: the quest for a human family," PhD thesis (London School of Economics, 2009).

Morgan, Lewis H., *Ancient society* (New York: Henry Holt, 1907).

Morris-Suzuki, Tessa, *Exodus to North Korea: shadows from Japan's Cold War* (Lanham, MD: Rowman and Littlefield, 2007).

Mosse, George, *Fallen soldiers: reshaping the memory of the world wars* (Oxford: Oxford University Press, 1990).

Mueller, Tim B., "The Rockefeller Foundation, the social sciences, and the humanities in the Cold War," *Cold War Studies*, Vol. 15, No. 3 (2013), pp. 108–135.

Oberdorfer, Don, *The two Koreas: a contemporary history* (London: Warner Books, 1999).

O'Brian, John Lord, "Loyalty tests and guilt by association," *Harvard Law Review*, Vol. 61, No. 4 (1948), pp. 592–611.

Ochman, Ewa, *Post-communist Poland: contested pasts and future identities* (New York: Routledge, 2013).

Oh, Je-do, "Gŏsujaŭi jŭngŏn (Testimonies by puppet individuals)," *Ban'gong jisik ch'ongsŏ* (Collection of anticommunist knowledge) Vol. 1, (Seoul: Hŭimang Publisher, 1969).

Park, Chan-sik, "1947nyŏn 3·1sagŏnŭi yŏksajŏk sŏnggyŏk (The historical character of the March First incident in 1947)," *4·3 and Peace*, Vol. 27 (2017), pp. 14–19.

Park, Chan-sung, *Maŭllo gan hankukjŏnjaeng* (The Korean War that went into villages), (Paju: Dolbegae, 2010).

Park, Chan-sung, *1919, daehanmingukŭi chŏt bŏnjjae bom* (1919, Korea's first spring), (Paju: Dasan Books, 2019).

Park, Hyun-jong, "Jipdanjŏk jŏnjaenggyŏnghŏmŭi giŏkgwa ginyŏm (Memory and memorialization of collective war experience)," Master's thesis (Chonnam University, 2005).

Park, Kyung-li, *Sijang'gwa jŏnjaeng'* (The market and the war), (Seoul: Nanam, 1993).

Park, Myung-lim, *Yŏksawa jisikgwa sahoi: hangukjŏnjaeing ihaewa hanguksahoi* (History, knowledge and society: understanding the Korean War and understanding Korean society), (Seoul: Nanam, 2011).

Park, Wan-suh, "Kyŏul nadŭli (A winter journey)," in Wan-suh Park, *Baebanŭi yŏrŭm* (The treacherous summer), (Paju: Munhakdong'ne, 1999), pp. 11–29.

Park, Wan-suh, *The red room: stories of trauma in contemporary Korea*, trans. by B. Fulton and J. Fulton (Honolulu: University of Hawaii Press, 2009).

Park, Wan-suh, *Who ate up all the shinga?: an autobiographical novel*, trans. by Y. Yu and S. Epstein (New York: Columbia University Press, 2009).

Park, Young-taik, *Gajokŭl gŭrida: gŭrimsokŭro dŭlŏon gajokŭi ŏlguldŭl* (Painting the family: faces of family that have entered into fine art), (Seoul: Bada Publisher, 2009).

Parthow, Joshua, "War pulls apart Afghan families," *The Washington Post*, April 11, 2011.

Putnam, Robert, *Bowling alone: the collapse and revival of American community* (New York: Simon and Schuster, 2000).

Pyo, In-ju et al. (eds.), *Jŏnjaeng'gwa saramdŭl: araerobutŏŭi hankukjŏnjaengyŏngu* (War and peoples: studies of the Korean War from below), (Seoul: Hanul, 2003).

Rho, Min-young and Hui-jong Kang, *Gŏ changyangminhaksal, gŭ ilhyŏ jin pp' iul ŭm* (Civilian massacre in Gŏchang, its forgotten cries), (Chongju: Onnuri, 1988).

Robcis, Camille, *The law of kinship: anthropology, psychoanalysis, and the family in France* (Ithaca, NY: Cornell University Press, 2013).

Roberts, Adam, "The civilian in modern war," *Yearbook of International Humanitarian Law*, Vol. 12 (2009), pp. 13–51.

Robin, Ron, *The making of the Cold War enemy: culture and politics in the military-intellectual complex* (Princeton, NJ: Princeton University Press, 2001).

Robinson, Geoffrey, *The dark side of paradise: political violence in Bali* (Ithaca, NY: Cornell University Press, 1995).

Ryang, Sonia, *Reading North Korea: an ethnological inquiry* (Cambridge, MA: Harvard University Press, 2010).

Ryu, Youngju, *Writers of the Winter Republic: literature and resistance in Park Chung Hee's Korea* (Honolulu: University of Hawaii Press, 2015).

Sahlins, Marshall, *What kinship is – and is not* (Chicago: University of Chicago Press, 2013).

Sahlins, Marshall, *Evolution and culture* (Ann Arbor: University of Michigan Press, 1960).

Saunders, Francis S., *The cultural Cold War: the CIA and the world of arts and letters* (New York: Free Press, 2000).

Schlesinger, Arthur M. Jr., *The vital center: the politics of freedom* (Boston, MA: Houghton Mifflin, 1962).

Schmitt, Carl, *The concept of the political* (Chicago: University of Chicago Press, 1996).

Schmitt, Carl, *Theory of the partisan: intermediate commentary on the concept of the political*, trans. by G. L. Ulmen (New York: Telos Press, 2007).

Schneider, David, *American kinship: a cultural account* (Chicago: University of Chicago Press, 1980).

Schweitzer, Peter P., "Introduction," in P. P. Schweitzer (ed.), *Dividends of kinship: meaning and uses of social relatedness* (London: Routledge, 2000), pp. 1–32.

Shimazu, Naoko, *Japanese society at war: death, memory and the Russo-Japanese war* (Cambridge: Cambridge University Press, 2009).

Shorter, Edward, *The making of the modern family* (New York: Basic Books, 1975).

Shryock, Andrew, "It's this, not that: how Marshall Sahlins solves kinship," *HAU: Journal of Ethnographic Theory*, Vol. 3, No. 2 (2013), pp. 271–279.

Smith, Hazel, *North Korea: markets and military rule* (Cambridge: Cambridge University Press, 2015).

Sponsel, Leslie E. and Thomas Gregor (eds.), *The anthropology of peace and nonviolence* (Boulder, CO: Lynne Rienner, 1994).

Stafford, Charles, *Separation and reunion in modern China* (Cambridge: Cambridge University Press, 2000).

Stangl, Paul, "The Soviet war memorial in Treptow, Berlin," *Geographical Review*, Vol. 93, No. 2 (2003), pp. 213–236.

Suh, Dong-man, *Bukjosŏn sahoijuŭi chejesŏngripsa 1945–1961* (History of the building of socialist system in North Korea), (Seoul: Sŏnin, 2005), pp.466–471.

Suh, Jae-il, Jŏnhyang'gongjakgwa ŭimunsa (Questionable deaths in ideological conversion attempts), *Ŭimunsajinsang'gyumyŏngwiwŏnhoi bogosŏ* (Report by the Truth Commission on questionable deaths), (Ŭimunsajinsang'gyumyŏngwiwŏnhoi [Korean Truth Commission on Questionable Deaths], 2014), pp. 586–622.

Suh, Jae-Jung (ed.), *Truth and reconciliation in South Korea: between the present and future of the Korean wars* (New York: Routledge, 2012).

Sylvester, Christine, "Experiencing war: an introduction," in C. Sylvester (ed.), *Experiencing war* (London: Routledge, 2010), pp. 1–7.

Szalontai, Balázs, *Kim Il Sung in the Khrushchev era: Soviet–DPRK relations and the roots of North Korean despotism, 1953–1964* (Washington, DC: Woodrow Wilson Center Press, 2005).

Tahiri, Hussein, "Divided Afghans will never accept one master," *The Sydney Morning Herald*, October 22, 2010.

Tai, Hue-Tam Ho, *Millenarianism and peasant politics in Vietnam* (Cambridge, MA: Harvard University Press, 1983).

Taylor, Amy Murrell, *The divided family in Civil War America* (Chapel Hill: The University of North Carolina Press, 2005).

Voglis, Polymeris, *Becoming a subject: political prisoners during the Greek Civil War* (Oxford: Berghahn, 2002).

Von Heyking, John and Richard Avramenko (eds.), *Friendship and politics: essays in political thought* (Notre Dame, IN: University of Notre Dame Press, 2008).

Williams, Robert R., *Hegel's ethics of recognition* (Berkeley: University of California Press, 1997).

Wilson, Peter J., *The domestication of the human species* (New Haven, CT: Yale University Press, 1988).

Winnington, Alan, *I saw the truth in Korea* (London: People's Press, 1950).

Winter, Jay, *Sites of memory, sites of mourning: the Great War in European cultural history* (Cambridge: Cambridge University Press, 1998).

Yoo, Im-ha, *Hanguk sosŏlŭi bundan iyagi* (Stories of partition in Korean novels), (Seoul: Ch'aeksesang, 2006).

Yoon, Jeong-ran, "Hankukjŏnjaenggi gidokkyoin haksalui wŏningwa sŏnggyŏk (The causes and characteristics of the massacres of Christians during the Korean War)," in Kyung-hak Kim et al. (eds.), *Jŏngjaenggwa giŏk* (War and memories), (Seoul: Hanulakademi, 2005), pp. 76–112.

Young, Allan, "W. H. R. Rivers and the anthropology of psychiatry," *Social Science and Medicine*, Vol. 36 (1993), pp. ii–vii.

Young, Allan, *The harmony of illusions: inventing post-traumatic stress disorder* (Princeton, NJ: Princeton University Press, 1995).
Young, Marilyn B., "Remembering to Forget," in M. P. Bradley and P. Petro (eds.), *Truth claims: representation and human rights* (New Brunswick, NJ: Rutgers University Press, 2002), pp. 11–21.
Young, Marilyn B., "Bombing civilians from the twentieth to the twentieth-first centuries," in Y. Tanaka and M. B. Young (eds.), *Bombing civilians: a twentieth-century history* (New York: New Press, 2009), pp. 154–174.
Yu, Young-ik, "Unam Rhee Syngmanŭi kaehyŏk, gŏnguk sasang (Syngman Rhee's thoughts about reform and state-building)," *Aseahakbo* (Asian studies journal), No. 20 (1997), pp. 7–45.
Yun, Taik-lim, *Inryuhakjaŭi gwagŏyŏhaeng: han ppalgaeng'i maŭlŭi yŏksarŭl chatasŏ* (An anthropologist's journey to history: in search of a red village), (Seoul: Yŏksabipyŏngsa, 2003).

Newspapers and Journals

Daegu Maeil Sinmun (Daegu Daily Gazette), July 10, 1950.
Daegu Maeil Sinmun (Daegu Daily Gazette), May 27, 1960.
Daegu Maeil Sinmun (Daegu Daily Gazette), June 16, 1960.
Daegu Maeil Sinmun (Daegu Daily Gazette), July 29, 1960.
Hankuk Ilbo (Korea Daily), December 8, 1961.
Jindotaimjŭ (Jindo Times), June 26, 2009.
Kŭmsugangsan, 10 (1990).
Kyunghyang Sinmun (Kyunghyang Daily), November 15, 2009.
Mal (Parole), March 2000.

Index

For EU product safety concerns, contact us at Calle de José Abascal, 56–1°,
28003 Madrid, Spain or eugpsr@cambridge.org.

www.ingramcontent.com/pod-product-compliance
Ingram Content Group UK Ltd.
Pitfield, Milton Keynes, MK11 3LW, UK
UKHW020306140625
459647UK00006B/64